Praise for *No Fear, No Failure*

No Fear, No Failure provides a practical, structured approach to diagnosing the challenges to innovation within your organization and within yourself. This easy-to-read book offers a road map for navigating and reducing, if not removing, roadblocks to change as well as a powerful set of tools for building a culture of innovation and entrepreneurship within your team and across your organization.

—Paul Russo, Founding Dean, Katz School of Science and Health;
Professor of Data Science, Yeshiva University

As a corporate leader who has navigated complex transformations, I've seen firsthand how fear of failure can stifle innovation and teamwork. *No Fear, No Failure* is a bold and timely call to action—an essential guide for executives and teams ready to replace hesitation with resilience, creativity and encouragement. Marchand offers practical strategies for building a culture where bold thinking thrives, mistakes are reframed as learning, and progress becomes the norm. A must-read for today's business leaders.

—Deborah Juantorena, former Vice President,
Enterprise Data Solutions and Engineering, Pfizer Inc.

As our keynote speaker for our Mastercard professional training seminars, Lorraine Marchand has inspired and energized our employees with her innovation mindset prescription for change. The ideas in her new book, *No Fear, No Failure*, which show how to help create a culture of innovation at the organizational level, are equally exciting and vitally important in helping managers and executives kindle and sustain that innovative flame in their corporations.

—Paul J. Bailo, Lecturer, Columbia University School
of Professional Studies; CEO, PiPCG

In this insightful book, you'll discover a wealth of practical tools, strategies, and case studies that illuminate the path to fostering a culture of innovation and organizational change. Each chapter offers invaluable insights to help navigate the complexities of innovation. With easy-to-use frameworks, diagnostic tools, and exercises, you'll learn how to overcome barriers, embrace uncertainty, and turn bold ideas into tangible results. Whether you're a seasoned entrepreneur or a corporate leader, *No Fear, No Failure* equips you with the knowledge and confidence to fortify your organization for the challenges ahead and unleash its full potential. Get ready to embark on a transformative journey toward innovation excellence!

—Deborah Y. Cohn, Interim Dean, School of Management,
New York Institute of Technology

This book is essential reading for boards of directors, CEOs, and their management teams. As a CFO, I have finally discovered a concrete framework in *No Fear, No Failure* that empowers leadership teams in any corporation to achieve exponential and sustained impact on shareholder returns while redefining the organization's full potential.

—Nisheet Gupta, chartered accountant and a seasoned CFO
and global finance leader

I've had the privilege of seeing Lorraine Marchand in action—showing students and professionals alike how to innovate. Her first book, The *Innovation Mindset*, is popular among students, and we use it in our courses on innovation and entrepreneurship because it is practical and inspiring. In *No Fear, No Failure*, she addresses the problem that blocks so many bright talented professionals from pursuing their dreams and hinders organizations from developing creative solutions—fear of failure. She doesn't just talk about it but provides a roadmap. Her "try, fail, learn" methodology and prescriptive framework offer a mindset shift that can create a growth-oriented culture and transform organizations. Her book is filled with relevant case studies and examples, making it dynamic, engaging, and easy to read. If you are ready to break through the fear and show your creativity, this is a must-read book. Get this book and get ready to innovate like a pro.

—Rana Khan, Inaugural Director, Bioscience Research and Education Center, Hood College, Frederick, Maryland; former professor and director, Yeshiva University, New York and the University of Maryland, College Park

In her new book, Lorraine Marchand maps out a path to overcoming the fear of failure that can hold back any business. Through insightful anecdotes and strategies, this book develops a framework for thinking about "intelligent failure" and empowering individuals and organizations to embrace change and allow passion and curiosity to thrive. *No Fear, No Failure* is a compelling and immediately useful read!

—Benjamin Newland, Principal, Newland Ventures; Chief Legal Officer, Kelix bioLimited; Director, Nightjar Coffee Limited

Lorraine Marchand has done it again. Her new book, *No Fear, No Failure*, a sequel to the successful *The Innovation Mindset*, is a powerful, practical guide that demystifies the innovation process in organizations. It provides a framework organizations can use to diagnose their culture and a prescription for driving growth over the long haul. Marchand masterfully bridges the gap between inspiration and execution, making this a must-read for entrepreneurs, business leaders, and changemakers.

—Natasha Srulowitz, Board Member, Soul Power Acquisition Corp., startup founder, investor and career advisor

In *No Fear, No Failure*, Lorraine Marchand introduces a groundbreaking guide to corporate innovation, skillfully weaving together the essential 5C's—Customer First, Culture, Chance, Collaboration, and Change. The book offers a fresh perspective on fostering a culture of innovation, providing insightful case studies and practical tools for organizations of all sizes to thrive in today's dynamic business landscape.

—Eric Piscini, CEO, Hashgraph

NO FEAR, NO FAILURE

NO
FEAR

Five Principles for
Sustaining Growth
Through Innovation

NO
FAILURE

LORRAINE H. MARCHAND
WITH JOHN HANC

Columbia Business School
Publishing

Columbia University Press
Publishers Since 1893
New York   Chichester, West Sussex
cup.columbia.edu

Cataloging-in-Publication data are available from the Library of Congress.
ISBN 978-0-231-21920-4 (hardback)
ISBN 978-0-231-56256-0 (epub)
ISBN 9780231565042 (PDF)

Cover design: Noah Arlow

GPSR Authorized Representative: Easy Access System Europe,
Mustamäe tee 50, 10621 Tallinn, Estonia, gpsr.requests@easproject.com

TO NOLAN AND ISAAC:

TRY, FAIL, LEARN

CONTENTS

FOREWORD

Advising Fortune 500 clients as the head of a multi-billion-dollar business, my life is anything but predictable. Yes, there are macro events and trends that make a big impact on my clients—COVID, geopolitical instability, and economic uncertainty to name a few. But one of the most striking and exciting observations I've made, as I speak with CEOs and analyze my clients' businesses, is the breathtaking speed of innovation. And it fills me with great hope for our future.

Of course, humans have been thinking of new ways to do things for centuries. But not at this pace. Let's look at a historical example, one that might initially seem obscure, but not to me. As an engineering student in my native Istanbul, I learned how, in the year 1698, an English military engineer and inventor named Thomas Savery patented the first steam-powered pump. Steam power, of course, would go on to drive the Industrial Revolution. But that was a century later. It wasn't until 1776, the same year the United States declared its independence, that another Englishman, James Watt, added a separate condenser to make steam engines more efficient. And *that*, not Savery's original invention, is what truly launched the technological revolution that would transform society in the nineteenth century.

Think about that: the world had to wait seventy-eight years for steam's industrial application; seventy-eight years before it could become a truly viable technology. Today, it would be unthinkable to wait that long for design iterations that could scale an invention. Now we measure the uptake of innovation in days. For example, according to *Time* magazine, ChatGPT achieved a hundred million users in November 2022 in only two months!

To compete in this lightning-fast innovation environment, organizations can't just wait for their own Savery or Watt to come along. For me, the key question is: How can a company *institutionalize organizational innovation*? How can it foster a culture of innovation to sustain a competitive edge and avoid becoming a corporate dinosaur destined for extinction? Research by the artificial intelligence (AI)-powered competitive intelligence platform, WatchMyCompetitor (WMC), found that about 52 percent of the companies that were listed on the Fortune 500 in 2000 had disappeared by 2020.

This is a sobering fact. What's keeping those in the C-suite up at night is the issue of relevance. How do we stay relevant to our customers? By adapting and changing and offering new and better products and services, yes. But to do that, we must foster and create a culture of innovation. How?

No Fear, No Failure can provide some answers. This book's author, Lorraine Marchand, is a former Big Tech and Big Pharma executive, as well as a professor of innovation and management at some of our country's finest business schools. In her first, award-winning book, *The Innovation Mindset*, she showed how to bring a good idea from inception to market. Here she looks at innovation from an organizational perspective. And she has developed a thoughtful framework after conducting over one hundred executive interviews; she has distilled her insights into an easy-to-follow and practical 5C's approach to organizational innovation.

Here we are also reminded that just as some people may be better "out of the box" thinkers than others, so, too, can organizations be classified by their level of innovativeness. Indeed, everyone reading this book will have a unique perspective because the approach to innovation varies significantly across four company typologies in different stages of maturity. Lorraine describes the start-up trying to survive and producing a working prototype as well as a Fortune 500 that must constantly replenish its billions of dollars' worth of products and services to stay on the list, as well as many other types of companies in between. Why is this important? A company's chronological age isn't indicative of its innovation aptitude. Quite the opposite: she shows us how start-ups can be old and stodgy and twenty-five-year-old corporations can stay hungry and curious.

Why the disconnect? The secret lies in the culture of innovation companies create.

Typically when we think of innovation, our mind's eye goes to Silicon Valley. There is a kind of ethos—as well as a popular mythology—that has developed about the start-ups that have proliferated in that area of northern California, a place that's become synonymous with innovation. You know the story. The start-up originated in the proverbial garage after the founder dropped out of an Ivy League school to bet it all on a dream. The company bootstrapped with seed funding from friends and family in pursuit of a risky opportunity. With luck and perseverance, the computer chip or the smart phone was created as a result, and the world is a better place. The end.

That's only part of the real picture, however. Less attention has been paid to corporations that are already operating at scale but need to add increasingly bigger revenues year after year to continue their historical growth pattern and avoid being classified as a dreaded *value company* with much less generous valuation multiples and an expectation of a dividend payout. What everyone seeks is the coveted *growth company* designation with an aspiration to enjoy higher multiples in valuation.

Lorraine's book addresses the existential question: How can large corporations institutionalize organizational innovation and thereby maintain their competitive edge and avoid becoming a corporate dinosaur destined for extinction?

Let's expand on what Lorraine calls the 5C's, starting with *Customer First*, where the innovation journey starts. In my experience of working with start-ups, the biggest challenge I see a founder struggle with is the articulation of what problem they are solving for the customer. Founders typically have a technical background, and the expression of value proposition from a customer point of view is outside their comfort zone. I usually ask them this question: "Imagine you are Steve Wozniak, the cofounder of a leading technology innovator and its renowned technical genius. How do you translate your technology to Steve Jobs's vision that focuses on customer's needs?" I usually get an introspective pause that tells me that they have not thought this through yet. And for the large corporations, it gets trickier if the employees in charge of innovation, such as research and development (R&D) or product development, are not connected to the customer-facing functions. I was in a similar role earlier in my career at a large pharma company, and I felt at times like a translator of product requirements from my team on the commercialization side to the scientists who had the unenviable task of discovering molecules with attributes that would help address unmet medical needs.

Culture, the second C, is the one that makes innovation sink or swim in the large company environment. My experience suggests culture is driven by incentives, and there is an intrinsic asymmetry of incentives in a large organization based on varying degrees of risk tolerance. For example, although the business side with little risk tolerance prefers a quick uplift in revenue driven by the novel innovation, the R&D side needs more runway and time to experiment for the new solution to meet or exceed customers' requirements. R&D has a much greater risk tolerance. Ultimately the winning culture of the innovation mindset philosophy—bringing both sides together—was best coined by a quote attributed to Nelson Mandela: "I never lose. I either win or learn."

Lorraine's next C is *Collaboration*. That is where things get interesting because the leaders of the organization must articulate a clear vision of why the team members are doing what they are doing. In my broad corporate experience across three Fortune 500s, a $50-billion-plus partnership, and a start-up, it goes beyond a well-thought-through motivational narrative. It also requires a key ingredient: trust in each other and the organization's *common purpose*, particularly around the customer, and a shared goal to grow the business. This also ties well to the common incentives in the second C, *Culture*, where the teams with different functional responsibilities understand their unique contributions and move as one toward the desired future state.

The fourth C, *Change*, is about getting the team members across the organization to mobilize the innovation mindset to transform the business. It's the most audacious C given that it requires team members to operate outside of their comfort zone. In my view, change requires a blend of IQ and EQ—emotional intelligence. The leader needs to compel the company to do things differently by demonstrating business rationale while at the same time overcoming reluctance to get the company moving to a new operating state. Prime examples in my experience are divestitures, post-mergers, and enterprise-wide technology implementations. Change is never easy, but change and adaptation are the key evolutionary skills that got us this far as humans.

Chance is Lorraine's last but not the least important C for sure. There are reams of stories about scientists getting lucky with some serendipitous invention, whether it is discovering penicillin, repurposing Viagra's indication from a heart medication to erectile dysfunction, which I was fortunate enough to launch globally early in my career as the global marketing director, or finding a better use of Post-it Notes when the adhesive failed to be strong enough for its initial intended purpose. When my team *humbly* says they got lucky, I often cite the words of one of history's most renowned scientists. During an 1854 lecture at the University of Lille, the French microbiologist and chemist Louis Pasteur said, "In the fields of observation chance favors only the prepared mind."

Mitigating intrinsic risks in innovation requires a culture of risk tolerance alongside the competence to pivot combined with a compulsive creative drive. Lorraine also posits that there is an algorithm for financially investing in chance or opportunity. I heartily agree. The most successful innovative companies dedicate a portion of their budget to investing in innovations that are a big risk but in the end often end up driving the company's growth five years later.

In other words, those who think boldly and act without fear of failure are the companies that keep up with the ever-accelerating pace of innovation. Mastering the challenges of organizational innovation is not straightforward. But after reading this insightful and provocative book, I think you will walk away with actionable insights to inform your own journey.

Arda Ural, PhD
Life Sciences Sector Leader, Ernst & Young LLC
New York, May 2025

The views reflected in this foreword are the views of the author and do not necessarily reflect the views of Ernst & Young LLP or other members of the global EY organization.

NO FEAR, NO FAILURE

INTRODUCTION

The phone rang. It was the VP of sales and marketing who had reached out to me on LinkedIn just a few days earlier. I was expecting his call—but I wasn't exactly sure what he wanted to discuss. A seasoned pharmaceutical exec, Howell said he'd read my book and now urgently needed to speak to me.

Urgent? I am, of course, always delighted to talk about innovation, about change, about new ideas—particularly with readers. Still, I couldn't imagine what the rush was. However, as he spoke, I could feel the excitement—and perhaps a trace of anxiety—in his voice.

"Lorraine, it's so nice to speak with you. I loved *The Innovation Mindset*, and that's why I'm calling."

He went on to tell me that his business unit, part of a pharmaceutical giant that I was familiar with, given my career in life sciences, was focused on a particular rare disease that could manifest itself in many ways. Although it ultimately would reveal itself as a neurological condition, there was typically a long path to diagnosis, which is difficult for the patient suffering from it. But it was also challenging for Howell and his team. Scientists at their company had developed a new drug capable of mitigating the symptoms. Howell's team was eager to get out in the marketplace and start visiting physicians to let them know about this breakthrough therapy.

But wait, which physicians? Who was the right practitioner to diagnose and treat a disease that presents itself with differing symptoms in various parts of the body? And once Howell's team had narrowed down their target audience, how could they communicate clearly the benefits of this therapy for a disease that's such a chameleon?

That was something Howell's group had to figure out. It would probably take some fresh, imaginative thinking—not to mention the kind of intense focus and passion that is intrinsic to the innovation mindset. Part of the process (discussed in my first book, which Howell had read) involved a clear identification of the problem— asking the right questions, observing and listening, developing solutions, and taking the best solution to the prototype stage for testing with customers.

"All of that would be really helpful to my team," Howell said. "When can you get here?"

On the morning of our working session, he picked me up at my hotel. After exchanging pleasantries, we got in his car and headed for the meeting at a local conference center.

"Lorraine, there was something I forgot to tell you."

Uh-oh.

"What was that, Howell?"

He looked a bit sheepish as he confessed that his company— the pharmaceutical giant—was thinking about closing his division. "We're under the gun," he said grimly. Now I understood the urgency.

"Just thought you should know," Howell said. "Because my group is going to need to start being creative and innovative . . . like, right away."

Okay, I thought. Game on.

The working session was at a hotel meeting space, an environment that is for me—like most consultants—all too familiar. Conference table, usually with a hodgepodge of controllers and remotes gathered in a pile in the middle. Big video screen. Whiteboard. Lectern. Laser pointer and a bottle of water for the presenter.

Facing me around the conference room table were members of Howell's team: A silver-haired gentleman. A young woman with short, cropped hair and a thin, silver nose ring. A woman of Asian descent who, I learned, had a PhD in biochemistry and had transferred to Howell's group from R&D. And a recent MBA grad—a Caucasian guy who had been texting when I got in and who, as Howell introduced me, removed his AirPods.

They were all polite but reserved—the usual and understandable stance for most attendees in this situation. They were here because their boss had told them to be here. I understood that. But I also detected, as with Howell, a sense of unease, as if they were waiting for me to give them an answer to a problem that had given them all some sleepless nights.

I started by posing a simple question—one that I often ask when I give workshops and presentations like this.

"On a scale of one to ten, with ten being a perfect score," I asked, "how would you assess your innovation mindset, which I define as insatiable curiosity, a passion for problem-solving, embracing change, and seeking diverse perspectives?"

I saw a couple of pairs of eyes widen. This is a question that requires a little thought and elaboration, which I quickly provided.

"All of those are important attributes for anyone who is looking to create a new product, or"—and I gave a knowing look to the six marketing people around the table—"for those whose job it is to figure out how to best communicate the benefits of a new product and successfully get that product in front of the right audience."

They knew I was talking about them, and I could see them straighten up in their chairs a bit. Sales and marketing people in pharma are sometimes looked upon as lightweights by those on the clinical side. But without them in a business, there is no business. These folks took pride in their work. And they also knew that there was a lot on the line with this new product—and thus a lot of pressure on them to come up with innovative strategies to get the product out into the marketplace.

"Okay," I urged, bringing them back to our little classroom exercise. "Who wants to go first. Who is a perfect ten on the innovator scale?"

Not a hand was raised.

That was predictable. Few people are bold enough in this kind of setting to say that they're a ten at anything, much less a concept that most people haven't thought much about. What are the attributes of an innovator? Are you born with them? Can they be learned?

I wanted them to think about that.

"You're all being modest," I said. "So, who's a nine?"

Half the hands in the room shot up.

"Wow," I said. "Well, obviously I'm looking at a lot of curiosity and passion here. I'm looking at some people who embrace change and seek out different perspectives."

Now, as their hands were lowered, I saw a glimmer of self-doubt in a couple of faces and could almost read the mind of one of the older men ("I've been going to the same diner for breakfast on Saturdays and ordering the same thing for twenty years; that's not really embracing change").

But the woman with the short hair and nose ring shot her arm back up.

"I'm one of those people who like to change things up," ventured Alyssa, a young, self-confident saleswoman. "I'd always rather find a better way to do things."

"Good!" I said. "That sounds like the innovation mindset to me. Okay, you've ranked yourselves nine out of ten when it comes to innovativeness. You're obviously good. That's why you're working for one of the largest pharmaceutical companies in the world. So, if half of you are a nine on the innovator scale, who's an eight?"

The other half of the hands shot up. I feigned shock. "You've got to help me understand this," I said. "I'm here to help improve your innovation acumen so you can do a better job solving your customer's problems and thereby drive better sales results, right? Yet none of you seem to need the help. You're all experts or close to being experts in the area of innovation. What gives?"

Adam—in his late thirties, I guessed, and dressed impeccably in a blazer, pressed slacks, and a shiny pair of brushed-leather Pradas on his feet—spoke up. "Actually, I was going to give myself a ten, but then I thought everyone would expect a lot out of me throughout the rest of the workshop," he chuckled, "so I settled for a nine."

"Good for you, Adam," I said. "If you can't believe in yourself, who can you believe in? But I'm still questioning why you need my help if you're all innovation experts. And why do you think you're having challenges selling your product to doctors, given all the innovative horsepower in this room?"

This was a question I genuinely wanted answered. Howell had told me what a crack sales team he had assembled. I assumed they were right in their self-assessment—they probably were open-minded to new ideas and creative ways to solve problems. But if that was true, why were they feeling stymied, and why were they performing poorly enough that their heads were on the chopping block?

As if reading my mind, Jim spoke up. He had sat quietly for most of the session so far, but now he spoke with a kind of wise authority the others recognized. With his streaks of gray hair, Jim seemed to be the senior member of the team, and I could sense the others respected him. They nodded as he spoke.

"The problem isn't us, Lorraine. Our team is innovative and creative. We have lots of great ideas for making our product attractive to doctors and patients and getting our message out to them. The problem"—he paused and looked around, as if making sure no one from top management was present—"the problem is this organization. It's huge, it's global, and it's bureaucratic. They're beholden to regulations and policies and filled with lawyers who have one hundred different reasons why they need to shut down our new ideas."

Heads were nodding vigorously now and hands shot up. I almost thought Jim was going to get a round of applause. Alyssa joined in.

"Jim's absolutely right. There's a lot of lip service paid to this idea of getting us to 'think outside the box.'" She drew air quotes around that shopworn phrase. "But when we do, the organization chases us back inside our boxes!"

Laughter. Yet, even the vice president, Howell, sitting quietly to my right, had to agree. "They're right," he said, when I asked him about this. "I encourage them to be innovative, but very often when we try to act on what they've suggested, we get shot down. I'll even sometimes try to go up the chain of command myself to get something green-lighted—which, as you know, is not always a politically smart thing to do—but it's a no go. You know what it's like. You've worked for a lot of big corporations."

I have, indeed. And particularly in the last few years, as I've been researching, writing, and teaching the principles of the innovation mindset, I've seen or experienced firsthand the problem that was frustrating Howell and his sales team.

"You're not alone," I said sympathetically. "We're going to talk about that, but first let's try a different question," I said. "I think I know the answers to this, based on what you've just said, but I'm going to pose the question anyway. We've talked about your attitudes toward innovation. But what about management's? On a scale of one to ten, how would you rate your company on their innovation mindset?"

There were snorts of laughter.

"Can we use minus numbers?" asked the feisty Alyssa.

"I'd give us a four," said Denise, a sales leader for the Midwest, as others nodded in agreement. "And that's generous."

"Yes," agreed Ken. "A three, maybe a four, certainly no more than a five. I've been here for a few years now, and it's always been challenging to get anything new and different approved. It's frustrating. And that's really why we need your help."

"Look," said Jim, the senior man, leaning forward on the table for emphasis. "This is an enormous global corporation, with a lot of a talented and smart people. But, for whatever reasons—fear of failure is probably a big one—we can't implement the ideas that we know can help increase sales. And if the organization won't support our ideas, they're never going to fly."

This was certainly not the first time I'd heard this lament. Employees whom I've interacted with in general find it stressful, difficult, and frustrating to advance new proposals and new ideas, or new ways of doing things, because of organizational resistance, rigid lines of authority, and other built-in obstacles common among companies whose culture is to play it safe.

It's true across industries. Take higher education—an area with which I also have significant experience and one that you would think would be most welcome to change. After all, aren't universities supposed to be the locus of new knowledge and new discoveries and incubators for new ideas? Yet, ask any professor or department chair at almost any college or university in the country and they'll tell you that it's nigh on impossible to implement change from the bottom up. "Too many rules, too many committees, too many layers of management," one administrator admitted to me. "I always have to stifle a laugh when I hear our provost or president drone on about our commitment to new ideas and busting silos and creating interdisciplinary partnerships. It all sounds great, but if you actually try to propose a partnership or a new initiative, you'll get shot down. 'That's not the way we do things' . . . 'We have to make change from the bottom up, not top down' . . . 'This will never work.' It'd be comical if it wasn't a sad testimony on the state of higher education."

Jim was right.

But why? What is it about the innovation process that is so concerning to large organizations (and some smaller ones, too)?

As we took a break, something Jim said stuck with me: the way he had managed to put his finger on the problem.

He'd talked about top management's fear of innovation and change. He was right. In my experience, it's fear that stifles innovation: fear of lawsuits, fear of change, fear of the wrath of superiors, fear of what will happen to you if you don't cover your backside.

Fear of all that.

But, ultimately, what paralyzes the innovation process is fear of failure.

And it's certainly not limited to the sales team in a struggling division of a major pharmaceutical company. Fear of failure pervades the halls of industry—every industry. I've heard similar frustrations expressed by employees of accounting firms and financial services companies, as well as universities and tech start-ups (yes, even high-tech firms are not immune to this).

Are you among the legions of the frustrated? Are you disenchanted with and disappointed by the culture in your organization when it comes to change? Would you like to be able to create and nurture new ideas despite the inevitable, knee-jerk reaction of many who would rather perpetuate the status quo?

Well, that's what we're going to address in this book. I'm going to arm you with a road map for change—change that can help you innovate within your organization, no matter how large, no matter how hidebound it is. Let me be clear: I'm not trying to turn you into some kind of internal activist, gadfly, or perceived troublemaker. I'm not McKinsey coming in to reorganize everything. And we're not promising that you can revamp long-held practices and deeply held beliefs overnight. But we can arm you with the strategies, tactics, and tools that can help you implement the innovations that will help you and your organization succeed—and do it in a way in which everyone benefits.

We can also help instill in you an attitude that is a direct outgrowth of the innovation mindset—an attitude that recognizes the obstacles every agent of change must face, but one that remains undaunted by them.

An attitude, an approach to doing things that has its own rallying cry:

No Fear. No Failure.

Everyone talks about innovation. We're a society that believes in new technologies and new ways of doing things. Better, smarter, faster, more efficiently. We live in a world surrounded by the products of innovative thinking—from the cell phone in your pocket to the electric car in your driveway. It's almost a cliché to talk about innovation being the "lifeblood" of most organizations. When surveyed, CEOs list innovation as their number-one priority. And yet, ask some of the employees at those very same companies about innovation, and they'll tell you they are often frustrated in their efforts to create change.

One reason is that, for many, innovation seems to be a bad investment: 94 percent of CEOs are dissatisfied with the performance impact they are seeing from the dollars spent on innovation, according to a McKinsey study cited in a *Harvard Business Review* article, "Breaking Down the Barriers to Innovation."[1] The article's authors write that, across business sectors, one survey after another finds that businesses aren't getting the impact they want, despite their spending. Employees are equally frustrated that despite all the innovation initiatives, their attempts to bring new ideas and products to the table are frequently blocked. According to another survey, failure, criticism, and career-impact concerns are holding people back from innovating in their companies.

And yet, companies that do succeed in creating a sustained approach to innovating see exponential growth. Those with strong innovation cultures outperform their peers by 3.5 times on financial metrics, according to another recent McKinsey report. Corporations with strong innovation cultures have better talent retention and success in new markets and emerging markets, according to separate articles in *MIT Sloan Management Review* and *Harvard Business Review*.

As I learned during my work with the under-the-gun pharma sales team whose experience I recount in this introduction, there are a lot of creative, talented, innovative, and extremely frustrated employees out there. In the talks and workshops I've done since *The Innovation Mindset* was published, I've heard time and again from large and small companies, across many industries, that are fearful of losing their innovative edge or have already lost it and don't know how to get it back.

Where is the disconnect? Why is something seen as so important by everyone—innovation—so hard for companies to accept or accommodate. What can be done to help individuals like Howell and his team, employees who are trying to be innovative to the benefit of their employer?

One big stumbling block is that companies hate talking about the "F" word. It's the word that haunts every in-house discussion about new initiatives and new ways of doing things, the word that informs every email shooting them down.

Failure.

That—our entire perception of failure—needs to change!

It starts with a recognition that not all failures are equal. Harvard Business School professor and author Amy C. Edmondson categorizes missteps in three classifications:

- Preventable failures in predictable operations
- Unavoidable failures in complex systems
- Intelligent failures at the frontier

It's that third kind of failure—intelligent—that probes the border of what is known. It's intrinsic to the innovation process. "Failures in this category," writes Professor Edmondson in the *Harvard Business Review*, "can rightly be considered 'good,' because they provide valuable new knowledge that can help an organization leap ahead of the competition and ensure its future growth."[2] Intelligent failure, she says, occurs when experimentation is necessary, when answers are not knowable in advance because the situation is new.

This idea—of failure as a necessity to advance knowledge and new ideas—is actually not a new one. Thomas Edison had plenty of his inventions flop (including an electric pen and a tinfoil phonograph). But those missteps didn't keep him from creating the spectacular inventions that make him one of the most significant innovators in American history. He dismissed those alleged failures in a now-famous quote: "I have not failed 10,000 times—I've successfully found 10,000 ways that will not work."

Modern-day titans of innovation have similar feelings about failure. "If the size of your failures isn't growing," wrote Jeff Bezos in a 2019 letter to shareholders, "you're not going to be inventing at a size that can actually move the needle."

In *No Fear, No Failure*, I will empower you to rise above the workplace fears that stifle our most creative thinking and keep us from saying, "There's a better way to do this." Based on my own research—interviews and a survey of 120 CEOs, executives, and senior managers in various industries; an innovation investment model developed with Bentley University's Center for Integration of Science and Industry; case studies on corporate innovation; and my own thirty-year career as a serial innovator, executive, consultant, and professor—I will show you what sustained innovation looks like and how to achieve it within your organization. In the following pages, we'll address the deference to sacred cows that trips companies up, and we will lay out a playbook for creating the kind of innovation road map that drives strategic growth over the long haul.

In *No Fear, No Failure*, I will also posit a typology of corporations and individuals in relation to their innovativeness and show how our principles can improve the success rate of each type. I'll explain the best ways to measure innovation, including failures, and how companies can establish metrics that matter, a topic that is underrepresented in the innovation literature. And because you can't talk about innovation these days without mentioning artificial intelligence (AI), I will include a special chapter on the promise (and hype) of AI, including insights from experts at IBM, Carnegie Mellon, and MIT. Over the past years, I've visited countries in Europe, Asia, and the Middle East and studied their approaches to innovation. I've discovered some interesting truths and new insights on creating a culture where innovation can flourish.

Using the same approach that I took in *The Innovation Mindset*—where we demonstrated the process of innovating to bring a new product or service to the marketplace—in *No Fear, No Failure*, I will provide you with a framework for the implementation of new ideas and for creating an organizational culture that welcomes and encourages change. Each chapter is rich with research, examples, case studies, and profiles of current-day innovators and their companies. The frameworks, diagnostic tools, exercises, and templates

I will provide can help improve innovation results and future-proof your organization.

The audience for this book is anyone in the business world seeking to create a climate of innovation: Are you an executive who wants to improve your organization's capabilities and drive new growth? Are you a midlevel manager who sees opportunities for change but doesn't know how to break out of the silo you're trapped in? Are you a student who wants to learn how to create new products in different types of organizations or someone who seeks to foment change in any organizational setting of any size, including the not-for-profit world and government?

Then this book is for you.

At its core is a series of principles that are at the heart of the innovative process in any organization.

THE 5C's OF CORPORATE INNOVATION

In *The Innovation Mindset*, we shaped our prescriptive materials around eight principles (or "Laws," as we called them) of innovation.

In *No Fear, No Failure*, the primary organizing principle is what we call the 5C's—ideas that form the foundation for effective innovation to be used by organizations, from corporations to small companies and start-ups, that want to make innovation a way of working and create a culture from which the organization can reap the benefits for years to come.

- Customer First: Executives talk a lot about being customer focused and customer oriented. The sad truth is that most lack a true understanding of who their customer is, much less the problems they should be solving for them. Innovators need to learn how to think in new ways about their customers and to understand the emotions guiding their decision-making. We look at the six killer questions you should be asking every customer as you launch new products and measure adoption. Who are some of the best companies when it comes listening to the customer?

And how do they apply the lessons they learn, even when the cold facts bruise their egos? The results may surprise you.

- Culture: How do you create a sustainable culture of innovation? It starts with fundamental objectives: Do your employees feel safe failing in your organization? Does leadership consider innovation a core value? What systems and processes are in place to integrate innovation into the way the company works? Learn a diagnostic tool for assessing the innovation DNA of your culture and methods for improving the mindset in your organization, including seeking diverse perspectives, teaching the discipline of constructive failure, and training teams to cocreate effectively. We explore why Jeff Bezos says that Amazon has had "plenty of practice with failure" and believes it is the "best place in the world to fail."[3] And we'll look at how Fictiv, a fast-growing mechanical parts sourcing company, inculcates innovation in the culture. In fact, the CEO sees himself as a culture "river guide" whose job it is to embed innovation in the company's operating system.

- Collaboration: Smart collaboration means applying a strategic approach to integrating business lines, services, and products to meet more of your customer's needs and to meet them better, exponentially increasing revenue. We look at several case examples where collaboration is paying off big financially, including in software and financial sectors, and we also describe how to encourage and facilitate collaboration, tactically, in a postpandemic world, where many employees will interact only through their Zoom and Teams accounts.

- Change: The ability to embrace and navigate change is like a muscle—it's the fourth C, and it's got to be developed and used to strengthen the adaptability of your organization and make embracing change a way of life. Although we profile small to midsize companies that are adept at change, we also highlight larger companies that have succeeded in embracing pivoting and making adaptability to change a criterion when hiring new talent. We learn how they test for innovative behavior in the interview process. PTC Therapeutics, for example, is a twenty-five-year-old company that has succeeded in creating a culture that embraces change. We'll look at how how they've done this. At the same time, there are start-ups that operate like stodgy bureaucracies. Why is that

Roadmap to Sustained Innovation: The 5C's

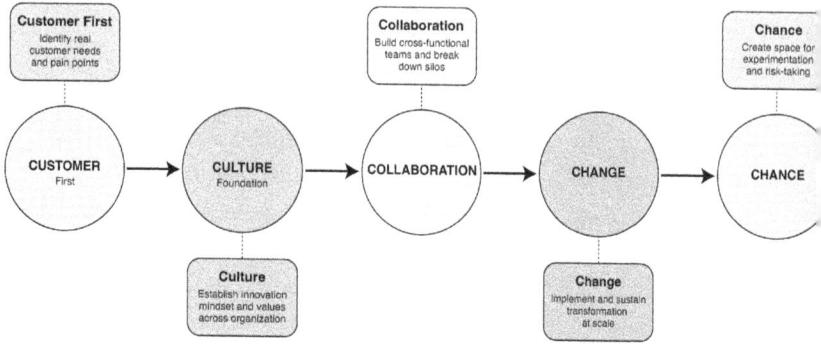

Figure 0.1 The framework of the 5C's provides a roadmap for sustained growth through innovation.

and what can we do to make them more curious and more embracing of change?

- Chance: Learn the 70-20-10 rule for investing in innovation and how to derisk any new product during the commercialization process. We examine companies that do this well, including Google and Johnson & Johnson, and those that failed to make investing in risk a strategic imperative integrated with business goals, with dire results.

To answer these kinds of questions and to better assess your organization's innovativeness, we need to first help you identify the kind of organization you're working for, which we do using a second typology that seeks to classify corporations by their attitudes toward innovation.

THE FOUR FACES OF ORGANIZATIONAL INNOVATION

Is your organization welcoming of change? Do they simply pay lip service to the idea of innovation, or do they put their R&D money where their mouth is? Can you shepherd a new idea through fruition in a company that is more risk averse? If so, how? And on the flip side, if you are in upper management and looking to change a culture, what is the kind of innovation-ready organization you should aim for in terms of allocation of resources and investment in innovation?

To answer those questions, we need to look at the kinds of organizations we're talking about. We've identified four general personas when it comes to corporate innovation. As a way of illustrating each, we spotlight four companies—each exemplifying one of the archetypes—that have agreed to share their innovation road map with us. You'll hear their stories:

- The Fearless Start-Up: A cybersecurity start-up is an example of a company with almost stereotypical innovation DNA. They were great at solving problems and creating solutions, according to the CEO. The challenge? Hiring the right talent at the right time to scale the business and attract capital.
- The Adolescent Up-and-Comer: This persona has a high innovation score but knows that its progress is being held back because it lacks process, discipline, and effective ways of collaborating. It's adding organizational muscle even as it maintains a highly innovative culture that is open to talking about failure. We talk to the CEO of a privately held, growing, technology-based company whose story of success and investment in scaling is a great example of how companies can professionalize their operations without compromising creativity.
- The Stodgy Old Bureaucracy: The fearful, mostly risk-averse corporation is—as you might guess—on the far right of the innovation continuum. It sacrifices innovation for scale, process, repeatability, and reproducibility. In the desire to please shareholders with expected results, it increasingly loses focus on the customer, becomes more internally focused, and loses its ability to change and pivot. There is an exhaustive list of companies in this category. We share stories of IBM, Novartis, Hewlett-Packard, Bayer, Dupont, and InfoSys, all working hard to revitalize the innovation mindset and spur growth.
- The 70-20-10 Innovator: This is the sweet spot. These companies follow the 70-20-10 portfolio approach to investing, which we explain

in the book, and have a process for moving worthy new projects through their pipelines efficiently. These companies report a 10–15 percent premium in price-to-earnings ratios over their peers, and their five-year growth rates are impressive. They embrace innovation in the culture and make it safe to fail. Examples include familiar names such as Google, Johnson & Johnson, and the remarkable Tata, sometimes called "The GE of India," a corporation that in a single, two-year period showcased 3,300 implemented innovations in various digital technologies. We profile a 170-year-old French water-hygiene company that has reinvented itself around the theme of sustainability and continues to flourish and grow.

I didn't need to ask Howell's sales team about where they thought their Big Pharma employer fit in that typology. I'd heard similar laments from employees across a wide spectrum of industries, large and small. The theme is familiar: it's difficult to advance new ideas and ways of doing things. There's resistance at every level, and there are too many levels. There are also those fears. Fear of senior management. Fear of lawyers. Fear of jeopardizing one's own career to bet on a long shot. Fear of internal resistance, fear of external disapproval. Fear of do anything but playing it safe. Fear of almost everything, instead saying no to new ideas—because that's so much easier.

All of these fears and all of these layers of management lead to companies, often swaddled in a thick cloak of legal representation, whose cultures are defensive, reactive, and suspicious of change. I've worked with my share of companies like this, including one that was cynically referred to as a "law firm that just happens to sell pharmaceutical products."

Howell's team was describing something similar. "Well," I said, "this is helpful to know. So you guys are innovative and creative, and you have some good ideas on how to get this drug into the hands of the patients who need it. But the organization is blocking you out of fear, some of it understandable, some of it knee jerk?"

"That's about the size of it," said Ken.

"Good, then we'll take a closer look at that shortly," I said. "In the meantime, let's look at how you're currently doing things in getting your drug to market and ways you can improve your results. Then we'll look at how to do all of this in a way that ensures you don't break rules, at least any rules that would get you fired."

I paused. Howell nodded his head adamantly in agreement. The rest of the group looked on somberly, skepticism still written across their faces. They had tried before and not succeeded. Could this time be different? But I had admitted to them that my strategy involved bending or bypassing a rule or two. They liked that. "If I have to, I'll hand-deliver our proposals to the CEO," said Alyssa, with a wink.

The team had to develop a strategy for marketing the new drug, which they did using the 5C's approach that forms the basis of this book. The first thing we tackled was the customer. How well did our group understand the audience they were trying to reach?

I posed the question. "Okay, so 'Customer First' is how we describe it in our rubric. And now I'll ask you to enlighten me. Exactly who is your customer here?"

"Doctors," said Ken confidently.

"Yeah," said the ever-wise Jim. "But which doctors? Are you talking to neurologists, cardiologists, rheumatologists . . . or maybe you want to just do an email blast to everyone in the AMA?"

A titter of laughter. "Seriously," he continued, "this disease manifests itself differently in every case, so we're not certain which specialist is treating which patients, at least not initially."

"You're right," said Kim, the woman with the doctorate. "I've been thinking about this. And I believe the customer is the patient—the patient taking the medicine."

"I don't want to be a cynic here," said Denise. "But isn't the customer whoever is going to be paying for this? And wouldn't that be the insurance companies?"

A lively debate ensued.

I finally interceded. "Okay, so how about this? For now, let's choose one of these customer groups, and let's define the problem we're solving for them."

The group got quiet.

"The problem, Lorraine, is that the customer doesn't know they have a problem," said Kim. "I mean, our job is to help inform the doctor and the patient that we have a drug that can transform their health. So we have to find them and then get to them with that message. And our company puts restrictions on how we get to the doctors and the patients and what we say to them about our drug. How do we fix this creatively?"

I smiled.

"Now we're getting somewhere," I said.

With me serving as the facilitator (and, when energies flagged, champion), the team identified everything we knew about their customers. I scribbled each bit of demographic and psychographic information and what we knew about diagnosis patterns on the whiteboard. But the team soon realized there was a lot they didn't know about their various customers and those customers' needs. That alone—the huge gap in their understanding—was an "ah-ha" moment. This team had confidently assumed they knew everything there was to learn about who they were selling to. Know your audience. That's rule number one for a salesperson, right? But now the team saw there was more research to be done.

It took a few more meetings—and some more spirited exchanges of views—among the team members, but before long, the team, recognizing that there were a number of potential customers for this new product, had narrowed it down to the one they felt they should target. It was Alyssa, the fiery young member of the team, who nailed it. "The problem is that the customer—the patient—doesn't know they have a problem," she observed. "Meaning, our job is to help inform the doctor and the patient that we have a drug that can transform their health. We need to address that creatively."

This was an important insight. Over the next few weeks, I gave the team assignments culminating in the development of a plan—based around the 5C's—to drive sales growth. The three-month plan incorporated what we'd learned about the customers and the appropriate messaging; the risks we might encounter and how to overcome the biggest one—resistance to change and fear of failure, internally and externally; an assessment of who in the organization would be our likely allies on the plan (and from whom we could expect resistance); and a road map addressing the potential obstacles along the way and how we could continue to innovate and pivot our way to success.

The plan and process were essentially the same ones I will guide you through in the pages of this book. And, I'm happy to say, it worked!

Not only did the team now have the ammunition they needed to convince management of their strategy, but also they had a detailed road map to implement their plans. When we had our final readout in December—three months after that initial workshop—the formerly somber faces were aglow with the satisfaction of success.

"I feel pretty good about this," admitted the veteran Jim, holding up a hard copy of the proposal he and the team had put together at the end of our time together.

"You should feel good about it," I said. "You all should."

"There are still some issues to work out," said a beaming Howell, who seemed a lot less stressed out than when I first met him. "But I feel like the organization is finally understanding what we're trying to accomplish. They like the approaches we've come up with and are committed to helping us succeed."

The role of the innovation-oriented management consultant is sometimes a frustrating one. In a project like this, I'd worked cheek by jowl with my client's team; gotten to know many of them pretty well; learned a lot about the marketing of treatments for rare disease; and seen at least some of the fruits of their labors.

But what I was really there to do was help instill in this team an innovation mindset and, using some of the principles that I will share with you in this book, give them a road map to navigating the all-too-common barriers in corporate innovation.

For them, this road map included developing creative ways of making the drug more affordable and accessible to currently diagnosed patients; using data and AI to better target patients for earlier diagnosis; and process improvements like enhancing the collaboration between rare disease sales and corporate functions and upper management. But I wasn't there for some of the key meetings with senior management as the team presented the plan I'd helped them develop. Some time later, I got a text from Howell:

"Success! We're moving ahead with the plan. Thanks, Lorraine."

I was proud of the team and exhilarated by the way they'd used the 5C's to not only identify the right audience but also successfully launch this new product—essentially saving their jobs. Within six months, they'd far exceeded their sales expectations. I'm happy to say that the rare-disease division at this Big Pharma corporation is no longer on the chopping block. In fact, they're now a golden franchise. Howell's budget was increased significantly.

In a phone conversation soon afterward, Howell signed off by reminding me what I'd told them at one of our first meetings. "Remember that, Lorraine?" he said. " 'No fear, no failure'? I wasn't sure then, but I am now. We put aside our fears and focused on what was best for our customers. We tackled the problem using that rubric you gave us, and you know what? We're a success!"

Now let's get to work and ensure your success as well.

1

FEAR OF FAILURE AND THE 5C's—
LESSONS FROM THE RISE AND FALL
OF IBM WATSON HEALTH

The success of launching a new product hinges on what I call the 5C's of successful innovation. Although there is some overlap, these are, by and large, distinct from the Laws of Innovation I posited in my first book, *The Innovation Mindset*. Those laws were designed as steps to help an individual bring their great idea from inception to market. The 5C's are principles that can help spark and nurture the flames of innovation on the organizational level. Heading the list of these principles is what I call a "Customer First" mindset.

Throughout my career, I've seen how that kind of mindset can be a catalyst for some of the most important and most enduring innovations. On the flip side, I have seen what can happen when the customer is second—at best—and it's a lesson I learned in a very unlikely place: IBM Watson Health, where I served as general manager. In the fall of 2020, I accepted an offer to become part of a new leadership team charged with mounting a turnaround of the business unit, which had been unprofitable since its inception in 2015. Watson Health was formed from the $4 billion acquisition of four companies, all with different forms of healthcare data and analytics, with a goal to make Watson a leader in healthcare artificial intelligence (AI). By 2020, when I joined, IBM had sunk an additional $3 billion into the business unit, with no improvement in results. IBM decided to stage a turnaround by bringing in a new leadership team to reduce costs and improve sales, with the goal of selling the company. I was there to grow the life sciences business and help with the exit to a strategic partner or private equity firm. Watson Health had some really smart and enthusiastic people, and none were brighter and more hardworking than the computer science engineers.

My colleague Raj headed the 250-person research division. When he invited me to join a Zoom meeting with him and his team of engineers in the winter of 2021, I anticipated a convivial, productive brainstorming session around new ways to harness the power of Watson, which had already become the most popular automaton in America since R2-D2 and C-3PO charmed audiences in *Star Wars*.

That morning, Raj opened up the Zoom meeting with his customary infectious enthusiasm. "Thank you for joining the meeting. Lorraine, the team is excited to discuss with you some promising innovations we've been working on in biotech."

With thirty years in pharma and medical devices, including roles at the National Institutes of Health, Bristol Myers Squibb, LabCorp (acquired Covance), and IQVIA (formerly Quintiles and IMS Health), I had been invited to this meeting in part because of my years of experience with biotech clients. "Given your experience," Raj said, "we are eager for your feedback on a specific project that is ripe for biotech customers."

It was hard not to share in Raj's enthusiasm. With a PhD in computer engineering, he loved coming up with new ideas for products and solutions and described his job as head of research at Watson as "the most fun job in the world."

And why not? At that time, everyone had heard of Watson. It was cool. It was the future. It seemed invincible. The supercomputer—named "Watson" after IBM's founder Thomas Watson Sr.—had been trained to predict word patterns and had demonstrated its prowess in a memorable appearance on *Jeopardy!* Over the course of three episodes of the popular quiz show that aired in February 2011, IBM's Watson DeepQA computer soundly defeated two all-time human *Jeopardy!* champions, Brad Rutter and Ken Jennings.

The computer's knockout blow came when, in Final Jeopardy, Watson correctly wrote the correct response to this clue: "William Wilkinson's 'An Account of the Principalities of Wallachia and Moldavia' inspired this author's most famous novel."

Watson had wagered $17,973, and so when it answered correctly—"Who is Bram Stoker?" (and indeed it was *Dracula* that he was inspired to write by reading Wilkinson's book)—Watson took its winnings to a total of $77,147 (later donated to charity), which was far more than the two humans took home. ("Quiz show contestant may be the first job made redundant by Watson," quipped Jennings after the show, "but I'm sure it won't be the last.")

The New York Times marveled at Watson's performance on *Jeopardy!*—and what it seemed to portend. "For IBM," wrote John Markoff, "the showdown was not merely a well-publicized stunt . . . but proof that the company has taken a big step toward a world in which intelligent machines will understand and respond to humans, and perhaps inevitably, replace some of them."[1]

Watson may have been cool, but it didn't come cheap. The hardware costs alone were $3 million. The machine itself was the size of a small room and could process the equivalent of a million books per second. Still, its success on *Jeopardy!* generated a lot of buzz. Watson was profiled on CBS's *60 Minutes*. It had much-publicized chats with Serena Williams and Bob Dylan. But amid all the promise and hype, many folks, both inside and outside of IBM, didn't know (or didn't wish to acknowledge) that it was a big reach to go from writing an algorithm to beat a game show contestant to applying Watson's powers for, say, cancer detection and treatment recommendations. (Watson Health was formed to harness Watson's AI prowess for the healthcare industry. Other uses of Watson were being applied throughout IBM.)

But those were the voices in the wilderness. Most of us weren't thinking about Watson's limitations at that point but were concentrating on its potential. Like Raj, we were all dazzled by the possibilities of this early form of AI.

From his Zoom background, a wall-sized bookshelf filled with textbook spines, I could see Raj was in his home office in New York. Yes, Raj, a leading researcher in AI, still loved to read books. "Raj, I see you're an art history buff in addition to a computer science geek," I teased. "Look at that shelf with all those books about Renaissance art."

Raj, in his mid-50s, with dark-rimmed glasses and a neatly manicured mustache, chuckled jovially. He had been educated in India before coming to the United States for his PhD at MIT. His research spanned AI and machine learning, cloud computing, quantum computing, and data analytics in healthcare. Ever since my arrival at IBM as general manager of life sciences, he had sought me out to share ideas. We both reported to the CEO, who encouraged us to collaborate on bringing new solutions to market that could grow the life sciences business. As general manager, I was responsible for the profit and loss, operations, and supporting sales and marketing of our products and services for our $150 million unit.

For someone like me, who has spent much of their career studying the innovation process, it was thrilling to be involved at this level and on this kind of cutting-edge technology with someone like Raj and his team at IBM.

IBM! There was a time in America when those three letters were synonymous with innovation, technology, and the best and brightest minds. Some of that aura had faded in recent decades, as high-tech giants sprang up on the other side of the country from IBM's headquarters outside of New York City. But IBM was still creating terrific products—Watson seemed proof of that—and still hired brilliant people like Raj.

"I'm ready to hear what you and the team are working on, Raj."

Raj explained that the team had been collaborating with a major US-based medical device company that wanted to measure function and mobility in people suffering from pain.

Based on those metrics, they would develop a pain severity algorithm that the device company planned to offer to healthcare systems treating patients suffering from pain and to biopharma companies developing pain-management therapies. The device company and Watson Health were working under the auspices of a cocreation agreement, a popular approach for working closely with clients on the design and development of new solutions. IBM and other tech companies regularly used these agreements to create new patentable solutions that the tech firm could then develop and market to other customers. I knew that, if and when this solution worked, it could have far-reaching implications for a number of pain-based conditions and generate interest not only from pharma but also from the healthcare system at large. The pain market was $69 billion, with a compounded annual growth rate of 5.8 percent, one of the leading growth markets in the life sciences and healthcare.

Raj was explaining this to the team, and I was listening, nodding along, until he addressed me and said something that provoked mild concern. "We want you to join the team as our commercial lead," he said. "We're hoping you can help us with our sales and marketing materials and introduce us to pharma customers in your network who have an interest in pain." He went on to tell us that his staff had already compiled a list of fifteen companies and had set up meetings with some of them.

"We'd love for you to join us, Lorraine," he said.

I put my hand up. "Raj, hold up, my friend," I said. "You're getting ahead of me. I have at least a dozen questions about the technology, the development plan, the relationship with the device company, what kind of prototype we're designing, and how we're going to generate data for a beta test." I went on, "While this is potentially interesting and a game changer, we are far from ready to start sales meetings with potential customers."

Customer First was a discipline I was trying to instill across the business. Since its inception in 2015—four years after Watson's triumphant performance on *Jeopardy!*—Watson Health had compiled a rather troubling track record for its new products, primarily due to a lack of understanding of customers' businesses and a confirmed market for the solutions. These glaring setbacks included a diabetes app with a major medical device manufacturer; a project with MD Anderson, a leading cancer healthcare system in Texas that had sunk $65 million into the cocreation of an oncology diagnostic tool that didn't work as planned and received extensive press coverage—all negative; and a clinical trials recruitment solution with Mount Sinai Hospital that also failed to achieve the desired results.[2]

The rush to cocreate solutions with a client without a disciplined plan and clear metrics on results had led to many commercial disappointments for Watson Health. I was here to fix that for the Life Sciences division, which served biopharma and medical device clients and was the fastest-growing division of Watson's business segments.

I didn't want to see another embarrassment for us. So, I outlined for Raj and his team the Customer First process we needed to follow.

First, we needed to observe the experience of patients suffering from pain and map out their diagnosis, treatment, management, function, and mobility—in other words, the patient journey. I asked whether they had done this with the client yet or whether the project been led by engineering to date.

Second, we needed to talk to customers—those who would both prescribe and pay for this pain-tracking device—to better understand if they viewed this as a solution they were willing to pay for. This meant focus groups and interviews with physicians, patients, regulators, and payers. We needed to also understand which types of patients would benefit and where this solution would fit in their lives.

Third, we needed to talk to pharma companies about their drug development efforts in general to see if a device like this would fit into their plans.

We needed to gather this basic information and learn more about our customers before we pitched this solution to anyone, especially pharma.

"Creating a solution with a customer to solve a market need they've identified is certainly a good way to approach innovation," I said. "But the customer has to be part of the process. We really need to know as much as we can about them. Given that the team on this project is composed only of engineers, I would say we have some customer research to do. We're still missing their perspective!"

Raj scratched his head, and his team nodded at my words. "We had a garage session with the medtech customer, Lorraine. You know, where we met in a room for a day and a half and brainstormed the solution. But you're right, it was with the engineering team only."

A "garage session" at IBM was a brainstorming technique adopted from the forty-year-old "design thinking" company IDEO's human-centered approach to innovation. At IBM, the process involved meeting with the client, aligning on business goals and objectives, and generating ideas to create a solution together. For example, we ran a garage session with a Big Pharma client who was redesigning their information technology (IT) department to include AI and digital technologies. These were exhilarating creative sessions, an ideal way to build rapport with a client and glean useful insights on their business, but honestly, I never saw much come out of the sessions. Too often, the ideas we generated required a lot of follow-up; both companies needed to get back to their day-to-day business of selling products and generating revenue, and all the genius that was sparked fell to the wayside.

Raj was bullish, however, about the value of the garage sessions for the launch of this new product. "My team thinks this thing has legs, especially since the client is willing to co-invest," he said. "And we are aware we need a business case and to show we can generate income, so that's why I had Suzanne schedule a meeting with a potential Big Pharma client in the pain space. We hoped you would bless our plan and open some additional doors."

I appreciated Raj's enthusiasm, but I tried to remind him that real innovation takes time and only reaches fruition after a series of steps.

"Raj, you're giving away too much too early," I said. "This is still at the idea stage. We don't even have a prototype." Talk is cheap, as the saying goes. I knew that any Big Pharma company would accept a meeting with Watson Health about an exciting new solution. But if that solution hasn't been fully thought out, if we don't have a well-cultivated understanding of who the patient is, who the customer is, what problem we're trying to solve, and whether someone is willing to pay to solve the problem, well then, we'd look foolish. I suggested to Raj and his team that we work on the answers to these questions and reconvene in a few weeks.

I know it's hard to believe that IBM, a 112-year-old company recognized as one of the top three trusted brands in the world, with a litany of firsts—the first record-keeping system, the first mainframe computer, the first quantum computer—could miss the need for solid customer market research in new product development. But in my three-decade career, I have seen this time and again, not only at IBM.

How does it happen?

Often, corporations spend more time looking inside than out—meaning they are focused on what's going on inside the company and not spending equal or greater time understanding customers, stakeholders, competitors, the market, and the environment. These companies develop a narrow view of the market, and they innovate based on an internal perspective of the problem when the heart of the innovation mindset requires that we understand what's happening around us.

It goes like this: The company believes that because they are cocreating solutions with a customer—let's say in a garage session like the one Raj mentioned—they have done sufficient customer research. They then succumb to pressure to get new solutions to market quickly to meet shareholder expectations. But most lack a disciplined process for seeing the innovative idea through to the commercial marketplace, which the 5C's address in this book. And the culture embodies wishful thinking, a can-do mindset, maybe hubris, even when the data tell them to pivot or halt their efforts.

They wrongly believe that if they throw more money and resources at the problem and stick it out a little longer, their luck will change.

In the case of Watson Health, they were dependent on Big Blue's capital. Watson Health wasn't singled out in the company's financial statements, so people outside the company didn't know Watson Health was losing money year after year. The CEO at the time, Ginni Rometty, described AI in healthcare—and cancer, in particular—as the company's moon shot and Watson as their best chance at having a big impact. Rometty was interviewed on *Charlie Rose* in 2015.[3] The company execs and managers took their marching orders and aggressively pursued becoming a leader in AI and healthcare.

In the case of IBM Watson Health's investment thesis (one of the 5C's we call Chance because it's associated with investment risk), they poured money into innovation, but their investment approach didn't align with strategic goals or follow a process, nor did it adhere to adequate metrics, all of which are critical to innovation success, as we'll learn later in this book. Some accused Watson of the old saying "overpromise and underdeliver," particularly in the project with MD Anderson.[4]

Based on articles cited earlier in *The New York Times* and *Slate*, MD Anderson sank $62 million into the Watson experiment, according to a public audit. What went wrong? The hospital lacked adequate patient data to run the algorithm. Much of the data was in doctors' notes, and Watson had not been designed for natural language processing at that level. Watson's team lacked an understanding of MD Anderson's situation and the capabilities needed to build the solution. An executive at MD Anderson was famously quoted in news articles as saying Watson for cancer "was a piece of s—t."

Quoted in a 2017 story in *StatNews* that detailed Watson's growing problems, a South Korean cancer specialist who used Watson was a little more subtle in his criticism. "Watson for oncology is in the toddler stage, and we have to wait and actively engage, hopefully to help them grow healthy," said Dr. Taewoo Kang.

Despite the doctor's kind words, I'm afraid Watson Health was already on its deathbed. The lack of customer understanding and confirmation of their business requirements was beginning to spark widespread grumbling in the medical community, and unwanted attention in the press was emblematic of a deeper issue.

"IBM, in its rush to bolster flagging revenue," wrote *StatNews* reporters Casey Ross and Ike Swetlitz, "unleashed a product without fully assessing the challenges of deploying it in hospitals globally."

How was this happening? Why was Watson launched without seemingly adequate research into the marketplace? The reasons are complex and multifaceted. But there's no doubt that some of the problems would have been avoided if the company had truly embraced a Customer First mentality.

WHAT IT MEANS TO PUT THE CUSTOMER FIRST

There are three steps for putting the customer first that would have helped Watson Health. Following these in your organization is the first step toward nurturing successful new ideas.

Observe needs and translate them into demand.

The great management guru Peter Drucker wrote about the need to observe how people work, identify their needs, and then translate that need into demand for something better. "The only purpose of business is to create and keep a customer."[5]

Design firm IDEO and its CEO, Tim Brown, spent a career popularizing human-centered design and integrating it into corporate strategy—but what were the results? If it's such a natural thing to do, why don't we see more successes on the level of Uber, Airbnb, iPhone, Fitbit, eBay, and PayPal? The problem is that conventional research methods don't uncover how people work and, importantly, how people work around problems to create jury-rigged solutions that satisfy them, at least for a time. So their needs may be obfuscated, obscured even from them!

For example, I would love to have a pair of lightweight running shoes to use when I travel. Most of the weight in my suitcase is from shoes, and the rubber in running shoes is a big culprit. I haven't found a shoe that meets my needs, and the rental of shoes when you travel never really took off. I work around this by using an old pair of lightweight orange track shoes when I travel. I carry my orthotics in a separate pouch to distribute the weight. This method reduces my luggage weight by almost two pounds.

If you surveyed me about running shoes, you might never know I need a better solution and would be willing to pay for it. Why? Because I consider my problem solved, even though it really isn't. (These track shoes are on their last leg, no pun intended, so I need a solution in a hurry.)

How do we identify the latent needs of people—needs they don't even know they have, like Steve Jobs with the iPhone? Or going further back, recall Henry Ford's famous (apocryphal) quote about the development of the automobile: "If I had asked people what they wanted, they would have said 'faster horses.'"

To truly identify need and convert it into demand, we must observe customers or people in the real world. In my first book, I said I demand one hundred customer interactions/interviews from my students and consulting clients, and I mean it.

Observe what people do more than what they say.

This is best done through what has come to be a buzzword, "ethnographic research," which anthropologists use to learn about people and cultures. In the business world, it involves watching a customer at work—what they do and how they act. One of my favorite examples of an ethnographic researcher in action is Phil McKinney, the former CTO of Hewlett Packard, who spent his weekends at Circuit City, watching customers in the electronics aisles so he could learn what they liked and didn't like by observing them pick up and handle devices. Many companies use a technique called "user experience testing," where they give a participant a problem to solve and see what they do. At technology companies I've consulted with, we bring customers together at the office or the lab and let them play with our solutions and products, watching them but also getting their feedback on what they like and don't like and why.

Apply empathy when designing new solutions.

Once we've observed the customer and how they work, we move on to the next step: empathy—connecting with people emotionally so we see the world through their eyes. Nitesh Bansal is bringing the Customer First experience he learned as senior vice president of the India-based software giant Infosys to R Systems, the global software company of which he is now CEO. "I spent the first three or four months in my new role meeting clients. I wanted to learn about their business needs, intuitively, first," he says. "Don't get me wrong. I looked at the numbers, so I know how much business they are doing with us. But I wanted to first understand their business from their point of view." Nitesh believes empathy is one of the most important customer research tools because, as he says, "it helps us understand what clients really need, not what we think they want."

Nitesh is right. Inside-out thinking gets a lot of companies into trouble. In the fifty customer meetings he held, he says he learned what his customers do and what R Systems does for them. He answered questions: Are we core or peripheral to their business? Are we a support function? How important are we to them?

Nitesh boiled those questions down to what he calls the Six W's:

- Why does the customer want this?
- What problem are they trying to solve?
- Why do they have this problem?
- Why hasn't this problem already been fixed?
- Why does this have to be solved now?
- Why do they think we can help?

Nitesh likes to share an example of this from his time at Infosys: a case study of a clothing retailer who wanted to install a store tracking system to discount their products at multiple stores at a specific time. The Infosys analyst who was assigned to the project couldn't answer the "Why and What" questions listed above, so he called the customer and interviewed him. The client told him that a particular clothing item was not selling, and they wanted to discount it. The analyst asked why the customer thought discounting across the board would work. He offered to help select the right stores where the excess inventory warranted a price reduction. It took him thirty minutes to write the additional software code to discount in some stores and not others. It worked—as it turned out, only certain stores needed to discount. Nitesh says, "The client wrote to us praising this guy. They said, his solution saved us a million dollars in a set of stores where otherwise we would have made an across-the-board discount but didn't." Nitesh adds, "Now, that's what we mean by understanding the customer, applying empathy. To me, that's the heart of Customer First."

Two of our 5C's, Customer First and Chance, affected the fortunes of IBM Watson Health, as did another: Collaboration. In business, collaboration is not defined as who gets along with whom. It's a strategic imperative. Collaboration can drive exponential growth when business lines, service functions, and other key stakeholders in the organization all come together around the customer, around the company's goals and objectives, to create solutions that make a difference. It's on display when a software company encourages cooperation among its software products, consulting services, and functions such as IT and legal to solve customer problems and grow customer share of wallet (the amount a customer spends with a supplier). It results in upselling, cross-selling, adjacent sales, and, importantly, happier customers and topline growth.

The problem at Watson is that the 7,000 people were working in a silo, albeit a large one, separated from IBM. Watson was in some respects a start-up, except that it was formed by the merger of four established companies, each of which had its own history, culture, and problems. When they were combined, there was no effort to integrate them and create a common vision and shared culture for Watson. The company became the sum of its parts. What's more, Watson was separated from the mothership operationally and from a market perspective, despite the fact that its budget came from IBM. There was inadequate collaboration with Big Blue. Often the Watson and IBM teams would find themselves competing for the same client. There were valiant efforts among senior leaders to address this gap and work together, but red tape and the lack of an incentive structure to ensure the right type of collaboration always got in the way.

Another of the 5C's is Culture—the environment that allows innovation to flourish or not. An important aspect of culture is making it safe for employees to try and fail, fostering ideas that emerge from analysts and managers, as we learned in our Infosys example with Nitesh Bansal. Data show that companies that embrace innovation—from the C-suite down through middle management and below—create a culture in which innovation is encouraged and celebrated. I like to refer to it as try, fail, learn.

Laurence Blumberg, serial entrepreneur and cofounder of Syntimmune, which was sold to biotech company Alexion for $1.2 billion, has experience creating a culture of innovation in start-ups, a very different proposition from dealing with a corporation. His innovation meetings were done over pizza. "We got the team together on Friday afternoons over pizza, and we just hashed things out," Laurence says. "We came up with our most creative ideas at those pizza meetings. The feeling was collaborative, open, even irreverent—and people's genius really shone through because they felt safe to express their wildest ideas."

By contrast, the Watson culture was transaction based. Despite the presence of smart and sociable executives like Raj, I don't think a lot of senior IBM officials would have been seen brainstorming with the entire team every Friday over pizza.

Another of the 5C's is Change. Maybe it all starts with a desire for change, which is why the 5C's are nonsequential and don't happen in a linear fashion. Change is an organization's ability to pivot as the situation dictates; customers, markets, and environments change, and companies need to adapt and show resilience and perseverance. They also need to embrace change from the inside—bringing all the voices to the table, like Laurence did. We know that a diversity of perspectives around the table is good for innovation. If you only work with people who think like you, you'll be in an echo chamber, getting approving nods to ideas you all agree on. Healthy debate without bureaucracy occurs when a team embraces diverse perspectives. Thinking out of the box means getting out of your box and checking out someone else's so you can understand how they think.

In the case of Watson, IBM waited too long to pivot and poured out a lot of capital and resources to meet Rometty's vision. By the time the board ran out of patience, Watson had been losing money for seven years. After IBM had invested billions in Watson, the company was sold for parts in 2021—for $1 billion.[6]

Watson is a case study of a company formed around the belief that if they had data, AI, and customer solutions in healthcare, they could create and dominate a new market—AI in healthcare. Remember the movie *Field of Dreams*, where Kevin Costner's character, Ray Kinsella, hears a mysterious voice saying, "If you build it, he will come"? When Ray plows under his cornfield to build a baseball field, the ghosts of famous players, including baseball great Shoeless Joe Jackson, magically appear, save the farm, and reconcile him with his estranged dead father. I tell my students to not fall in love with their own idea and succumb to the *Field of Dreams* trap of innovation—build it and they (customers) will come. But in many ways, Watson Health did just that.

In addition to wishful thinking, some, including commentators in the media, have posited that Watson Health lacked a shared vision of exactly what they were creating, spent too much money on projects, lacked a disciplined approach to innovation, and didn't manage innovation strategically. The vision for AI was immature and not based in reality—one can't go from writing software to outguess a trivia game to diagnosing cancer and recommending the best treatment. It's a testimony to a failed business case and operating model, as noted in the articles in *The New York Times* and *Slate*.

Many have learned valuable lessons from the Watson Health story, especially me. It's why we chose to highlight, in this book, innovative companies that are doing things the right way. That's what you'll find in our Champions of Change profiles, including the one in this chapter about innovator Erez Naaman of Scopio Labs.

CHAMPIONS OF CHANGE

Lessons from Fearless Founders and Enterprising Executives

Erez Naaman
Cofounder and Chief Technology Officer for Scopio Labs, Tel Aviv, Israel

The passion for innovation, says Erez Naaman, "is really what defines me." His curious, inventive nature was demonstrated at an early age: As a boy growing up in the suburbs of Tel Aviv, he carried around a notebook—observing, thinking, and wondering about the world around him. And he had a goal: to write down an idea for one new invention a day.

"Some of my ideas were funny," he recalls. "And some were actually invented by others afterward." In the former category was an automatic salt-and-pepper shaker that hung on springs and dispensed a specific amount of both condiments. In the latter category was a flashlight with an additional switch that could be hit to trigger a small siren. (This was later developed by others for use in neighborhood watches of warfare-related attacks.)

Erez's talents led to his acceptance into Talpiot, an elite Israeli Defense Forces academy. Talpiot recruits the brightest students but also stresses independent and original thinking. It was the perfect innovator incubator for Naaman, who, after graduating from

Talpiot and Hebrew University, served eight more years as an officer in the Israeli Air Force. After retiring at the rank of major, he went to work as vice president of engineering and business development at OrCam, a leading Israeli high-tech start-up.

In 2014, he and Itai Hayut cofounded Scopio Labs, a company he describes as focused on "digitizing microscopy and bringing it to the modern age by providing access to rapid diagnostic tools for the first time."

In 2022, Scopio accomplished a string of notable achievements, including a $50 million Series C investment round and US Food and Drug Administration 510(k) clearance of its X100HT device, allowing Scopio to address the needs of labs of any size. In quarter 3, Scopio signed a global distribution agreement with Beckman Coulter, a global leader in clinical diagnostics, a huge vote of confidence in Scopio's Full-Field digital cell morphology platforms as the new market standard, replacing the use of the manual microscope, which had been the gold standard for decades.

In 2023, *Fast Company* named Scopio Labs to its prestigious list of the World's Most Innovative Companies.

Erez offered some thoughts on how to foster innovation in your organization:

Looking to create a culture of innovation in your organization? Then hire innovative people.

Sound obvious? No, says Erez. "It's not typically an attribute that job candidates are asked about. When you want to hire someone, you check for technical skills; you want to know if they work well in a team. But people who really think creatively, people who can really generate new inventions are few and far between. You need to make sure you're looking for that kind of person."

To help identify those people, Erez says he often asks job candidates the following question: Can you give me a situation where you encountered a problem and solved it in a creative manner? "Creative people will typically offer several examples that are truly unique within five or ten minutes," he says.

Another option is to ask an open question that requires creativity and imagination to answer. One of Erez's favorites is: You have a barometer and need to measure the height of a building. How many ways can you think of to do it? "There are at least six solutions I'm aware of," he said. "Most people come up with two."

Hands off, management!

Once you've found the right people, you need to put them in the right environment. "You can't micromanage innovative people," Erez says. "And you should encourage them, and give accolades for their successes, but you can't punish them for mistakes. That's part of the process."

Some innovate; others implement.

Although everyone can become more open to change, not everybody is born inventive or creative. "You can't expect to have a company that is entirely filled with innovative people," Erez says. "You need those creative minds, but you also need those who know how to implement and manage those ideas." Thus, he says, the idea of creating a culture that is entirely based around innovation is both unrealistic and impractical. "Most organizations have different subcultures," he says. "It's a matter of finding the right people." One common denominator, however, should be self-improvement. "Everybody in the organization should be encouraged to keep getting better."

Put it in a box.

"People don't innovate in an open-ended space," Erez says. "If I tell you, 'Come up with an innovative, life-changing idea,' it would be hard. It's like, 'Tell me a funny joke.' We freeze up. Where to begin?" The enlightened manager, he says, will create boundaries: a framework within which ideas can be focused. "If I create a box in which you're supposed to innovate, it's much easier." He offers this example: "What if I tell you, 'When I go to the doctor and they take my blood, it takes so long for them to get results and figure out what's going on. Can you come up with an idea to fix that?' Now you can immediately come up with specific questions. Now we have a framework for our thought process."

Say "yes" to new ideas—no matter how far-fetched.
Erez has a specific rule about brainstorming sessions at Scopio: "You never say 'no,'" he says. "You don't disqualify any idea, no matter how outrageous. If someone says, 'I have an idea: Let's harvest green cheese from the moon,' you don't respond by saying, 'No, that's nuts . . . the moon is not made of cheese, and how would we harvest it anyway?'"

Instead, says Erez, all ideas must be welcome. "If you start saying no, people stop coming up with innovative ideas. They start going with the safe answers. I try to be adamant about the fact that there really are no stupid ideas. When you manage the room in a brainstorming session, it is like an improvisation exercise. The right response is, 'Yes, and. . . .'"

For more information, see https://scopiolabs.com/.

2

THE 5C's: CUSTOMER FIRST—ASKING THE RIGHT QUESTIONS

I t's not often that college students are asked their opinion, so when I queried Scott on his thoughts about higher education, customer service, and innovation, he sounded happy to be asked—and had plenty to say.

Scott, who is in his forties and the father of five children, is a member of that increasingly large cohort at colleges today—the adult learner. According to some estimates, these students compose nearly a quarter of the undergraduate population in America. Generally defined as those age twenty-five and over, adult learners are typically working full-time jobs while juggling classes, usually at night, weekends, or online, to finish a degree that might help them advance up the ranks in their careers or perhaps blaze a new career path.

Scott's path was, well, rather innovative. A native of New York, he graduated high school in 1991 and immediately landed a job at a telecom company in New Jersey. "My job was fixing computers," Scott recalls. "Back then, you didn't need a college degree for that."

He repaired those old mainframes well enough to get hired by a medical device company. "My job there was backing up tapes," he says, with a chuckle. "Something else we don't need to do anymore." (Thanks to that little thing called the cloud.)

But while Scott was moving up the ranks of the IT industry, he was still eager to learn—to acquire not only the skills that could help him in his career but also the kind of worldly knowledge that comes with a college education. With encouragement from a mentor, Scott earned his associate's degree in graphic arts from a regional school designed for first-generation college students and adult learners. "My favorite subject was philosophy," he says. "It had absolutely nothing to do with my job, but it really opened up my mind." Scott then did a stint in IT at a state agency in New York and was recruited to a university in New York, where he was eventually promoted to a senior position in IT.

As an employee of the university, Scott took advantage of a tuition-remission program that allows employees to attend classes for free. He earned his bachelor's degree in history in 2020 and is now pursuing a master's in a career-related area, data analytics, while working full time in IT.

I applaud Scott's commitment to lifelong learning and his determination to expand his horizons, intellectually as well as professionally. What made his ideas particularly valuable to me was that he sees higher education from two perspectives: from that of a high-ranking college administrator and that of an adult student, taking online classes leading toward his master's degree.

When we sat down for a Zoom call in the middle of the spring semester as part of my research for this book, I learned that Scott was eager to share his perspective. "As a working adult student, I see several design flaws in higher education," he said, looking rather professorial himself with his reddish-blond beard and black-rimmed glasses and speaking with the command and authority of someone who knows their subject well.

First and foremost: "Registering for courses is time-consuming and inefficient," he said. Not an uncommon complaint; I hear that from my students frequently. Class information is incomplete, and sometimes, classes close or are canceled and students are not notified. Sometimes it's even as simple as students not knowing what classroom they're supposed to go to. (A teacher colleague of mine recently sat in an empty classroom on the first day of a semester, wondering where the students were. They finally arrived en masse, apologizing that the room listed on their schedules was incorrect, and the whole group had to march over to the registrar's office to find out the correct meeting place.)

Scott's second objection was another one that students have been voicing for decades: unrealistic expectations of the time that they can devote to their schoolwork, expectations that are rooted in faculty's lack of awareness (or disinterest) in the realities of their students' lives. He offered an example. "The professor for one of my classes assigned us four textbooks. Four? I barely have time to read one!" Indeed, some professors seem not to realize that alternative student populations—adult learners like Scott, international students, and first-generation students—might require alternative pedagogical approaches. It's not a question of these students being lazy or unmotivated to read. Heck, like many adult learners, Scott is juggling a job, family responsibilities, and his schoolwork. He is a good time manager and a hard worker. Must we put up additional obstacles to his academic success?

Yes, students need to learn the material. But they shouldn't have it fed to them in a cookie-cutter way, and the demands of working students' lives needs to be considered. As a wise educator once said to me, "You don't teach the subject, you teach the student."

And that led to Scott's third (and, I thought, most insightful) criticism: "Every course is so different in the way it's organized," he said. "I understand that you can't teach an English class the way you might teach a chemistry lab, but there should be some general consistency. Each instructor requires different learning software and different types of assignments." Scott had two ready examples for this point. "In one of my classes, I had to use four different types of software," he said. "I'm an IT guy, so I know that the material could probably have been consolidated onto one or two platforms. That would have taken a little extra work the first time for the instructor, but it would have made life a whole lot easier for us students."

Inconsistency is rife when it comes to grading as well. "Many professors include class participation as part of their grading," Scott said. "That's fine, I get that. But one of my professors used our participation on an online discussion board for that part of the grade. I'm sorry, but a live Zoom class and a digital discussion board are two very different environments. I don't think it's fair to grade participation the same way in both."

While I also see some of these issues from the instructor's point of view, I couldn't help but nod as Scott ticked off his well-thought-out criticisms.

"Okay, well, I see we've been able to isolate some problems," I said with a chuckle, as Scott grinned.

"Uh-oh, hope I'm not getting anyone in trouble," he joked.

"No, no," I said. "This is how positive change starts. With constructive criticism. But, Scott, you are someone who has had management and higher-education experiences, and I'm curious: What do you think needs to be different organizationally? What outcomes are you looking for?"

I've got to hand it to Scott. He wasn't just there to complain. He had come to our interview prepared. Along with the list of problems, he was able to tick off a list of improvements that, in my opinion, could be made at his college and at many colleges and universities in America: better student support for administrative matters, more affordable technology that hosts all readings and assignments in one place, a universal software system for online learning, and opportunities to interact with peers and build a network to foster learning outside the classroom.

What Scott was really talking about though was a Customer First orientation, one of the most important of our 5C's. Until recently, higher education rarely even used the word "customers" to describe the people who pay the bills: students and their families. And perhaps because, traditionally, they were dealing with a population of young adults, colleges tended to treat these customers as if they were still in high school, largely incapable of making their own decisions.

To be sure, there are many passionate and caring people working in colleges who always have the students' best interests at heart. And, to be fair, many institutions have heard this or similar messages and are working to improve these areas. But, traditionally, the customer in higher education is not treated like those in any other business. And now that customer is changing. Many college students are adults, like Scott. Many are the first in their families to attend college. Others come from backgrounds that have not prepared them well for the rigors of academia. Still others are looking for very specific educational credentials to help propel their careers, not necessarily the traditional four-year degree. Servicing these new categories of students will require fresh thinking. And as with any other innovation, what's really needed to make that happen is a deeper commitment at the organizational level.

I asked Scott about the trend among some universities to create schools of professional studies to better meet the needs of adult learners. His response should be posted in the conference rooms and C-suites of every college and university in America—or at least those committed to improving their product.

"Any college specializing in the needs of adult learners, to be successful, is going to need a model that is very different from conventional college programs and processes and procedures. It needs to have the freedom to create its own way of working—a way that is designed for the working adult. It can't get held back by the traditional university bureaucracy."

That's a customer talking. And Scott put his finger on a problem that can stifle creative thinking and innovation in any organization, not only those in colleges and universities.

"DEATH BY A THOUSAND EMAILS: HOW ADMINISTRATIVE BLOAT IS KILLING AMERICAN HIGHER EDUCATION"

That was the headline of a 2024 article in *The Bowdoin Review*, in which writer Lance Dinino reports on a dubious first achieved by a bastion of American higher education, Yale University. This New Haven, Connecticut–based pillar of the Ivy League can now count among its ranks more administrators than students (5,460 of the former to about 5,000 of the latter).[1]

That truly is an astounding and (in my opinion) deplorable statistic. Imagine if Starbucks had more store managers than consumers of its coffee; if Honda had more sales personnel than buyers of its automobile. They'd be out of business! But some in higher education seem to think that this kind of inverted structure is sensible and sustainable.

It's not.

"Like many of its peer institutions," Dinino wrote, "Yale faces an epidemic of administrative bloat: a self-perpetuating ecosystem of expensive career administrators who are far removed from the classroom. In the last three decades, the number of administrators and managers employed by American colleges and universities has ballooned, dwarfing the growth of student and faculty populations."

In other words, while their customer base is changing, organizations in higher education have been creating a new, multilayered bureaucracy that has little to do with understanding, much less addressing, the needs of those customers. This new, top-heavy structure is hardly conducive to fresh thinking, but it is a symptom of a larger issue.

As someone who has served on the front lines of higher education for fourteen years—and at some nationally prestigious institutions like Columbia, Princeton, the Wharton School, and more recently, Yeshiva University and Moravian University's new School of Professional Studies and Innovation—I've had the opportunity to observe firsthand, from the classroom perspective, how the current educational system is failing to meet the needs of its customers. And as anyone knows who has had to alter a grade, battle a bursar, or change their class schedule around, when it comes to servicing and assisting these customers, colleges generally get a poor grade in customer service.

So where does one start to change this fundamental aspect of higher education and of other large industries where rigid thinking holds sway? When I wrote about the need to understand the customer in *The Innovation Mindset*, I asserted that first we need to ask ourselves this question: "What's wrong with what?"

Meaning, what specifically are the problems that prevent a more Customer First mindset from flourishing, and in what areas of the organization are these obstructions happening?

Let's pose that question here: What are colleges not doing to better enhance and facilitate the needs of changing student populations? The article in *The Bowdoin Review* pinpoints one: an unwieldy administrative structure that diverts resources, time, and attention from the academic side. But there's another problem that most college customers—students and their parents—would point to: cost.

According to the Education Data Initiative, as of May 2024, the average cost of attendance for a student living on campus at an in-state, public, four-year institution was $27,146 per year, or $108,584 over four years. Out-of-state students paid an average of $45,708 per year or $182,832 over four years. For private, nonprofit universities, the bill was $58,628 per year or a staggering $234,512 over four years. That's far beyond the means of most families and another reason student debt became such a huge and politicized issue.

Another challenge is that the entire higher education process is organized around an arcane system of credits, coursework, and complex scheduling logistics that seem based not on the needs and wants of customers but all too often on the interests (and convenience) of faculty and administration. Also, although this is changing in some disciplines, much of the content taught in curriculums today is still highly theoretical and not designed to give students the experiences, insights, and skills needed for today's fast-changing, technology-driven working world. One of my undergraduate students at Wharton shared his concern about the relevance of his education at one of America's premier business schools: "We're training to be 'spreadsheet monkeys,'" he said disgustedly. "And we'll probably be displaced by AI soon after we graduate, if not before. But nobody seems to recognize that, or if they do, it's certainly not reflected in how we're being taught."

I was keen to understand more about the flaws in the education system today and do my part to help craft a new solution. In March 2024, I started a new role as professor of practice and business program director at Moravian University's new online School of Professional Studies and Innovation (SPSI).

Let's take a closer look at this private liberal arts college nestled in the bucolic Lehigh Valley, near the Pocono Mountains in eastern Pennsylvania. Moravian was established in 1742 by members of a Protestant church of the same name. It is the sixth-oldest university in the United States, and although its origins are as a theological seminary, it considers itself an innovator in higher education, having created what we would now call one of earliest co-ed campuses back in 1759.

The area in which Moravian's campus now sits is named for the Lehigh River that skirts its boundaries. It's best known for its precolonial and industrial history and as being the home to Crayola Crayons, Martin Guitars, and craft beer. But while much of the area's economy was once tied primarily to the smokestacks and foundries of now-defunct Bethlehem Steel, the region has bounced back: healthcare, IT and software, manufacturing and engineering, and education are among the vibrant new industries that have helped shake the rust off the Lehigh Valley and transform it into one of the fastest-growing regions in the Northeast. It accounts for $43.3 billion of economic productivity annually, according to the Lehigh Valley Chamber of Commerce.

Moravian's School for Professional Studies and Innovation is designed to serve those working in these new industries; they are its new customer base, so to speak. "The university offers a seamless and innovative customer experience for adult students returning to complete their degrees by handling administrative tasks such as registration and payment assistance efficiently," says Deirdre Letson-Christofalo, EdD, associate provost and dean of the school.

"This frictionless support ensures that students can focus on their studies without the stress of managing bureaucratic and administrative hurdles."

The school is also doing something that's vitally important to a Customer First orientation: They're listening to the concerns of their customers—adults students like Scott. "We're helping to create a consistent experience across courses, using one universal type of technology and software," says the dean. The new program also emphasizes the practical over the theoretical: "We want to help the learner to learn, and to be able to apply their new knowledge immediately, so our faculty are practitioners from industry who can share their real-life experiences with our students."

Moravian's new initiative is certainly not the only college program that is adopting a more "customer-friendly" approach (a term that is probably still anathema to many in higher education). Interestingly, this shift toward addressing the kinds of concerns voiced by students like Scott has been most evident not in graduate programs but in community colleges—the two-year institutions that now represent the fastest-growing sector in higher education, according to the National Student Clearinghouse Research Center. One of the most successful of these is a college few have likely heard of: the Lake Area Technical Institute in Watertown, South Dakota, which has close ties with local and regional industry (and designs its curriculum accordingly) and holds its students accountable, as if they were in a job setting. It works. The two-year college boasts an astounding 99 percent job placement rate—in large part because they recognize that they serve two customer bases: the students they educate and the local industries that will hire them. This, the college's president Michael Cartney told *The New York Times* in 2017, is the secret to their success. "We view college as a pathway, not a destination."

Moravian's Dean Letson-Christofalo takes a similar view. "We're designing education around the student as opposed to the student having to fit into a box we created, which is the way education has traditionally been designed," she says.

That's not to say every college program must be vocational, that studying the classics and the arts isn't valuable. And I agree that at least part of the goal of college should be to broaden students' worldviews. But new thinking is needed, and that new thinking needs to start by giving higher education a "C"—meaning a more customer-centric approach.

Moreover, this is not just an academic, ivory-tower debate. It's becoming a question of survival. According to a 2024 study from the Hechinger Report, colleges and universities are closing or merging at the rate of about one per week. The contributing factors, wrote *Forbes* magazine in a response to that alarming report, "are by now all too familiar—sagging enrollments, decreased tuition revenue, inflation, soaring labor costs, and unsustainable debt often taken on in futile attempts to build or spruce up facilities that might attract more students."

Underlying many of those reasons for failure is a chronic lack of focus on customer needs.

CUSTOMER FIRST DOESN'T MEAN ASKING THE CUSTOMER TO TELL YOU WHAT YOU SHOULD DO

Despite the growing list of colleges closing their doors, Customer First innovation in higher ed is happening—sometimes within the walls of a college (such as at Moravian) but often outside the campus.

The four-year-old start-up company Extern is one example of the latter. The problem they are addressing is what founder CEO Matt Wilkerson calls "a supply shock in the economy," one that's developed because companies aren't providing enough work experience training for college students. If you peruse entry-level job listings, you'll learn, as LinkedIn recently published, that nearly 40 percent of entry-level jobs require three or more years of work experience. College students I mentor comment on this "chicken-and-egg" problem all the time. How do I get work experience unless I have a job, and how do I land an entry-level job that requires three years of experience as a fresh college graduate? They have a good point.

Matt says undergraduate and graduate student frustration is at an all-time high and Extern's timing couldn't be better. "Traditional students in undergraduate programs need job experience integrated with their academic curriculum, and internships are hard to come by, especially for students from marginalized communities, rural areas and local colleges," he says. "Extern's mission is to create a new way for students to get on-the-job experience while in college." How do they do this?

Extern invented a new form of real work experience called the remote or virtual externship. Instead of focusing on on-site work at a company, it created a remote platform that can match students with various employers. It works with the employer to design a project for students that is useful to both them and the employer. For example, a project they did with *National Geographic* involved students from around the globe investigating water hygiene and other sustainability initiatives in their home countries. The magazine gathered useful information for an article on global sustainability initiatives, and the students learned about sustainability in their home countries.

Then Extern manages the students and the project, creating a completely turnkey operation for the client companies. It integrates work experience with the student's classroom learning so there is alignment between learning objectives in coursework and the professional experience the student gains. Their platform unites students, companies, and higher education institutions around the credential that matters most: professional experience.

On behalf of client companies, Extern had created and delivered more than 75,000 externships as of December 2024 in which students and career switchers from all backgrounds enhanced their skills, built their résumés, and launched their careers with real-world work experiences. Extern has teamed up with global brands, Fortune 500s, corporate foundations, investment funds, start-ups, and more to deliver these expert-led, learning-integrated projects to students. Nearly half of these students have gone on to land internships and full-time jobs with Fortune 1000 organizations alone.

It's too early to comment on how Extern and Moravian's School of Professional Studies and Innovation will play out in the long run. Both are clearly innovators in the field of education who understand the importance of a Customer First mentality. Still, we can learn something from them—how their approach can be applied to other organizations, including for-profit companies, about the dos and don'ts of good customer service, informed by effective customer research.

"TELL US WHAT WE WANT TO HEAR!": THE EPIC FAIL OF CUSTOMER RESEARCH

Many companies and organizations in various industries believe they have adopted a customer-centric approach—and they pride themselves on giving customers what they ask for. Organic fast foods, water bottled at the source in throwaway plastic bottles, natural pain relief products with few side effects, longer-lasting electric car batteries. The thinking is that giving customers what they say they want guarantees success. How do we know what they want? By asking them to describe it to us. And by asking them questions that (subconsciously or not) are really designed to provoke answers that tell us what we want to hear. We share this information with R&D, who then busy themselves developing concepts and prototypes. And then we're surprised when, after incorporating all this customer-research insight, the product or service is finally introduced and the market's reaction is a resounding flop!

Why? Because companies ask the wrong questions and expect the right answers—meaning the answers that confirm management's previously held opinion. This undermines not only innovation but also, ultimately, the bottom line. Shortly, we'll offer you some better questions to ask customers as part of your research.

But the first step is to understand the distinction between being customer driven and being informed by customer input.

The balance between the two is important. Any new product or service must achieve business goals along with customer goals, and it's a delicate balance to integrate the two so that your customer loves your solution and your company can make money at the same time.

Anthony W. Ulwick says customers should not be trusted to come up with solutions; they aren't necessarily expert or informed enough. Ulwick, author of the book *What Customers Want*, points out that what customers typically say they want is based on what they have already experienced. They can't be expected to imagine products or services based on emergent technologies, new materials, or processes that they wouldn't necessarily be aware of. For example, what customer would have asked, in a focus group, for the microwave oven, Velcro, Post-It Notes, or the iPhone? It's true even when the customer is a business. For example, at the time the transistor was being developed, radio and television manufacturers were still requesting improved vacuum tubes.

Ulwick goes on to point out other risks of being overly reliant on what customers say they want. This can result in incremental improvements over true disruption that can leave the field open to competitors. This was the case in 1973, when Kawasaki introduced its Jet Ski. At the time, the company dominated the market for recreational watercraft. When it asked users what could be done to improve the Jet Ski's ride, customers requested extra padding on the vehicle's sides to make the standing position more comfortable. It never occurred to the customers to tell Kawasaki they wanted a seated watercraft. The company focused on giving customers what they asked for, while other manufacturers began to develop models in which the customer can sit down and enjoy the ride. Those competitors have long since bumped Kawasaki—famed for its motorcycles, which are never ridden standing—from its leading market position.

Meeting customer demands to the letter also tends to result in "me-too" products. Customers merely ask for missing features that other manufacturers already offer. In the mid-1980s, for example, market studies conducted by US automakers Ford, Chrysler, and GM revealed that customers wanted cup holders in their vehicles. Because Japanese manufacturers had provided this feature for years, when American companies finally added the frequently requested cup holders, none gained an advantage. Customers merely said, "It's about time."

Another danger arises in the common practice of listening to the recommendations of a narrow group of customers, often called "lead users"—customers who have an advanced understanding of a product and are experts in its use. Lead users can offer product ideas, but because they are not average or typical users, the products that spring from their recommendations may have limited appeal. Consider what happened to U.S. Surgical, a medical instrument manufacturer now owned by Tyco. Acting on recommendations from lead-user surgeons, U.S. Surgical introduced a set of instruments that could rotate and move in many directions. The instruments were unveiled with great fanfare at a national medical show in 1991. Although the initial excitement led to some orders at the show, reorders amounted to less than 5 percent. The reason: The lead users were simply too sophisticated. Although most surgeons applauded the improvements, they found the new instruments too difficult to use.

Finally, attempts to give customers exactly what they say they want can lead to the creation of products that they're not really interested in paying for—no matter what they said in a focus group or survey. Software companies, for example, operate sophisticated user laboratories and employ keystroke-tracking technology to build incremental improvements into their products. Yet most users avail themselves of less than 10 percent of the software's overall capability—and grumble when they feel forced to pay for upgrades.

Instead, research should focus on the problem and the customer's desired outcomes—that is, the problem they are trying to overcome and what they want a new product or service to do for them that's better or different. Maybe customers want a friction-less educational experience like Scott, the working adult learner from Moravian; or maybe they want a more structured internship experience, one that is more project oriented, can be completed remotely, and in which there is a structure to assist, as Extern tries to provide.

Understanding your customer's needs, interests, desires, and problems is, of course, a fundamental part of the innovation process for any organization. The form the solutions take, however, should be up to you to figure out. Don't expect the customer to tell you.

PRINCIPLES FOR EFFECTIVE CUSTOMER RESEARCH TO HELP GUIDE YOUR ORGANIZATION TO REAL INNOVATION

Let's now look at a methodology for conducting research that can help you better understand the customer's perceptions and needs, without expecting them to provide the solutions. These are the kinds of questions your organization should be asking if they want insights that can lead to genuine customer-focused innovation—and not just confirmation of what you already think they should want.

Principle 1: Start by Defining the Problem, Not the Solution

Customers don't have enough information to evaluate a solution. Why should they? They're not working in your office, devoting their lives to thinking about your product or service. They're interested in solutions to problems; they're interested in products or services that will make their lives easier or allow them to accomplish things more effectively. When conducting research, many interviewers start with what should be one of the last questions: "How do you like my new product . . . my solution to your problem?" Instead,

they should first ask questions that will help them better understand what those problems are. I posit that there are six "killer"
questions that need to be asked in order to get their opinions on
your proposed solution. Let's pose these questions through the lens
of Geoffrey M. Roche, formerly head of strategy, planning, and business development for the Pocono Medical Center (now part of the
Lehigh Valley Health Network). Geoffrey, currently head of Workforce Development at Siemens Healthineers, explains the problem
he was tasked with fixing back in 2011.

At the time, the Pocono Medical Center served the needs of
local residents and tourists visiting the popular waterparks and ski
resorts in the Poconos. "It was the waterpark capital of the world,
and we were seeing over 90,000 emergency room visits a year at
a thirty-bed emergency room," Geoffrey explained. "As you can
imagine, this was very taxing on the clinical team and expensive to
maintain. We needed a new solution and fast."

To arrive at that solution, Geoffrey and his team first needed to
answer the following questions:

Who is the customer? It may be hard to believe, but this fundamental
question can sometimes be hard to answer. For example, if you're a
biopharmaceutical company bringing a new drug to market, is your
customer the patient who will be taking the drug, the physician pre-
scribing the drug, or the policymakers approving the drug's distri-
bution? In many cases, it's all three! At three different stages in the
drug-launch process, the customer will be patients, physicians, or
policymakers, and you need to listen and understand the needs of
each and address them in a way that gives each what they need. In
the case of the Pocono Medical Center, Geoffrey's customers were
the hospital administrators concerned about the operational and
financial implications of the demand surge for emergency room
(ER) services during tourist season; the ER team seeking relief
from the patient burden on their facility; patients; and tourists and
local residents, who expected responsive, high-quality care appropriate to their medical needs. Geoffrey's solution had to address

the needs of the medical center, his main customer, but in a way that also ensured the needs of the ER staff and patients were being addressed. It also needed to help improve the reputation of the ER because a competitor healthcare system was building a new hospital ten miles from Pocono Medical Center.

What kind of work does the customer do? The premise of design thinking, a popular methodology, is the use of social science research techniques, such as ethnography—observing the customer in their natural habitat (living, working, and playing) in order to get a 360-degree view of them and their needs. When Geoffrey was analyzing possible solutions, he visited the resorts to better understand how they were designed, where the entrances and exits were located, and how many people came in and out at various times of the day. He went to the ER to examine patient traffic, and he learned about the patients in the ER and the kinds of issues that typically brought them to the hospital. He also analyzed data on the park visitors, including age ranges, seasonal spikes in visits, length of time in the park, and length of stay in the area.

How well do you understand the customer's current business situation? Geoffrey's customer, the Pocono Medical Center Emergency Room, was designed to treat 65,000 patients a year or 178 patients per day. They were well equipped to handle emergencies, but much of their patient traffic needed treatment for scraped knees and elbows, dehydration, bruises from falls, and other non-life-threatening issues. These minor injuries were a distraction from the more serious issues ER personnel were trained to triage.

What is the customer's pain point? "Pain point" is a common way to refer to the problem the customer is experiencing—and that you are determined to solve. Pocono Medical Center was facing tremendous financial pressure and strain on the physicians, nurses, and team maintaining an ER that was already seeing more patients than it was designed to handle. Their goal was to reduce ER visits by 40 to 50 percent and to only see patients experiencing true medical emergencies. At the same time, they wanted to ensure that tourists' and residents' healthcare needs were being properly triaged and tended to.

How big is the problem? "Problems," as we know from life as well as business experience, are relative. Some impact only a few individuals; some have a severe impact on a broader population. Some are really more minor annoyances that can be easily addressed without enormous expenditures of time and money. Others may require a solution that takes a greater commitment of resources. So we need to first stop and objectively assess the significance of the problem. When Geoffrey was looking at the impact of ER visits on the hospital in the Poconos, he learned that the cost and labor burden of caring for those 90,000 patients a year in the ER was significant—40 percent more than the 65,000 patients the center was designed to handle, outstripping the hospital's budget and resources. So it was a big problem that the healthcare system and the resorts needed to solve right away.

What solutions have been tried and what were the results? As innovators, we are so eager to ask customers what they think of our solution that we fail to recognize that they have choices. They can stay with the status quo, use a competitor's solution, or even come up with one of their own. In the ER example, the center's only option at the time was to treat all patients, from those with minor bruises and scrapes to people with life-threatening injuries. That wasn't a satisfactory solution and everyone knew it. "We knew we had to expand the emergency room to 43 beds by using capacity at the hospital that was no longer needed," Geoffrey says. "But even that wasn't enough to really address the problem." Geoffrey and the executive team came up with a creative solution: they opened new urgent care centers conveniently located near the parks and educated patients on when to use them for care. And because Geoffrey and the team wanted to go above and beyond and offer concierge healthcare to tourists, they installed kiosks at the parks and offered a mobile app to help direct people to the urgent care centers instead of the emergency room and to allow patients to preregister for their visit. They called it PoconoRapidCare.com.

What does the customer think of your solution? The final question is the one all too many product developers start with. Geoffrey only asked this question after he'd asked the previous six—and the responses were positive and significant. "We reduced ER demand by 20 percent when we launched the urgent care concierge service. Consequently, we grew demand for the urgent care centers by 20 percent, so they were happy." The Pocono Medical Center and the ER were pleased with the lightened load; the resorts were happy because they could boast of great concierge healthcare services. And patrons of the parks were satisfied, knowing that if they needed medical help, a care center could be quickly located and a visit scheduled on the app.

Principle 2: Articulate the Customer Outcome

Once we've gone through the steps of observing the situation, listening deeply to understand the problem, and asking the customer the right questions, we're ready to define what the customer needs or wants. What do they want that's different from their current experience?

Let's go back to the story of Moravian University's new approach to professional education. Dean Christofalo's team at Moravian translated the educational experience or outcome desired into this outcome statement: "We want to address the evolving needs of adult learners in the workforce by creating frictionless access to education."

In the case of Extern, the remote internship facilitator, the team is designing the outcome around the user—the extern (or student) is at the center of the work experience. They are saying, in effect, "We want to create a platform that unites students, companies, and higher education institutions around the credential that matters most: professional experience."

In both examples, the area of need and the desired outcome are clearly stated but not the specific solution and its features. Those will be articulated at the next stage of the process.

This kind of thinking is evident with innovative companies in all kinds of industries, as we learned from our interview with Christopher Harrison, former global product manager and business unit president at Stanley Black & Decker. Chris, who is currently an advisor to Bain & Company and board director in the building products space, oversaw an important product category for the company called "Striking & Struck," which includes hammers, chisels, and shaping tools. His customers included retailers—primarily the hardware and DIY stores around the world that sell tools. Chris was tasked with leading global product teams to develop and deliver products to these customers. "We held regular focus group sessions where we would include the product teams, customers, and end users," he recalled. "In one instance, I wanted to prove a point to a Home Depot buyer about a particular DIY hammer we wanted them to carry that would retail for under $10.00. They were already selling a low-price-point, private-label hammer for several dollars less that they were sourcing from overseas. It really popped, with the signature Home Depot orange color, and was a high-volume seller for them. We knew ours was better, and we were confident that end users would be willing to pay a few dollars more for a higher-performing, more durable tool. But we had to prove it to Home Depot."

Instead of doing a phone survey or conducting a more traditional focus group, Chris and his marketing director decided to go directly to the source. They visited approximately a dozen Home Depot locations around the country and stood in the parking lot, holding both hammers. "When customers approached, we just held the hammers up, and politely asked them to hold each, one at a time. I'd then ask them, 'Would you be willing to pay $9.99 for this (yellow) hammer versus $6.99 for this (orange) one?' I didn't provide any other information. I simply let them examine the two products and decide for themselves."

Now that's hands-on end-user research! And it was focused on giving these customers the outcome they wanted—better value with a high-performing, long-lasting DIY product experience. Ultimately, the vast majority of the hundreds of Home Depot shoppers polled said they'd prefer the slightly more expensive yellow-and-black hammer over the orange-and-black Home Depot version. "That turned out to be a key factor in the decision process for Home Depot," Chris said. "Our hammers did very well for them, and we gained more shelf space at the higher price points as well."

Let's look at one more example. As a principal designer for GE Healthcare, Doug Dietz had been designing diagnostic imaging equipment for more than twenty years when he realized that young patients' actual experience of this cutting-edge technology, in this case the MRI machine was, well, awful. Children were often so terrified by the prospect of lying alone inside the MRI machine, which is huge and noisy, that they often had to be sedated just to get through the experience. Doug realized that what kids and their parents wanted—the desired outcome, so to speak—was a diagnostic experience that was not scary and that might even be pleasant and fun! Doug put together a team of experts to solve this problem, including staffers from a local children's museum, kids, and hospital staff.

The goal was not only for children to lose their fear of the MRI machine but also to make the procedure enjoyable—a tall order, for sure, but one that Doug was committed to achieving. He visited preschools and kindergarten classrooms and engaged the children in drawing their favorite adventure stories. Based on his interaction with them, he got the idea for designing the MRI like a pirate ship, complete with gangplank and portholes. The result was an innovative, design-driven solution that utterly transformed the experience for children. At a TedX San Jose event, Doug described the reactions he overhead when the new MRI debuted at the Children's

Hospital. "I heard a little girl say to her mom, 'That was fun! Can we come back tomorrow?'"

How gratifying that must have been for Doug, who, in addition to holding over twenty patents, is now a consultant, helping organizations think more creatively about customer solutions. His mission: "I hope to help folks amp up their creativity and innovation practices in order to make the world a better place."

Principle 3: Swing the Hammer! Define, Test, and Refine the Solution with the Customer

Just because your solution is on the market and customers are buying it, don't assume you're done! Many companies have precipitated their own demise by becoming overly confident in their ability to predict what the market and customers want. We can cite such high-profile companies as Blockbuster, Nokia, and Kodak—not to mention various telecommunications companies—who didn't see customer dynamics changing and didn't pay attention to competitors addressing customer needs that they didn't know existed.

Other companies have become complacent, forgetting about the customer and the need to delight them. A former executive of Dupont explains that, in the early 2000s, the corporation was losing its focus on the customer in exchange for quarterly earnings. "We brought on our own problems by being satisfied with being good enough, and our customers noticed," she recalls. "It became much harder to sell Dupont's products during that stretch of time."

We related the story of Chris Harrison and his colleagues fanning out to Home Depot parking lots across the country to show the DIY giant that their customers were willing to pay a little more for a Stanley-branded product with a higher level of performance and longevity. Mindful of the risk of taking one's eye off the customer, Chris says Stanley Black & Decker worked very hard to stay in tune with theirs. "We talked relentlessly about our customer and our end user," he says. "While our customers were extremely valuable retail partners like Home Depot, Lowes, and other smaller, two-step destinations, we understood the person swinging the hammer was the one who mattered most in the end."

Who's swinging the hammer among your customers or end users? Identifying them, asking them the right questions, and listening to what they say—without letting them dictate your solutions—are the first steps in successful change. Indeed, you could say that the process of innovation begins with identifying the outcomes customers want to achieve; it ends in the creation of items they will buy. When desired outcomes become the focus of customer research, innovation is no longer a matter of wish fulfillment or serendipity; it is instead a manageable, predictable discipline.

CHAMPIONS OF CHANGE

Lessons from Fearless Founders and Enterprising Executives

Catherine Reynolds, Entrepreneur-Philanthropist
Chairman and Chief Executive, Catherine B. Reynolds Foundation

"Who is Catherine Reynolds and why has she been giving away millions of dollars?" That was the question correspondent Mike Wallace posed in a December 2002 story on CBS's *60 Minutes*. It was about a woman from a family of modest means who helped create a $200 billion per annum industry that many wouldn't think of as innovative in any way, shape, or form: finance—specifically, the financing of higher education. Meaning college tuition and how to pay for it.

We talked earlier in this chapter about the need for change inside academia and the need to make education accessible and affordable. Catherine recognized three decades ago that the best way to democratize education for students and their families was to create a new financial infrastructure. She set out to build that novel infrastructure under the auspices of EduCap, which disrupted higher ed and spawned today's $200 billion US private student loan industry.

"I came from a family that highly valued education," recalled Catherine when I spoke to her recently. "We weren't wealthy, but we were surrounded by books, art, and music, and getting good grades was a high priority. We were taught that education was the key to a better life."

Catherine, who grew up in Jacksonville, Florida, also knew that this key to a better life was something not everyone could afford. After graduation from Vanderbilt, she moved to Washington, DC, where, in 1988, she met an interesting man with an interesting idea: Reverand John P. Whalen was president of Catholic University of America in Washington, DC, and chairman and CEO of the Consortium of Colleges and Universities of DC, Maryland, and Virginia—the first private entity to provide student loans for middle-income families at the thirteen colleges and universities it represented. "Father Whalen identified the need for middle-class families to get loans for college tuition, and I figured out how to create a sustainable business," Catherine said with a big smile. "It was a challenge."

At the time, the only federal loans available were for the 15 percent of the population defined as needs based. Another 10 percent of students were the children of the wealthy, who didn't need any help. But there was a big group in the middle that had no support system for financing their child's education.

Father Whalen was impressed with the young accountant and suspected she could do more than help his organization prepare financial statements. He hired her as their comptroller. "When I started, I realized they were technically bankrupt, meaning they hadn't filed for bankruptcy, but they were close," she says with a laugh. "He forgot to tell me that."

Unfazed, Catherine went to work. She was determined to build a sustainable financial model that would help middle-class students access loans for their education. One of the many innovative aspects of the model she created involved partnering with the

US Chamber of Commerce. She recalls pitching them on the idea: "Your platform (of employee benefits) serves an educated workforce, and our platform is designed to serve an educated citizenry. How about if we offer our program to members of the Chamber as an employee benefit and advance both our missions?"

The Chamber embraced the idea and promoted the loan program in corporate materials it provided to its members. Lunchrooms across America boasted posters asking if employees needed money for college and directing them to the EduCap toll-free number. In effect, the Chamber served as EduCap's marketing channel, helping them target the right audience—namely, credit-worthy individuals who had income to pay back their debt. Catherine notes that, at the time, there was no precedent for credit-worthy people being given long-term loans and therefore no history of how those loans would perform. The default thinking was that student loans required a government guarantee. EduCap challenged that thinking by providing long-term loans to corporate employees, credit-worthy individuals who could pay back their debt without a government guarantee. "That helped us de-risk the program," Catherine explained. "The employees had jobs and could pay their bills, so they were less risky an investment than if we went directly to families and students in the general population. We knew the employees had a paycheck and were credit-worthy—we knew they could pay us back."

Once Catherine's team built the model, they approached Norwest Bank as the first underwriter. Norwest appreciated how creative the model was, and they especially liked how the "halo effect," as Catherine described it, reduced loan risk. She explains, "Because employees got a loan marketed to them through a company benefit program, they were committed to pay it back on time for fear the company would find out if they missed a payment. That was not a consequence of our program course, but it had the unintended benefit of ensuring the program had better performance and payback." And in fact, the loan program had less than a 1 percent per annum default rate—unheard of.

A FISTFUL OF FIRSTS FOR EduCap

The infrastructure Catherine established to finance higher education meets the very definition of innovation—that is, to create a new solution that solves a customer's problem and one they are willing to pay for. But EduCap was so much more. It established a model that has been the progenitor of the modern-day student loan program. Consider the series of "firsts" in Catherine's model:

- The first student loan with no government guarantee or safety net
- The first student loan program ensuring that the financial needs of both the lender and borrower were met
- The first student loan program of amounts up to $100,000 with long-term, fifteen- to twenty-year repayment terms and no collateral. At the time Catherine launched EduCap, the only private loans available were short-term signature loans with collateral such as CDs.
- The first program to use technology to gather data that could be analyzed to create underwriting discipline, derisk and price loans, and even help identify students for loans
- The first loan program to work with the financial rhythm of the family. At the time, federal programs allowed students to defer payments while students were in school. But students faced sticker shock when they graduated because of the accumulating interest. Catherine explains, "We didn't want families to experience that sticker shock, so we required payment of at least the interest on the loan beginning thirty days after the loan was administered. We described it as the cost of a daily cup of coffee." What happened was another pleasant surprise. Fifty percent of EduCap's portfolio chose to pay more than the minimum. EduCap had the data to prove it, providing yet another opportunity to build the confidence of banks in the program.
- The first loan application program for the digital age. Catherine's use of the technology at the time made the loan application experience private and easy—able to be done from the comfort of one's own home.

The student loan program was eventually acquired by Wells Fargo for a sum rumored to be around $800 million. A significant amount of the proceeds established the Catherine B. Reynolds Foundation, which continues to support many education-related causes. That's part of the story that *60 Minutes* reported. But for our purposes, I want to go back and look at how Catherine's success story is rooted in the main focus of this chapter: Customer First.

Mission driven

In my first book, I talked about what I called the Laws of Innovation. The first law held that a successful innovation must solve a problem. There was clearly a problem here and one that Catherine felt passionate about. "I believe in education," she says. "I believe that every student who wants to go to school should have that opportunity, and that finances shouldn't be the reason they don't." Passion counts. Drive counts. Commitment to a mission—not just to make a profit but to make an impact, a difference—that counts, too.

Decoding customer motivation is key.

Catherine and her colleagues used the digitally based student loan application data to glean understanding and insights about the attitudes and behaviors of the stakeholders they were serving. The testing not only revealed a triangle of customers—the student, the parent, and the employers—that were key to the success of the process but also provided something truly insightful. "We learned that there was a code of honor among these folks around the value of paying for education," she says. "We heard many of the parents-employees say that they would rather have missed a credit card payment than skip a payment for their child's tuition." Catherine also learned that families were embarrassed to borrow money for their child's tuition and having to discuss their personal finances with loan officers. They loved the private digital application process—it put dignity into the process of applying for a loan. Those are the types of insights that only come with in-depth, qualitative customer research and with listening to the customer.

The numbers don't lie.

Catherine didn't expect a major bank to make a bet on her idea simply based on a novel idea. They needed data. And Catherine had that covered as well. This aspect of her customer research didn't involve just speaking with the customer. Instead, she was able to analyze loan applications and create an objective picture of the loan programs' financial and market fundamentals. The data were compelling and, in tandem with the insights gleaned from the qualitative research, impressed the bank and other underwriters. "We had a disciplined, evidence-based process for pricing risk, selecting borrowers, and addressing the needs of our marketplace. Our offering ensured clarity, transparency, and ease of interacting with each other. Tech was a huge component, but we never lost sight of the human touch—our call center was staffed with highly trained, empathic professionals."

Believe in your customers, believe in your idea, and believe in the possibility of change.

The focus of this book is on innovation at the organization level. In Catherine's case, she had to persuade dozens of organizations—not only the bank but also major employers—that this idea had merit and that helping finance college educations for their employees and their children was a safe and worthwhile investment. It wasn't always easy. "Honestly, I ran into a lot of status quo thinkers," she says. "A lot of resistors. But we knew what we were doing was right, and we also had confidence that our model was sound."

Stick to your guns.

Undaunted Courage. That is the title the historian Stephen Ambrose gave to his 1997 bestseller about the Lewis and Clark expedition that explored the American West in the early nineteenth century. In a less dramatic but very significant way, Catherine demonstrated that same quality. She was undaunted by the naysayers and unintimidated by those who said that a woman in what was then a man's world of high finance couldn't possibly pull a multibillion-dollar package like this together. Although Catherine had support from her husband, Wayne, and her family, she believed in herself and believed in her idea—in part because she knew that the people involved, the families who benefited, were as committed to their children's education as she was committed to making EduCap the success it became.

Catherine's innovation story doesn't end here. She went on to create a college technology loan program with computer manufacturers including Apple and Microsoft. She and her husband Wayne continue their philanthropic work through the Catherine Reynolds Foundation and an educational initiative called the Academy of Achievement. And she continues to innovate. Recently, she cofounded VitaKey, Inc., with Dr. Robert S. Langer, a biotechnologist and chemical engineer at the Langer Lab at the Massachusetts Institute of Technology. VitaKey's first-of-its-kind technology delivers targeted and time-controlled release of micronutrients, macronutrients, and probiotics and can be used at every link in the food chain. It has the potential to be a game changer in ensuring quality and cost-effective access to nutritious foods globally.

You can learn more about Catherine B. Reynolds and her work at the Catherine B. Reynolds Foundation website (https://cbrf.org).

3

THE 5C's: CULTURE—INNOVATION FOR THE LONG HAUL

Gavin thoughtfully pondered my question, setting down his fork and squaring his arms around his plate, which boasted a healthy array of fresh raw vegetables and cooked grains. We were meeting over lunch at a popular restaurant in the suburbs of Philadelphia to discuss a talk on innovation I was scheduled to deliver to his legal services team at the company's upcoming annual off-site meeting. "Gavin, how would you describe your company's culture and what about it is working?" I had asked. Culture is a hot topic in business circles these days and was on the minds of the employees at PTC Therapeutics as they anticipated the company's founding CEO of twenty-five years stepping down and the chief operating officer taking the helm. It was all happening at the very same off-site meeting for which I was preparing my talk.

"PTC has a strong entrepreneurial culture, and our founding CEO is a big reason why," Gavin said. That CEO established and has maintained the company's values, behaviors, and rituals. He emphasized experimentation, high performance, and transparent communications. But now the CEO was stepping down, and Gavin, understandably, was wondering how that carefully nurtured culture could be maintained under the new regime. That's why I was there. "How do we maintain our spirit of innovation as we transition to the new CEO and align with his vision? Do you have any tips for us?" Gavin asked.

I did—in fact, that was the purpose of my talk: I needed to offer advice on how a twenty-five-year-old biopharma company could maintain an innovation mindset for the long haul. It's a challenge many companies face. When we examine cultures of companies that sustain high performance and drive growth year after year, New Jersey–based PTC is doing a lot right. At just under a billion in annual revenues and a thousand employees, the company is a leader in rare-disease drug innovation. They have a history of firsts—the world's first approved drug for a severe form of muscular dystrophy known as Duchenne; the world's first approved gene therapy directly infused into the brain; and a unique RNA-splicing technology enabling the development of novel therapeutics for the underlying causes of neurodegenerative diseases. Their core values reflect that spirit, emphasizing attributes of intensive collaboration, scientific expertise, cutting-edge biotechnology, and a relentless focus on the patient. According to Gavin, everyone from the administrative assistants to the executives are encouraged to offer their opinions and defend their point of view. "It is a safe place to experiment," Gavin assured me.

Their story is iconic. What company wouldn't want to emulate PTC? Surely it should be easy for them to maintain their innovative culture. But as we know from a multitude of failed cultures and companies throughout history, complacency is the enemy of innovation, and I applauded the employees' interest in preparing for a major leadership transition.

Now it was my turn to ponder Gavin's questions. Culture and innovation, I thought. What experiences from my own thirty-five-year career were relevant to Gavin's situation? I didn't remember culture being talked about as I started my career in the late 1980s, first in academia and eventually with publicly held companies. Was I clueless at the time, or was culture a subject that had only developed over the past thirty years? In fact, I may have been clueless about a lot of things as a twenty-something professional, but I was correct in my observation that culture is a relatively recent focus of business. Clearly, it has gained momentum in the ensuing years, as we'll learn later in this chapter.

Because culture is a relatively new concept in the lexicon of business, let's offer a definition, one that we'll explore and build upon later in this chapter.

And to answer the question of how we define business culture, let's first look at the definition of the word "culture." Those in the business of compiling dictionaries seem to go into overdrive with this word. Merriam-Webster has nearly a dozen definitions and subdefinitions of culture. On these and other lexicological sites, "beauty culture," "youth culture," "pop culture," and "cancel culture" are also listed as variations of the central concept.

Let's keep it simple. One widely cited definition describes culture as "a way of life of a group of people—the behaviors, beliefs, values, and symbols that they accept, generally without thinking about them, and that are passed along by communication and imitation from one generation to the next."[1] Innovation culture is defined as a workplace environment that encourages employees to share creative ideas and solutions. We'll come back to innovation cultures and how to recognize them later in this chapter.

In my own career, I've experienced a variety of cultures, as most of us have—from soul-sucking and demoralizing to inspiring and transcendent. As someone who embraces an entrepreneurial mindset, culture has always mattered to me, even before it became popular and I knew what it meant. I became good at recognizing, mostly intuitively, the environments where I could flourish and do my best work and ones where I needed to fit in a box, shut up, and get the job done. (I seldom lasted long in the latter.) But looking back, I always assumed I was the outlier—a natural change agent—who didn't fit in. I didn't realize until many years later that by examining an organization's culture, I could choose companies that were a good match for me, rather than just me being a good fit for them, something I readily encourage my students and mentees to do with great deliberation.

When one thinks about academic and government organizations, we naturally assume we'll encounter a staid, bureaucratic culture that doesn't embrace change or innovation. But that's not necessarily the case. I learned a thing or two about experimentation and change management, two critical components of innovative cultures, in one of my first jobs out of college, as a medical writer and eventually director of public affairs at Eastern Virginia Medical School (EVMS) in Norfolk. EVMS is renowned for a series of firsts in medicine. The first baby born by in vitro fertilization was delivered at the Howard and Georgeanna Jones Institute for Reproductive Medicine, established at EVMS in 1978. EVMS was also a site for one of the first clinical trials for the implantable insulin pump, and it was a research site for one of the first Lasik surgeries and cochlear ear implants.

Even the founding of EVMS was a novel, entrepreneurial endeavor. Concerned that the nearest major medical center was two hours away in Richmond, the Hampton Roads community wanted to establish medical research and clinical care capabilities in their region to address a physician shortage. A small group of physicians and business and civic leaders donated and raised money from the community and secured a small state grant to establish the school in 1973. Interestingly, the first students to graduate from the school, in 1974, were not physicians but rather art therapists, and the school remains renowned for its art therapy program. Around 1985, they recruited a new dean and president to expand the school's research program to attract grants, graduate students, and faculty and to advance care in the region. This mandate was embraced by the new dean and president. And all stakeholders, whether they were in bench or clinical research or were legacy or new to the school, were expected to get on board.

As a newly minted medical writer with a degree in journalism and biology from the University of Maryland, I joined the office of public affairs as writer in 1985. My first assignment was to interview every department head about their research plans. What an exciting project! The interviews were going well as I made my way through basic science departments in microbiology and immunology and clinical departments in ophthalmology and otolaryngology, but I had an unexpected response when I sat down to interview James P. Baker, head of internal medicine.

Dr. Baker was a pleasant-looking, middle-aged man with short brown hair wearing a white coat with his name embroidered above the pocket. He sat back in his office chair and looked at me evenly when I asked about his research. "Number one, who did you say you are? Number two, on whose authority are you asking me about my research program? And number three, do your superiors understand what we do in internal medicine? We take care of patients in underserved communities in eastern Virginia. We are not here to do research." He went on to say that although the school had attracted a number of celebrities, like the Joneses, for their work and research in reproductive medicine, those working in the trenches of basic clinical care were the unsung heroes.

Looking back, I'm sure I tripped over myself apologizing. I recall that the interview lasted only a few more minutes as Dr. Baker went on to describe what he called a research-like example of clinical care they were delivering to underserved patients in Northampton County, one of the poorest counties in Virginia. Dr. Baker has since passed, but the James P. Baker Award was established in his honor to recognize outstanding graduating residents in internal medicine. Presented annually by the EVMS, the award is bestowed upon a graduating internal medicine resident who demonstrates the ideals and skills of "the complete and caring practitioner of internal medicine."

Stunned after that experience, I debriefed with the director of the department, asking what I had done wrong. "You didn't do anything wrong," Sheila chuckled kindly. "We probably should have prepared you for Dr. Baker." I learned that not everyone, particularly those in clinical care, had embraced the new administration's research mandate, and some felt slighted by the fanfare being displayed toward the new incoming faculty. Fortunately, the new president was a seasoned administrator adept at culture change. In one meeting,

I witnessed him giving the resistors this advice: "The train has left the station so enjoy the ride or get off at the next stop!"

And I should note here that Dr. Baker was absolutely right in what he said (even if he could have demonstrated a little more patience with an eager young staffer). His department was responsible for training students and residents to provide care to the poorest of the poor in the area.

I'm sure Dr. Baker himself was a beloved practitioner—and his short-tempered response to my questions was an example of his passion for delivering the best possible care for the community. And yet here was clearly a "culture clash." But it was also a failure on the part of top management at the time to ensure that one of the organization's most prominent and respected voices had been brought on board with the new mission.

It was one of my first experiences with organizational culture— one that was in transition, embracing experimentation and new ways of working. The medical college hadn't yet gotten all of its employees aligned with the new direction. It had failed to reach a consensus with its employees. As my experience showed, the organization was struggling with change management. EVMS has recently experienced another major change. It has merged with Norfolk-based Old Dominion University. Academic mergers are a common occurrence given the challenging financial times both academia and healthcare organizations are facing. And like every merger, this will also challenge and perhaps change the existing organization culture.

When I moved to the for-profit side of the business world, I found that sustaining a culture of innovation in for-profit, publicly held companies wasn't that dissimilar to academia—key tenets were embracing experimentation and encouraging diversity of perspectives, coupled with a leader with a vision and commitment to ensuring that innovation flourished. I learned a lot about innovation and culture at Cognizant Technology Solutions, an Indian American IT consulting and outsourcing firm, founded in 1994 in Chennai, India, by Dun & Bradstreet and Satyam Software. When

I joined the company in 2015, CEO Francis D'Souza had built the company into a $19 billion global powerhouse in IT, and his commitment and plan to make Cognizant a leader in IT innovation was working well. Frank did two things that stand out to me as creating a culture where innovation could flourish.

First, he established and funded a bold initiative—an internal venture-capital investment program—to cocreate solutions with clients who would use the solution for a period, say three to five years, at which time they would transfer ownership of the solution to Cognizant to offer at an enterprise level to all of its clients. This co-investment worked well for clients who had limited budgets and risk tolerance. It allowed them to try new things because Cognizant footed much of the bill, but it also enabled Cognizant to create new products and services alongside a customer so they knew the products and services were designed to address the customer's need.

For example, we cocreated a platform for a pharmaceutical consortium, called TransCelerate, to make it easier for companies to work with physicians. Eventually, Cognizant offered the solution to the pharmaceutical market directly, knowing the bugs had been worked out and there was a well-established market for the product. When I joined the company, I brought deep pharma experience and was able to help the company land a $35 million initiative with the pharmaceutical consortium. But this required a little "change management" of its own. We had to unseat an established supplier—an IT consulting firm that had been on retainer with the consortium for years. That's its own story! Once we won the business, I led the initiative and learned a lot about the benefits and nuances of working directly with customers to build new products. Some of our customers reminded me of Dr. Baker. They didn't agree with changing the way clinical trials were managed and initially resisted the new platform. We had to work every step of the way to show them the benefits of the technology and how it would improve the workflows of physician researchers and their staff.

The way D'Souza incentivized innovation was also interesting. He wanted ideas for the venture capital investments to come from every division and department, and he let the business leaders decide which ones had the most merit. Although there was an expected return on these investments, he didn't insist that the numbers alone should determine what got funded. There were several factors that went into choosing the most interesting projects. (In chapter 6 on chance and making investments in risk, we'll examine how companies like Cognizant use a portfolio approach to manage innovation.)

D'Souza also recognized the importance of diversity to sustain a culture of innovation, and he knew the Indian-male-dominated company needed to change its face in the market. In 2015, only 18 percent of US employees of Cognizant were women.

Fortunately, with the support of D'Souza, human resources and the CFO, an American woman who had joined the company early in its founding, created a women's affinity group. They called it WIN (Women Information Network), and its purpose was twofold. First, although it existed as a community for women employees and clients to benefit from guest speakers on leadership, work-life balance, and effective communications, its brilliance was subtle. Its other purpose was to generate greater awareness on the part of male leaders in the company on how to collaborate effectively with women clients and coworkers, thereby improving business development and delivery outcomes. I spoke about innovation at one of the WIN conferences—which, I should add, featured a keynote by American endurance sport racer and motivational speaker Robyn Benincasa, whose lively talk about competing in the epic adventure race known as the Eco Challenge demonstrated female leadership and team building. Another well-known motivational speaker shared her story of overcoming oral cancer and learning to talk again, and a famous woman psychologist from Manhattan taught meditation skills. Executive men from sales were placed strategically at tables with female clients where they co-led tabletop discussions on the empathy and listening skills required for effective consultative selling.

I applauded the efforts of WIN to create a more communicative and collaborative culture and noted an increased awareness among both men and women around the challenges and opportunities of intragender communications. As with most culture initiatives, this one lasted until the CFO retired and the human resources leader moved to a new role outside the company, but by then, diversity was improving, so one could say the initiative had the desired impact.

Many people from Western cultures take gender diversity in business for granted, but we need to remember that not all cultures are the same. In a course I teach at a university in Saudi Arabia on behalf of an education technology firm, the intragender makeup of the student body is the first experience some of the men and women have ever had to work with the opposite sex. One male student told me, "I was very uneasy coming into this course because I have never worked with women." I noted that when the women spoke, he cast his head down, unable to look them in the eye. Three weeks later, this individual was transformed and said the best thing he learned in the course was how to work with women peers. "I learned so much from my women colleagues, and I gained new communication skills that make me more confident in business."

Looking back at what I learned at Cognizant, I was able to advance the culture of innovation both by creating a new solution for clients that solved their problem and created a revenue stream for the company and by encouraging more of a voice for women and demonstrating the benefits of diversity to the executives, including those who needed to better relate to women clients. Both experiences served me well in future roles, including teaching in Saudi Arabia.

An example of a third type of an innovative organizational culture is also one of the best I ever worked for. Porter Novelli was a culture of creativity and caring. It was founded by colleagues who met in 1972 while working for the Peace Corps. Jack Porter and Bill Novelli began what would become one of the nation's largest and more respected public relations agencies to create something different, something new. With a spirit that Bill Novelli would later call "adventurous and entrepreneurial," Porter Novelli focused on a client roster of not just corporations, governments, and wealthy individual but also social causes.

This was decades ahead of its time—long before social marketing, long before giving and philanthropy became such important parts of the portfolio of almost every organization, as they are now. When I joined in the late 1990s, we launched major public health campaigns with the National Institutes of Health and other federal agencies for managing cholesterol and blood pressure and encouraging young people not to smoke. And not only did we feel good about having worked for such important causes, but management also celebrated our ability to develop impactful campaigns and PR materials for every client, whether it put money into the coffers of the agency or not.

The leaders of the DC office created a culture that was high energy, recruited dynamic talent and invested in them, encouraged diversity, and were strongly entrepreneurial. Even after the company was eventually acquired by Omnicom, a global marketing communications holding company, the agency maintained its entrepreneurial spirit. I remember bringing Porter Novelli a new business idea. With the president of the office and head of healthcare at my side, we took the train to New York City, where I presented my idea to the operating partner at Omnicom. It was a testament to their belief in me and willingness to take a risk on a new idea. We created a new business unit based on my expertise in clinical research and the needs of biopharma customers. I got a taste for being an intrapreneur, building a business within a business. I vowed to create the kind of culture and be the kind of leader I experienced at Porter Novelli.

As I said earlier, it's not easy to define culture. This is also true of innovation culture. But I like this definition: Fostering an innovation culture involves a conscientious and systematic tapping into the company's talent in order to develop new solutions that help customers solve problems. Let's return to the question Gavin posed about culture and my advice on maintaining an innovation mindset. The talk I gave at that PTC Therapeutics meeting became the progenitor for this book.

Earlier in this chapter, I suggested that culture was a recent phenomenon of the modern workplace. What was work life like before culture became a "thing"? Throughout much of recorded history, most people worked in the same place where they lived. Going to an office outside the home or the farm didn't exist. Researchers at Australia's Swinburne University of Technology trace the office of today back to medieval governments, trading companies, and religious orders—places where a lot of writing and record-keeping was needed.

In a 2018 blog post on LinkedIn, Leslie Aun wrote, "Open offices that are so much in vogue these days may not be quite as modern as we might think. In Botticelli's painting of St. Augustine, the sixth-century Benedictine monk is depicted working in a space that bears more than a passing resemblance to a 21st-century workstation."

But, she continues, "educated elites like Augustine were very much the exception. It wasn't until the 17th century that lawyers, civil servants and others in the emerging professional class began going into an actual office each day in major cities like London, Paris, and Amsterdam."

Aun—a strategic communications executive based in the Washington/Baltimore area—tells us that the trend continued throughout the Industrial Revolution as both jobs and workers migrated from farms to factories in increasing numbers. Over the following century, home-based crafts and trades would give way to mighty office towers and sprawling corporate campuses, and the organizational norms, attitudes, and behaviors that we now identify as "corporate culture" began to gain the attention of business leaders and experts.

The Functions of the Executive, written in 1938 by Chester Barnard, is widely credited with being the first book to outline theories of "cooperation and organization." While the book was hugely influential in the development of management theory, it's interesting to note that it does not once use the word "innovation." And there is only one mention of "invention." So the concept of an innovative culture was not something that Barnard and other management theorists of his day emphasized; we don't know whether they thought it was less important than other management principles or a topic about which little was known. More than thirty years later, Roger Harrison introduced what he called "organizational ideology," and although many of his theories still resonate today, no one paid much attention to them or him at the time. It would be another decade before corporate culture hit the big time with the 1982 publication of Tom Peters and Robert Waterman's blockbuster book *In Search of Excellence.* Often seen as an innovative book in itself—in part because it broadened the audience of those even interested in reading about management theory—the famous principles of excellence that are the prescriptive core of the book included some that are absolutely consistent with the development of an innovative culture ("Stay close to the customer"), as well as some that, in their interpretation, might seem inconsistent with an innovative mindset ("Stick to the knitting," meaning companies should do what they're good at and not become distracted by diversifying into totally different activities or enterprises).

An increasing body of research shows that when culture is properly aligned with leadership and strategy, it can unleash tremendous energy within an organization and enable it to thrive. As Peter Drucker famously put it, "Culture eats strategy for breakfast."

So why do so many companies fail to get culture right when the price for getting it wrong can be so steep—not just in poor morale but in lost productivity, poor financial results, losing competitive advantage, and in the worst cases, accusations and lawsuits that can destroy in a few weeks what took decades to build?

There are plenty of theories. *Zero One* blog author Tom Kaneshige says it's because a company's culture "is really a collection of micro cultures that may or may not align to the macro culture." These micro cultures prevail because most people care far more about their colleagues and their day-to-day work environment than "any sweeping corporate goals" handed down by management.

Bryan Walker and Sarah Soule take a similar view in their June 2017 *Harvard Business Review* article on leadership, "Changing Company Culture Requires a Movement, Not a Mandate." A company's culture, they argue, lives in the "collective hearts and habits" of its employees and their shared perception of "how things are done around here." Cultural change "requires a movement rather than a mandate," with leaders inspiring within their employees "a deep desire, and even responsibility, to change." This can be done by framing the change within the organization's broader purpose in order to "conjure individual emotion and incite collective action."

And then there is the plain old failure to make it a priority, as Jack Weiss, former CEO of WAM Systems, a supply chain planning and visibility software solution for the chemical industry, admitted. "I wish I had paid more attention to culture as we were building the company," he says. "The fact is we were always resource and budget constrained, and we hired people opportunistically as we needed them. We never felt we had the time to ensure that values, behaviors, and rituals were established and aligned with our hiring practices."

It's worth noting that it can be tricky to navigate culture in a global business where there are geographic and ethnic differences. Culture should be the common hearth around which everyone gathers. But bringing everyone together may require some give and take. Armin Spura, PhD, CEO of Bioduro-Sundia, a biopharma contract research and manufacturing organization headquartered in the United States and with a large operational footprint in China, explains, "Bioduro is innovative, and at least in part it's because we are a very multicultural organization, supported by a large contingent of staff based in Shanghai and Beijing, which is one of the most dynamic clusters of service innovation in the world. They frequently provide new ideas to improve customer satisfaction and operational productivity, but the new ideas need to be generated within a certain framework. You have to follow their process."

A deeper look at Armin's commentary on the service-sector innovation emanating from China is provided by a report by Emily Weinstein, published by Brookings.edu in January 2022, "Beijing's 'Re-innovation' Strategy Is Key Element of U.S.–China Competition." Weinstein writes that government backing and incentives for research have enhanced China's innovation potential. On the research front, Beijing has attempted both to improve its basic research ecosystem and to bridge the gap between basic and applied research, spurring innovation in the process.[2] Clearly, the Chinese government is a powerful influencer of culture and seeks to influence and control innovation and decision-making.

In addition to following processes to vet innovations, Iris Wilson-Farley, a human resources executive for American and Japanese manufacturing companies, explains the temporal and risk-management differences between American and Japanese cultures. "One of the things that's been interesting as we operate within a Japanese-owned company is time frames," she says. "Japanese culture tends to look at time on a much longer scale, and so the willingness to accept incremental innovation is greater with our Japanese colleagues, whereas colleagues in the US tend to want to get it done now and explode in the market."

Iris points out that risk tolerance is one variable aspect of organizational culture—as she has experienced herself. "The willingness to step out and take a risk seems to be greater among my North America–based colleagues than Japanese colleagues." That can be frustrating to the Americans, she acknowledges. "On the flip side, the Japanese approach makes financial sense. Sometimes caution is better." She references the old maxim of carpenters: "Measure twice, cut once." Same here. "But the benefit is, when the product is launched, it is really ready to go."

If you and your organization are ready to go—ready to become a more innovative culture and to reap the rewards that will bring with it—here are some key steps you need to take first.

SIX STEPS TO HELP YOU DEFINE AND DEVELOP A CULTURE OF INNOVATION IN YOUR ORGANIZATION

Step 1: Conduct a "Cultural Audit"

Like a financial audit, a cultural audit is an assessment of the health of your culture: where it stands and what, if anything, is missing. Although you don't have balance sheets to review in an audit of corporate culture, there are other indices that can give you a good picture of your values and whether your employees recognize and incorporate them into their work. Here's how to get a better handle on the state of your organization's culture:

Define it. How well-defined is your company culture? Where is it defined—on your company's website, in your human resources manuals, or over casual conversations in the coffee room? How specifically is it expressed, and are these standards, beliefs, and codes being articulated for your new hires?

Understand it. How would you assess your employees' current understanding of your company culture? Take a poll of your workforce or hold informal, off-the-record chats with a few of your workers. Do they have reasonable knowledge of your brand values?

Read your press clippings. How does your company look to the outside world? How is it described in your promotional materials and in your press coverage? Understanding how the rest of the world perceives you—and through what channels—should provide you with some cultural clues about your own organization.

Keep it consistent. Even if your workers understand your culture, they may not enforce it or "live and breathe" it consistently. If that's the case, it's time to look in the mirror: Can you think of one specific action or initiative you've taken on the job in the last few months that exemplifies your organization's culture? Do your company's executives seem to adhere to your ideal culture? How about your employees?

If the results of your audit suggest a risk-averse, by-the-book company and you want to infuse it with the spirit of a start-up, you know you have your work cut out for you. But perhaps the audit will show you that there are pockets of employees with terrific, new ideas but, for whatever reason, they're disinclined or afraid to advance them, champion them, or even suggest them. Identifying those employees, empowering them, and encouraging them—and their ideas!—are key steps toward making a shift to a more innovative culture.

Step 2: Welcome Diverse Perspectives and Encourage Employees to Step out of Their Box and into Someone Else's

Welcoming diverse perspectives in the workforce stimulates innovation by challenging status quo thinking, encouraging fresh perspectives, and promoting critical thinking and problem solving. Forbes. com cites research showing that diverse groups of people who have different backgrounds, experiences, and perspectives generate more innovative solutions than homogeneous groups.[3] Consultants like to challenge people to "step outside of their box." I modify that adage by adding that people should step outside of their box *and step inside someone else's box to see a new perspective*. Diverse thinking—exploring different viewpoints—on a team unlocks the potential for innovative products, solutions, and approaches. Other benefits include better financial results, enhanced employee engagement and productivity, stronger employer brand and reputation, and expanded cultural competence and global perspective.

So how do you get started?

Creating a culture of innovation starts with the right talent and that means the right recruiting and hiring practices. Experts warn against letting unconscious biases that favor the familiar influence hiring decisions. The tendency to hire people with interests and backgrounds similar to those of the people doing the hiring can lead to a high degree of homogeneity and groupthink—not what you want if you're looking to stimulate creativity. According to innovation strategist Alex Gonzalez, it's dangerous "not to bring a multitude of voices, values, thought mechanisms, needs, and belief systems to the innovation gallery."

Many organizations are employing proven methods to prevent different forms of unintentional bias from influencing hiring decisions. Best practices include standardizing the selection criteria to provide a comparable experience for all candidates, blind résumé evaluations, interviews conducted by a diverse panel, and more.

Clay Shedd, former director of executive education at Columbia Business School and now a consultant to UCLA's Anderson School of Management, points out that if you want to build an innovative team, you don't have to wait for human resources to start culling through résumés. "You can do it with employees already in the company," he says. Chances are that the varied perspectives required to mold an adventurous, creative culture are already part of your organization. Just remember that it takes many types. "You don't want to over-index on creativity or risk-taking," he says. "You need a devil's advocate. You need people who are risk averse, just as you need the risk-takers. So I would say try and build your team with those different perspectives in mind."

Second, leaders should look for opportunities to be good role models by encouraging collaboration on projects across departments and functions. When I was leading a cross-functional team at IBM Watson Health with the goal of engaging diverse perspectives in critical thinking about the design of a new product, I started by assessing the current team and ensuring we had the right complement of perspectives. We had a few gaps to fill. We needed engineers with different technical specialties, user-experience designers with accessibility (physical mobility limitations), market professionals with different cultural backgrounds, and account managers who understood the needs and preferences of all customer types. When I convened my cross-functional collaboration team for the project, I didn't start with a group whiteboard session, which I knew would be dominated by a few voices and lead to groupthink. Rather, I asked individuals to complete a brainstorming exercise independently in writing. I collected their ideas, and we discussed them one by one, categorizing each on a whiteboard according to where it fit—technical, marketing, and user experience, for example. Working as a group, we challenged each idea with an aim of improving it in some way. We didn't dismiss anyone's idea; we found a place for all of them at that stage of the process. Next, we developed a customer empathy map to ensure we brought all perspectives to bear on our understanding of the customer and their needs. The outcome is that we designed a product that was appropriate for multilingual wheelchair-accessible patients with neurological disorders. We couldn't have done that without all the perspectives in the room contributing. Everyone felt good about the process—we innovated as a team and succeeded in designing an important product for people suffering from neurological disorders. I then led the team on a reflection exercise where we examined the innovation process—what worked and what could have gone better so we could ensure an even better experience and improved results next time.

As an educator, I encourage diversity and inclusivity in my classroom to foster creativity and openness to new ideas and cultures. My students come from diverse ethnic, racial, and socioeconomic backgrounds, and I have an opportunity to place them on teams and demonstrate how they can leverage their different perspectives to develop more innovative solutions to problems we explore in class. One team working on a college mental health app learned that the stress students face has a cultural element. Students from Southeast Asia were more concerned about their parents' reactions to their grades than other students, and the solution they designed helped address those fears.

So are diversity and inclusivity important to fostering a culture of innovation? From students to newly minted employees to mid-level and senior executives to board members and company presidents, the answer is a resounding yes. We need inclusivity at all levels to foster innovation in the culture.

Step 3: Make It Safe to Experiment and Fail

Amazon has been declared one of the best workplaces for innovators because they empower every employee to be an innovator. Simply put, the organization creates an innovative culture by employing a unique idea-submission framework. They call it the PRFAQ format. That's Press Release/Frequently Asked Questions. The format is described as "a press release that outlines the vision for a product at launch, an FAQ that explains the customer benefits and answers theoretical customer questions." It's essentially writing a press release introducing your new product—justifying its need in the marketplace and who will benefit from it and why. These ideas are continually evaluated and also shared with other innovators at the company. Once an idea is fully formed and approved, it can then receive funding for launch. Some of Amazon's most lucrative products have been created via this process, including Prime Now, Amazon Go, and Alexa. (Alas, Alexa seems blissfully unaware of the process that led her to creation. When asked, however, she helpfully offered to help the questioner construct a list.)

The PRFAQ format also reminds us of a key point: even Amazon's legendary innovations are the result of a systematic, organized process. "Creativity can be messy," wrote Gary P. Pisano in a 2019 article in *Harvard Business Review*. "It needs discipline and management." Without discipline, he says, "almost anything can be justified as an experiment—discipline-oriented cultures set clear criteria."

However, providing a formal process alone won't create a culture of innovation. Management must still be the driver.

As Amazon's founder, Jeff Bezos, has famously said, "Experiments are by their very nature prone to failure. But a few big successes compensate for dozens and dozens of things that didn't work." His attitude toward experimentation indicates a clear strategic view, one that has spread throughout Amazon. Management must continuously encourage innovation and treat it as one of the organization's core values for it to truly become a part of an organization's DNA.

Clay Shedd agrees with the Amazon approach to innovation, and he describes what happens when companies require innovation but fail to define it or describe their expectations to their employees. "My coaching clients say, 'I'm supposed to focus on being imaginative, or innovation. And we don't quite know what that means. It's not really defined to us.' And I've seen what happens when people experiment and things don't go well. The company forgets that it was an experiment, and suddenly it's 'why did this go wrong?' and a finger-pointing exercise versus 'what did we learn from this?'"

Clay's next point should be written on the whiteboard of every corporate conference room: "Corporations think nothing of throwing people into roles without having a chance to sort of practice it (the new role) or time to figure out how to be successful. We would never do that to a baseball player or a concert pianist, but we do it to executives all the time."

Step 4: Reward Innovative Thinking

Julie Hermans explains, on the Qmarkets website, that one of the best ways to encourage innovation is to incentivize it. But, as she points out, it doesn't have to be with big bonuses or raises.

She uses as an example Josh Boehm, a former employee at SpaceX, who talked about how he was sparked to think creatively every day he went to work—and it was his "office" that inspired him! "The environment of working in a rocket factory is amazing on its own," he told Hermans. "We could watch camera feeds of the factory floor from our desks and were encouraged to explore."

The facility—and by extension, the organization—has been built with innovation in mind to facilitate creativity and curiosity at every turn.

Coming up with nonmonetary incentives for your innovative employees is not a one-size-fits-all process. In my own experience leading teams, I've learned that not everyone is motivated by money. For many years, I took it for granted that the best motivation for a team was salary increases, bonuses, and gifts. And, yes, those should be part of any incentive scheme. But humans need more—they also need recognition and opportunities for professional growth. Balancing the tangible with intangible rewards and recognition is the best way to incentivize innovation, growth, and productivity for the long term.

What kind of incentives would work best for your organization? Only you can answer that—but whatever they are, they should balance reward and recognition, and your incentive program should motivate the team to perform.

Step 5: Dream BIG and Give People Room to Create

In studying the science of productivity, Pulitzer Prize–winning reporter Charles Duhigg came across hundreds of examples demonstrating that "stretch goals" are the foundation of soaring innovation.

These were described in the *Harvard Business Review* as not merely challenging objectives but something bigger. "We're talking about management moon shots," wrote Sim B. Sitkin, C. Chet Miller, and Kelly E. See in a 2017 issue of the *Review*. These, they said, are "goals that appear unattainable given current practices, skills, and knowledge. In the parlance of the business world, these are often referred to as stretch goals."

An example of this kind of a "management moon shot" today streaks through the cities and countryside of Japan at almost 200 miles per hour: the Shinkansen—the famous Japanese "bullet train," developed just in time for the 1964 Olympics and to meet the needs of a country rebounding from the devastation of World War Two. The idea of a super-fast train line built in one of the most geologically unstable countries in Asia was initially greeted with skepticism—as was the idea that Japan (not yet the great economic superpower it would become) could actually build it. And at the time—the beginning of the Space Age—railroads were already being seen as a dying technology, but not to the visionaries in Japan who defied the skeptics and created a rail line that, to this day, is the envy of most of the world.

It succeeded not just because of its efficiency and speed. It seems that the dreamers of high-speed rail in Japan tapped into the dreams of a nation. "The bullet train was built to move people at high speeds from one city to another, but it also moved people's hearts and minds in more subtle ways," wrote Jessamyn Abel in her book *Dream Super-Express: A Cultural History of the World's First Bullet Train.* "It conveyed meanings, instilled feelings, and evoked emotional responses."

Innovation occurs when employees are encouraged to stretch their minds and imaginations, to aim higher than most would consider reasonable. And although it's tempting to spotlight spectacular "moon shot" innovations—like the electric light bulb, the iPhone, or the Shinkansen—as examples of stretch goals, Clay Shedd points out that even those working in more prosaic industries can dream big. "One of my coaching clients who was very good at package goods design wanted to align the packaging of their food products more tightly to the company's commitment to socially responsible investment," he says. "That required a really different way of management thinking." But in this case, "his boss loved it. He took a chance, made an investment and it paid off for both."

That's innovative culture in action—not only in the creative thinking of Clay's client, the package designer, but also in his boss's reaction. He knew that he wouldn't be penalized for signing off on something that might have seemed a stretch for the company at the time—a foray into social marketing.

Step 6: Make Innovation the Culture of All—From HR to the C-Suite

At an organizational level, major barriers to creating a culture of innovation include the rigid hierarchical nature of many companies and departmental silos that are antithetical to the free flow of knowledge. However, as the website Big Think + notes in a 2023 article on innovative culture, "Innovation requires champions and cheerleaders at every level and function in the organization."[4]

Eliminating these barriers and encouraging cross-directional collaboration starts at the top. "You can reinforce the cultural benefits of innovation parenting by opening up organizational space," suggests Dr. Waguih Ishak, chief technologist at Corning Research and Development Corporation. Doing so will "allow innovators to bypass barriers and hierarchies that often sap creativity."

In a 2017 article in the *McKinsey Quarterly*, Dr. Ishak related an example of how silo-busting collaboration can be sparked. It happened when he gave permission to one of his scientists to attend a conference in Japan that was somewhat outside of his area of expertise. When he returned, "he barged into my office with a fierce determination to immediately begin work on a new (at the time) kind of laser that promised dry low-cost computer interconnection."

The scientist had met the inventor of the laser at the conference and realized that his own skills weren't a direct fit to adapt it for commercial use. With Dr. Ishak's help, he assembled a group of engineers with the proper backgrounds in this area, and he reached out to other researchers, outside of Corning, who were studying similar technologies. The interdisciplinary team would eventually succeed in a big way but only because he, his team, and Dr. Ishak had been willing to break out of their hierarchies and established chains of command. "If he had not insisted on going to the conference; if I hadn't broken the rules and let him travel; if we hadn't given him the resources to start the work . . . we would not have been the first company to develop this widely adopted technology."

So if you want disruptive innovation, you'd better be prepared to disrupt your own rules, your own structures, and your own comfort zone. And you should make the ripening of an innovation culture in your organization the responsibility of the entire organization— and hold yourself and the C-suite accountable.

But don't stop there. Everyone should have a stake in the organization's efforts to create a culture of innovation. Consider how a company that has become one of the most well-known brands in

America in the twenty-first century—a true innovator in the way we watch movies and TV—ensures that the spirit of innovation permeates every aspect of the organization.

"Netflix is innovative in how they treat employees," says Clay Shedd, who has studied the streaming service. "They remove barriers and obstacles. It's that simple." The head of human resources at Netflix summarized it concisely in an interview, according to Clay. "She said, 'We're going to treat people like adults,'" Shedd recalls. "That's it. They had a rule book in HR that was probably two pages long, as opposed to the 5,000 rules that you typically find in a corporation." The concurrent slimming down in HR, overall, "made a big difference in how Netflix was able to move and pivot and go go go go go."

Clay had one more revealing insight from his interview with the HR head at Netflix. "She said, 'We want to be the company where it's good to be from, the company other companies want to hire from. That's what we want.' And that's what they became."

CHAMPIONS OF CHANGE

Lessons from Fearless Founders and Enterprising Executives

Dave Evans
CEO and Cofounder of Fictiv, San Francisco Bay Area, California

"Custom-manufactured parts done right" is part of Fictiv's promise. But innovation is at the heart of Fictiv's business. The company declares it in so many words on its website: "Fictiv has engineered a new approach—one that streamlines workflows to eliminate the barriers to innovation and unleashes the creativity of engineers."

The sense of possibility and of optimism and the forward-looking spirit ("Build the Future with Us!" is their hiring slogan) are all a direct reflection of Fictiv's cofounder and CEO Dave Evans, a guy whose enthusiasm for what might, at first glance, sound like a less-than-sexy industry is downright infectious.

Evans, who earned his BS in mechanical engineering at Stanford, was inculcated in a culture of innovation from early on in his career: he was the first hire at Ford's Silicon Valley Innovation Lab, a part of Ford's Global Research and Advanced Engineering Division.

He cofounded Fictiv in 2013 to help eliminate a major bottleneck in new product development: custom mechanical part sourcing. Dave and his team engineered a new approach, streamlining workflows and eliminating barriers in a process that was often slow, cumbersome, and fraught with delays and miscommunication.

The goal of his new system, he says, was to "unleash the creativity of engineers."

The result, *Forbes* magazine says, was "like Uber for idle manufacturing machinery. The company matches manufacturers with customers to provide rapidly produced parts and prototypes within 72 hours."

Over the last eleven years, Fictiv has manufactured more than 35 million parts for early-stage companies and large enterprises alike, helping them innovate with speed and agility.

The company is now valued at nearly $200 million. Dave and his team have accomplished the goal of unleashing creativity and opening up new pipelines for innovation. Dave himself was recognized for his early-career success by being named in 2018 as one of the *Forbes* 30 Under 30 and, in 2021, was recognized with a Manufacturing Leadership Award for his contribution to digital transformation within the industry. Given by the National Association of Manufacturers, the Leadership Award honors those contributing to excellence in manufacturing, which Dave has done in large part by putting great emphasis on a word one doesn't typically associate with manufacturing or heavy industries: culture.

In fact, as Dave told me in no uncertain terms, that's his primary role: "My job as a CEO is not to set budgets," he asserts. "It's not to build the product road map, it's not to hire people or raise money. I drive culture. That's all I do. I'm a culture champion."

Here are some of Dave's tips for creating a culture of innovation in your organization.

Find your cultural river guides.

Dave suggests looking at culture as something foundational to every organization. "Culture is the operating system for your company," he says. "Culture is how your employees know what to do, how to comport themselves, what kinds of attributes are valued and encouraged."

Workers shouldn't have to guess about the cultural mores of their organization. That needs to be communicated, not necessarily through complex written rule books but often by example and by interaction with key people—Dave calls them "river guides"—who personify your culture. "These are the people in your organization who exemplify your core beliefs. They're talking about it, they display it, they live and breathe it."

Identifying, empowering, and encouraging these individuals can help build and maintain the sinew and bones of your organization's culture.

Recruit with culture in mind.

This is as important as salaries, incentives, and bonuses—because none of that matters if someone is hired by a new company and feels out of place. How can you stoke the flames of innovation and creativity with someone whose top priority is updating their résumé? "Our culture is a differentiator," says Dave. "We're trying to create a rich, cultural environment that attracts a specific type of person and detracts another type of person," he says. Being able to clearly define that culture goes a long way toward ensuring a good fit with a prospective employee. "You know you've got a good culture when folks come there, and they've found a home, and they're like, 'This is my group of people.'"

Consider the Pancake Principle.

Identifying and instilling a sense of culture—among current and future employees—doesn't have to involve complex analytics or a long, drawn-out process. Early on in Fictiv's development, Dave and his colleagues learned a simple but effective technique for gauging whether someone was the right fit.

They just broke out the maple syrup.

"We were an early-morning start-up," recalls Dave. "Most of us were in the office every morning by 8 a.m. So with new hires, when we found someone we liked, after they'd go through a technical interview, we would invite the candidate to come have pancakes with us. This was a way to get a sense of how this person would get along with us, in a slightly more informal setting."

"Pancakes," as the periodic breakfasts were called, started with Dave and five members of his early management team. The company grew. The frequency of the breakfasts grew. Before long, "we were making pancakes three times a week," Dave laughs. "We had gluten-free pancakes, we had maple syrup or we had other types of syrup. We had keto-diet pancakes. Pancakes were out of control!"

The tradition spread as Fictiv grew internationally—eventually to countries where pancakes with syrup are usually not on the breakfast menu. Dave recalls having a call with his GM in China, and it was mentioned that they were having a meeting over dumplings. "I said, 'Dumplings?' He said, 'Well, you guys do pancakes, so we have dumplings.'"

Dave applauded the move. After all, the focus shouldn't really be on the pancakes or the dumplings. "It's about the cultural experience," he says.

Model innovation by example.

You want innovation? Dave's advice is to start by looking in the mirror and asking yourself: "What rituals are you doing every single day that reinforce the mindset of innovation you want your people to have?" In other words, demonstrate through your own example and those of your cultural "river guides."

For executives, the creation of a culture of innovation should be a fundamental part of your mission. That means more than foosball machines in the office, happy hours at the local pub, or even gluten-free pancake breakfasts! Those might be some of the conduits for helping maintain a cohesive organizational culture, but it has to be something more, something deeper. "I think many leaders and business books get this wrong," Dave says. "They talk about culture, culture, culture, but they don't talk about it as a product or an operating system."

That is good advice from an innovative culture champion! If you want more effective and profitable innovation from your organization, you must commit to creating a culture that values innovation, rewards innovation (without necessarily penalizing failure), and encourages innovation—at every level, in every way.

Just as Dave Evans has done so successfully with Fictiv—while enjoying a few pancakes along the way.

For more on Dave Evans, see https://www.fictiv.com/about-us.

4

THE 5C's: COLLABORATION—WORKING TOGETHER FOR A COMMON PURPOSE

We've all been there. A call from an unhappy client late on a Friday afternoon threatens to interrupt your weekend plans. In my case, it was 6:30 p.m. on the Wednesday before Thanksgiving, and I was just heading out to brave the traffic on Interstate 95 South toward Maryland. When I saw my client's number pop up on my mobile phone, I hesitated. Should I let it go to voice mail and deal with it after the holiday? What if it was urgent and required getting in touch with other executives in the company over the holiday? I pride myself on being responsive to my clients, and I really liked Anne, the new CEO of a well-known patient foundation focused on a rare disease. She was a highly accomplished business leader— the first woman CEO of a major marketing communications agency that she had led to impressive growth over the twelve years she was at the helm.

When she left the agency in 2017, it was to accept an important and challenging role: to transform a well-established, mission-driven organization, established in the 1950s, into a modern foundation. One of her chief goals was to create a sustainable annuity of funding to "future-proof" the organization, as Anne put it. This was an increasingly attractive concept among patient foundations: The idea was to leverage networks, subject-matter expertise, and data assets not-for-profits could offer to the commercial marketplace. Loathe to describe it as "commercializing their offerings," which is how I explained it to colleagues, the foundations preferred to say they were creating an annuity to sustain their organization for years to come.

The more innovative foundations were partnering with bio-pharma to develop lifesaving drugs, collaborating with investors to create venture funds, and establishing networks with academic centers to support research. The Multiple Myeloma Research Foundation (MMRF) is a prime example. They have committed more than $500 million to research, supported more than a hundred clinical trials, and helped to bring more than fifteen drugs to market, tripling the life expectancy of myeloma patients, according to the MMRF website. Having worked with this organization as a consultant, I can attest to the success of their model. In fact, it is one many foundations seek to emulate.

Anne was also very familiar with MMRF's founders and their work, and she acknowledged that she and the board wanted to replicate that kind of success.

Anne was well known in the world of advertising and marketing communications, where I first met her, but not in the world of patient advocacy. I wondered how her high-energy, "get it done at all costs" personality would mesh with the traditional bureaucratic organization and its board. Would she be able to turn the *Titanic* around, or would the inertia wear her down? We've all seen cases of the new, vibrant CEO valiantly trying to make a Big Bang change—something genuinely innovative that everyone says they want—only to butt heads with the "we've always done it this way" crowd.

"Hi, Anne. Calling for my sweet potato casserole recipe?" I joked cheerfully.

"Yeah, sorry to call right before the holiday, but you're my last meeting of the week and the most important, so I saved the best for last," she joked back. But then I heard the frustration in her voice. "I'm calling you because I need someone I trust and who has our organization's best interests at heart."

Okay, she had my attention.

Anne gave a short soliloquy about how she came into the organization with a mandate to establish a game-changing electronic patient registry and dataset for neuromuscular diseases—one that could answer research questions and help physicians and pharma take treatment and care to the next level. She was right. The registry and data products we were planning to create were an innovative idea, clearly needed by the community, and the time was right because the technology had evolved to make collecting and analyzing data possible. This was a perfect opportunity to create the financial annuity she and the board wanted. It was also the right initiative for broad collaboration among several different stakeholders across the healthcare ecosystem, which is why my company was excited to be leading this initiative. Anne emphasized, "My team and the board are behind me on this. Launching this dataset is our most important goal this year."

She paused. "But here's my problem," she said.

("Okay, here it comes," I thought.)

"None of us know the first thing about running a registry," Anne continued. "That's why we hired you guys. For us, this is a huge investment of time, resources, and capital. So you can understand why I'm disappointed."

Disappointed? Even though that wasn't aimed at me, it stung. I prided myself on regular, prompt communication with Anne.

"When I get invoices and don't see progress commensurate with what we're spending, I'm disappointed," she continued. "In fact, as you may know, we have had some major slip-ups." Anne went on to explain that she expected more transparent and frequent communications with my firm, support that coordinated with other parties involved with the registry, and a more seamless customer experience for the doctors inputting data, not to mention her staff who were managing things behind the scenes.

"Your company has an outstanding reputation, and we were so excited to be working with you when we launched this initiative," Anne concluded. "But it's been six months, and I feel like I'm not a very high priority to you guys."

Truthfully, Anne's foundation was a small organization of around $60 million and not a multibillion corporation like so many of the clients at the global contract research organization (CRO) I worked for. But that was certainly no excuse for what she was describing—lackluster service. I winced as Anne politely went through her list of criticisms. I was thinking about the extra time and effort I knew the team was putting into this project, which she wasn't aware of, but I was determined to make things right.

She summarized what was required from her end to "reset the table," as she put it: "We need a collaboration model that considers our strengths and weaknesses," she said. "One that marries our competencies—strong relationships with the patient and physician community—with your capabilities—technology, data, and the commercial chops to create a sustainable revenue model. Can you help us reestablish this relationship, Lorraine, and get it on track for the greatness I know it can produce?"

Anne was not a CEO and professional communicator for nothing. She had eloquently reamed me out. I took a few minutes to let her comments sink in. I promised to do what I could to kickstart our business relationship and to develop the kind of arrangement I now understood she was expecting.

I knew what we had to do next. What was needed was the establishment of a genuine collaboration with a key customer where we could cocreate a new data-driven model for developing lifesaving therapies. It was an exciting opportunity for all those involved, and I wanted to do my part to lead it.

Let's put a capital "C" on that word: Collaboration. It's one of our 5C's—a key to innovation. But the way it's understood and utilized among today's companies is very different from the way corporations viewed collaborations in the past.

Collaboration in business is the practice of working together with internal and external stakeholders toward a shared goal by optimizing resources, creating value, and solving problems to create something new.

Said another way, innovation-driven collaboration combines diverse perspectives, skills, and experiences to create something new, something better than any one of us could make individually.

In fact, collaboration is now so integral to the process of innovating that some would argue that the very act of working together to achieve a defined and common purpose is itself a form of innovation. A provocative 2016 *Harvard Business Review* article, written by Ernst & Young thought leaders Jeff Liu and Paul Brody, bears the headline: "Is Collaboration the New Innovation?" In the article, Liu and Brody declared that "we are on the dawn of a golden age of business innovation," that the dynamics of corporate innovation have changed fundamentally, including the very idea of how organizations become more innovative. "Typically," they wrote, "an incumbent leader hoping to jumpstart innovation would acquire it." But the speed of today's digital economy, they argue, has led to an ever-shortening innovation cycle that "can make partnership structures like joint ventures and M&A [mergers and acquisitions] too slow, costly and cumbersome, even for the largest companies."

Instead, they postulated, a new kind of alliance was being formed: what the authors called an "industrial mash-up," in which a company shares an asset or capability with one or more partners "in ways that create new possibilities for all."

Making such an arrangement work, Liu and Brody wrote, requires collaboration and a mindset shift, from industries based on sole control to those anchored in collaboration and partnership.

"Increasingly, a large industrial company cannot think about itself as simply a company," says Gary Hamel, a faculty member of the London Business School and the director of the Management Innovation eXchange. He says, "It needs to think about itself as a node in a much broader network, and it needs to see 'competition' as not simply about how we build market share but about how we capture innovation share from across a very broad ecosystem." By partnering, you can leverage another organization's competencies and capabilities in a different area and move faster, nimbler, and more efficiently.

This was the challenge that Anne posed to me in her pre-Thanksgiving phone call about the need to better harmonize our respective strengths in the design and development of a state-of-the-art neuromuscular disease patient dataset.

Collaborate! Or I should say, "collaborate more effectively in order to innovate."

It's not that I hadn't worked on teams in the past and enjoyed some very productive collaborations with colleagues in various disciplines. But before businesses went global and became technologically based, and certainly prior to the COVID pandemic, external collaboration was not a business necessity as it is today. Corporations could easily house all their knowledge, know-how, expertise, and client prowess inside their four walls (even the term "four walls" is now archaic, as nearly 30 percent of businesses operate online, according to IBISWorld.com). Still, their external focus was on keeping competitors off guard and building market share with customers. As businesses became more dependent on each other for supply chain, talent, and access to new markets, business models evolved toward specialization—doing what you do best even better—and identifying partners to outsource the functions and activities that weren't core to your capabilities and competencies. And the term co-opetition emerged—partnering with companies in some product lines and competing in others. Think Google and Apple and how they cooperate on apps but compete on smartphones.

Other collaborations are formed by partners deemed unlikely partners—until you examine the synergies that enable them to create new products and services and ways of doing things. I like this example of external collaboration in smart manufacturing in the auto industry—the partnership between Bavarian Motor Works (BMW Group) and Nvidia, the Santa Clara, California–based technology company with annual revenues of $60+ billion. In 2020, BMW announced that Nvidia is integrating artificial intelligence

(AI) and advanced robotics into BMW's manufacturing process, according to Nvidia's website.

Key aspects of this collaboration include:

- AI-powered logistics: Utilizing Nvidia's AI platforms, BMW aims to optimize its supply-chain and logistics operations. This includes real-time data processing and predictive analytics to improve efficiency and reduce downtime.
- Robotic automation: The partnership leverages Nvidia's expertise in robotics to develop smart, flexible manufacturing systems. These systems can adapt to various tasks and improve precision and productivity on the assembly line.
- Virtual factory planning: BMW and Nvidia are working on creating digital twins of the manufacturing facilities. Digital twins are functional computerized models of a physical object and a staple of smart manufacturing. They allow for better planning, simulation, and optimization of production processes before implementing changes in the physical world.

The BMW-Nvidia partnership represents interdisciplinary collaboration at every level—and it highlights how external partnerships can drive innovation in smart manufacturing, combining expertise from the automotive industry with technology from a leader in AI and computing.

This is just one type of collaboration—or, per the *Harvard Business Review* article, industrial mash-up—where industrial partners team up to create a new application of an existing technology and the sponsor company pays another company for its know-how. An interesting data point helps underscore the increasing focus on intracompany collaboration in innovation—the evolution in patent filings. In their book *Smarter Collaboration*, Harvard Law professor Heidi K. Garner and consultant Ivan A. Matviak studied the role of collaboration and innovation among professional services firms for more than a decade. In their historical analysis of patents, they compared the 1970s with today. What did they learn? In the

1970s, 60 percent of US patents were awarded to individual inventors. Nowadays, that number has reversed: 60 percent of patents are issued to teams—groups of people working together within and across academia and corporations. "The other thing we noticed," says Heidi, "was the more diverse the backgrounds of those teams, the more successful their innovation."

There are other collaborative business models where the focus is on creating a new product or even a new sector—outcomes possible only if all stakeholders in an industry work together. Terri Hall Zecchin is an executive partner at Gartner Research, where she advises clients, large and small and across industries, on ways to improve their sales and marketing outcomes. For this interview, she spoke to me through the lens of her former roles: vice president, Global Strategy Alliances at Redhat, an IBM company, and former corporate vice president, Global Business Unit Alliances and Solutions, at Advanced Micro Devices (AMD), a $30 billion multinational semiconductor corporation. AMD develops computer processors and related technologies for business and consumer markets. Terri has an impressive career in software business development, creating both new ways of working with clients and new ways of selling. While she is a fan of solving a client's problem and designing solutions that fit their needs, she said this approach to business development is often difficult to achieve organically. (As I told Terri, that doesn't surprise me one bit!)

Terri explained how she collaborated with external stakeholders to create a new market for the 64-bit chip. After leaving IBM in 2000, Terri joined AMD to lead a sales team focused on selling 64-bit chips to IBM for servers. But—and this is a big "but"—at the time, there was no 64-bit operating system (OS). "We had a next-generation 64-bit chip but limited demand—we were ahead of the market with this product," Terri exclaimed. The only way to sell these new chips was to generate demand. The only way to generate demand was to incentivize the giant software companies to make an operating system that needed a faster chip.

"I decided, with the support of my boss, to create the demand, to essentially create the market for our chip," Terri explained. Believing in the power of piloting an idea first, Terry started with a small set of partners with whom she knew she wanted to collaborate— Microsoft, Red Hat, and German-owned SUSE—to accelerate their development of an OS that needed the 64-bit chip to run. She chose her collaborators carefully: "SUSE was the first to release its 64-bit OS, and the others quickly followed, giving us a competitive advantage in the market. Additionally, I collaborated with database companies like Oracle to highlight our chip's superior performance." As a result of Terri's successful sales and marketing collaborations, AMD's stock quintupled. "We gained market share from Intel until they released their own 64-bit chip eighteen months later." Now that's an impressive outcome!

But I couldn't let Terri off the hook so easily. I wanted to know more about how she pulled off this collaboration. Having worked at IBM and being familiar with Redhat, I recognized how challenging it must have been to get these corporate behemoths to work together toward a common objective and outcome. "At first, it was just me, with the support of my boss, working with the big OS manufacturers like Microsoft to get everyone up to speed on the development of the 64-bit OS," Terri says. But once the president and the chief technology officer understood the impact the market opportunity was going to create for AMD, they got on board, and Terri had all the support she needed.

"I've always had this philosophy: Even when you work for a big company like IBM, you must prove something will work first," says Terri. "I never said, 'Give me twenty-five people and a million dollars.' I always said, let me take the first step and show some progress and then ask for the bigger investment." That's great advice for would-be innovators—and that's exactly what Terri did. Once AMD started to see the positive results of working with collaborators to build demand, they were willing to add more staff and pursue additional partners, like Oracle. They added staff to the Microsoft team and started working with the Linux companies to move faster. Reflecting on her success, Terri adds, "We then started to think about how to create a collaboration model so we never had to be in this position again."

That's what companies mean when they talk about continuous improvement. "We knew what features we were going to be putting into the chip," Terri says. "It takes eighteen months to get a chip to market, so let's start talking to them ahead of time and making sure they're starting to build the compatible features into the software."

What started out as "Terri's project" evolved and grew until the entire organization was focused on the software ecosystem and making sure that AMD and its partners were in sync with each other.

As Terri pointed out, in a highly technical field like software development, no one person can know everything, and no one company can dominate the market. Instead, success often comes from working together to solve common problems and create better products for everyone.

Terri has a good takeaway to pass on to collaborators. "I knew a solution was never created by just one company. I learned that at IBM. Other companies had other parts of the solution. I always approached technology innovation from that standpoint—that one piece of technology is not a solution."

That perspective became a game changer for AMD.

Software professional Jonathan Matthews's March 2023 blog post on LinkedIn reminds us of another useful example of external collaboration that I'd like to reference. He explains that, in the early days of the web, different browsers implemented HTML and CSS in different ways, leading to compatibility issues and frustration for developers. To solve this problem, a group of developers came together to create the World Wide Web Consortium (W3C), which sets standards for web technologies. By collaborating on these standards, developers can create websites and applications that work across different browsers and platforms, making the web more accessible and user-friendly.

Another example of collaboration in technology is the development of open-source software. This is software created by a community of developers who work together to create and maintain code that anyone can use, modify, and distribute. By collaborating on open-source projects, developers can build on each other's work, share knowledge, and create software that is more secure, reliable, and customizable than proprietary alternatives.

Now let's go back to Anne's foundation and the case for collaboration. In this case, we had a highly attractive opportunity to collaborate with our customer to cocreate a new data solution for the neuromuscular patient community. And to implement this customer cocreation, we needed to collaborate internally to create a new solution and business model. I discussed the pros and cons of this collaboration opportunity with executives at my company. At the time, I was in the consulting organization of our CRO, and although I wasn't the central point of contact for the client or our internal team, I was in the right position to play such a role, which was eventually part of the collaboration model we created. I hadn't read Heidi's book at the time, but her rationale for the benefits of a true collaboration found their way into my proposal to the executive team anyway—call it intuition or good business sense.

Anne didn't mean to ruin my Thanksgiving that night when she called to share her concerns. But as my family and I enjoyed our meal (I'm happy to say my sweet potato casserole went over big!), I was already thinking about how we could salvage and rebuild our relationship.

By the Monday after Thanksgiving, I had a plan in mind. The first thing I wanted to do was acknowledge to Anne that she had been heard. We did that face to face, in a strategic-planning meeting between Anne and her people and our executives.

We discussed the frequency of our communications to make sure, as we embarked on this collaboration, that she did not feel lost (as she had told me during our phone call) and that she knew we had her best interests at heart.

Then we talked about how we could work better together: who would do what—for example, lines of responsibility—what the pricing would be for the newly created offerings, and how revenue would be shared. As important as the model for developing and marketing the data asset was, it was the process of rebuilding the relationship that mattered most. A collaboration is something you build over time, but it's also a way of working together—and that requires an alignment of values, behaviors, and expectations and creating your own new culture together.

We discussed the complexities of culture in chapter 3. At one level, a collaboration between two innovation-minded companies is like a "culture mash-up." That includes the creation of a set of norms to guide the new team's work and relationship. Some of the new norms we created for Anne's foundation included attending and contributing to the foundation's annual fundraiser, presenting progress reports to Anne's board regularly, sharing the podium at conferences, and cowriting publications. We invited Anne and her senior staff to meet some of our other biopharma and healthcare clients and to learn more about our company's initiatives and relationships in the sector of data and AI. We shared more of the intangible resources and benefits my company could offer: access to thought leaders, genomic experts, genetic consortiums, and business partners. This built trust that we were "all in" with Anne.

Then we set about creating a new operating model to implement our cocreated innovative data solution.

One of the first things we did was create one central infrastructure, with my consulting team in a coordinating role, to help manage the partnership internally. This included what may seem like minor things—like developing one invoice to make it easier for the client to understand and pay their bills. Even that, we learned, had been a source of frustration for the customer. They were receiving several invoices from different business units within my company each month, none of which were consistent or easy to understand, leaving their CFO to figure out what work went with which invoice.

We then identified how to make the pie bigger so everyone could benefit. After all, we were a for-profit company and needed to make a margin to keep pace with our financial obligations to the company and our shareholders. So was this collaboration necessary to bring an innovation to market? You betcha. But it had to be designed in a smart way so that it benefited the company financially and fit with the way we were organized and staffed. If we had charged for each business line supplying services to the client, the budget wouldn't have worked for Anne's patient foundation. But in our case, because we were dealing with a not-for-profit, we did some work gratis or at a reduced rate. We also made trade-offs because we were their commercial partner and received revenue when we sold their data.

Let's examine what each party needed financially to make the return on investment (ROI) work. My company had an innovative idea—to create a business unit to work exclusively with patient foundations to collect, curate, and sell their data to pharma on their behalf. We created a platform and a data-licensing model and set up a royalty stream for the foundation in return for their data. From our lens, we viewed the data as valueless sitting on forms in a data repository. It had to be culled into an electronic record where it could be cleaned, combined, analyzed, and turned into a product that pharma and researchers could use to answer questions, perform research, and include in filings to the Food and Drug Administration. So we needed to be compensated for investing to make this data valuable.

The foundation had invested upward of $10 million in the patient registry. Essentially, they'd bet the ranch on this. They needed to see results from this collaboration. We helped them hire the right people to work on this project to bolster their internal know-how.

The time we spent reengineering the collaboration was, I think, well worth it. I got fewer distressed calls from Anne and then none at all and, finally, a call saying, "Lorraine, thanks." The patient registry was eventually established, a revenue stream was created for the foundation, and my company had a satisfied client and a new capability to offer other clients.

If that's your goal—an innovative new product that your company or client is happy with—you need to start finding allies and partners and learning how to collaborate to innovate. My experience with Anne was one of many innovative collaborations I've been involved with. Some, like this one, were successful; some not. Here are a few things I've learned, as an executive and consultant, over the years. You can use these items as a checklist to test the strength of any business alliance into which you're about to enter.

CAREFULLY CHOOSE YOUR COLLABORATOR

Entering a collaboration can be akin to getting married. You need a lot of time together to make sure you have a good match. So that you don't enter a collaboration only to have to restart it, like we did with Anne's foundation, assess the areas below as you're vetting the new partnership. It will save you time and headaches later.

How Are You Going to Split the Orange?

You may have heard this famous adage in the field of negotiations. Two people wanted to buy the last orange on the market shelf. One buyer was willing to outbid the other until a passerby noticed the altercation and asked them, "What do you want to use the orange for?"

The first customer said, "I want the peel to make orange zest for a cake."

The second customer said, "I want the pulp to make orange juice."

"Easily solved," said the passerby. "Split the orange, with each of you taking the part you need." Similarly, in a collaboration, what does each party need and want to ensure success? In the case of Anne's foundation, they wanted a high-quality registry and data that could be used by the community to improve care and therapy for patients. They wanted a revenue stream to offset their investment, one that would continue funding the organization into the future. My company wanted to sell datasets to biopharma and add revenues to their data business. We also want to show the market we had a new capability other clients could use. So, we "split the orange," and we both got the data we needed and achieved our objectives.

What Is Each Party's Risk Threshold?

How does each party view risk in the collaboration, and what is their risk tolerance? This is a critical question that can be challenging to resolve if companies are very different, as was the case with a multimillion-dollar patient foundation that generates income through donations versus a multibillion-dollar company with complex legal and financial structures and requirements. In this case, the risk that Anne needed to manage was reputation and brand—her foundation wanted to keep the respect of its physician and patient community at all costs. My company needed to manage financial risk—to replicate this model with other foundations and to prove that it was financially lucrative and easy to implement so it could be scaled.

How Will Control Be Divided?

In every collaboration, parties may need to control different aspects of the business or activities. This has to be worked out in advance to avoid confusion once the project is underway. In the case of the foundation, because its relationships with physicians and patients were of utmost importance, it wanted to control access to these stakeholders. Anne and her colleagues didn't want our company to communicate directly with either. This was difficult at times but an important part of the partnership terms. By the same token, our company wanted to control communications with biopharma about the data to ensure that questions were being answered correctly and pricing was consistent.

But by having these discussions in advance, both sides were able to give the other strategic control over the areas most important to them in the collaboration.

Do the Organizations Share the Same Values?

You can't forge a strong collaboration without trust. Agreeing on shared values is a good starting point. A set of mutual values provides confidence that the organizations think and act similarly and gives you a basis for settling any issues. In the early days of my firm's work with the foundation, we didn't have trust or open communications. That explains Anne's call over the Thanksgiving holiday to the one person she trusted to help reset the relationship. When we restarted the collaboration, we discussed shared values and even committed to them in writing: open communications, transparency in business discussions, and integrity in how we treated each other. We used these terms in our discussions to create our own lexicon for working together.

How Does Each Organization Communicate and Govern Collaborations?

It's helpful to develop a governance structure and communications plan early in the relationship. The plan should answer questions like the following: Who's overseeing the collaboration? What is the path for escalating risks before they become issues? How often does the executive team meet and what do they discuss? What tools will be used to communicate daily, weekly? The best collaborations have all this laid out from the start.

Do We Have the Right Talent to be Effective?

Talent is clearly critical to a successful collaboration. Do you each have the right people in the right roles doing the right job? This may cause you to think differently about how you resource and run the collaboration, as opposed to internal projects. For example, we needed a nurse to oversee the data collection at the sites, but in this case, we needed someone who understood the foundation's registry and the neuromuscular diseases it covered and who had experience working with a small not-for-profit. The first person we chose to monitor the study was too hands-off and had to be replaced with someone who was very responsive to the foundation. Lack of communication and transparency had been one of Anne's concerns—so we needed to make sure she and her team were informed every step of the way.

Do the Cultures Mesh?
Is a "Cultural Mash-Up" Possible?

We talked about culture earlier in this book and defined it as shared ways of thinking and working. Culture can be a challenge—in this case, in particular, we were trying to integrate a not-for-profit foundation and a for-profit company. The foundation was guided by what was best for the patients, but within the organization, departments competed for budget, resources, and the board's approval, so the data-collaboration project was the envy of some. Fortunately, Anne stayed firm and navigated internal resistance to the project. In my company, the culture valued internal collaboration and put clients and patient needs first, but our departments' financial incentives around who got credit for the sale, for example, didn't encourage internal collaboration. We couldn't fix that in the short term, so individual business leaders figured out how to work together, sometimes sacrificing their budgets for the good of the bigger program.

How Do Decisions Get Made?

Every organization has its own decision-making structure—and in the case of a collaboration between one company that is large and one that is small, those structures are going to be very different. How do decisions get made in each of the collaborating organizations, and how long does it take? Do those directly involved in the collaboration have decision-making authority? In the case of Anne's foundation, we had direct access to the decision-maker, but on a day-to-day basis, we had to work through her team, who in turn needed to get to her. This caused delays in decisions that slowed us down. Our company's decision-making model was not without challenges either, particularly because five departments were involved in the initiative and each had to be consulted about budget, resourcing, and strategic decisions. We ultimately created processes to streamline communications and decision-making, but it took some time.

We've examined a number of examples of external collaboration to demonstrate how everyone can win—the companies and the customers—when external collaboration is done right.

But there's an internal dimension to collaboration, as well. This requires getting teams inside a company to create new products and services. In our previous example, Terri had to first collaborate internally at AMD with her boss, the executive team, and sales colleagues to create the market demand plan before she could then approach her external collaborators and implement.

Where's the proof that internal collaboration drives growth in a sustainable way, you may ask?

Let's look at a simple example: real estate. Anyone who has ever bought a house or rented an apartment knows that the realtor company can offer just one service—let's say, renting a property. But what happens when it combines its rental service with financial services, property-management services, and even strategic planning? In *Smarter Collaboration*, Heidi Garner demonstrates that revenues were 7.1 times higher for accounts served by three business lines than for those served by just one. Customers served by five business lines generated 20.4 times higher fees than those served by just one business line.

Sounds like a no-brainer, right? Why aren't we all doing this? The answer is that expanding a company's line of products or services is more sophisticated and complex to implement than you might think. It's not simply a cross-sell—as in, "Do you want waffle fries with that?" at the Chick-fil-A window. It takes coordination and cooperation with everyone in the company—for example, financial incentives have to be aligned with the participating departments. But once you get the formula right and get the teams on board, the benefit, in addition to revenues, is more information about a client, which means more opportunities to deepen and broaden the relationship—and that's pure gold! All these teams engaging with the client provide a unique perspective on the customer's needs and wants, how decisions are made, and who else your clients are working with. And when you address bigger, more complex issues across a company, you get access to the CEO and the board, which gives you more insight into strategy, budgets, and mission, and you can play an even bigger role. I saw this firsthand in several companies where we bundled data and software products and services and sold to large corporations at an enterprise level, meaning our products and services were used by many departments in the company, not just one, so we had large master agreements with the head of procurement.

THE INSIDE-OUT RULES:
HOW TO FOSTER INTERNAL COLLABORATION

A sustainable model and culture of innovation start from the inside. Fostering a collaborative culture in your organization can be challenging, but it's essential for driving innovation. Here are some tips on how to achieve it within your organization, including the use of software collaboration tools from Atlassian's website, Atlassian.com.

Set clear goals and expectations. To collaborate effectively, everyone on your team needs to understand what they are working toward and how they are expected to contribute. Be sure to set clear goals and expectations for each team member and communicate these goals regularly to ensure everyone is on the same page.

Encourage diverse perspective. Collaboration thrives on diversity, so be sure to encourage diverse perspectives and backgrounds on your team. Consider hiring people with different skill sets and experiences and create opportunities for team members to share their knowledge and expertise with each other.

Foster open communication. Open communication is essential for collaboration. Encourage team members to share their ideas, feedback, and concerns freely, and provide opportunities for regular check-ins and feedback sessions. Consider using collaboration tools like Slack or Trello to facilitate communication and keep everyone on the same page.

Emphasize teamwork. Collaboration is all about teamwork, so be sure to emphasize the importance of working together toward common goals. Consider implementing team-based incentives or recognition programs to encourage collaboration and recognize team members who go above and beyond to support their colleagues.

Encourage experimentation and risk-taking, which are fundamental to innovation collaborations. Innovation often requires experimentation and risk-taking, so be sure to create a culture that encourages these behaviors. Provide opportunities for team members to try new approaches and ideas, and create a safe space where failure is seen as an opportunity to learn and grow.

Democratize innovation and collaboration will follow. We've discussed in this book the problem that arises at companies when innovation is a task meant just for certain people, like research and development teams or "chief innovation officers," or when innovative thinking is only encouraged at certain events, like retreats or brainstorming sessions. These approaches tell the rest of the organization that their ideas are not as valued and limit input from individuals who may have unique and valuable perspectives to share. Instead, the defining feature of a collaborative culture is the belief that innovation is every employee's job, not just the purview of a few. That belief has to manifest in the way the business operates day to day. For collaboration to thrive, leaders must believe that everyone has the capacity to innovate and create and must give their people the autonomy to try and to fail without fear.

Put ideas first. How do you empower all team members to contribute when some are naturally more assertive in meetings, especially in this new world of hybrid work where remote employees may feel less connected? At Slack, team members are now asked to generate ideas before meetings. "They put all the ideas out on a table in a virtual room, and then you have a conversation," says Brian Elliott, executive leader of the Future Forum at Slack. Elliott says this practice limits "groupthink" and allows all voices to be heard. Within a few months of doing this, the company saw concrete business benefits. For example, its pace of releasing new features accelerated as internal teams were "finding ways to do it better," says Elliott.

As we saw in chapter 3, with their PRFAQ approach to new ideas, Amazon believes in the power of the written word. Here's another example of how what the company calls its "document culture" is being used to help generate collaborative ideas.

Before meetings at Amazon Web Services, participants put their ideas in memos. The start of the meeting is silent while the team reads each other's memos, and then discussion begins. Writing forces people to organize their thoughts, and readers must focus on the quality of the idea rather than who's offering it, says Stephen Brozovich, principal evangelist at Amazon Web Services' HR Transformation division. To increase the focus on the ideas themselves, the memos are anonymized. Document-based meetings also improve hybrid work, when collaboration happens between people who are on-site and off-site. These meetings "change the voices heard in the room, because they aren't dominated by those who are centrally located," says Brozovich. The inclusivity benefits are clear, as this model allows input from individuals regardless of location or personal circumstances, such as childcare responsibilities.

Even virtual meetings have inclusivity benefits, notes Molly Hellerman, global head of innovation programs at Atlassian, a collaboration software company that sells the popular platform Jira. "In our research about how meetings are run, we've found they tend to be more inclusive when we see each face individually," Hellerman says. For example, there is no head of the table. To further promote inclusivity, some managers time how long each person speaks, and some impose a rule that says if one participant dials in, everyone does—even if they're on-site.

Tear down boundaries. Innovation that drives growth over the long term is best achieved when decision-making is delegated to agile, cross-functional teams "with high levels of autonomy," according to a study by Forrester Financial. But the effort stalls when useful information is hoarded by designated "innovation teams" and people don't collaborate. To encourage broader collaboration, companies must tear down information silos. Teams must be willing to share their works in progress and be open to input from throughout the organization, according to collaboration software company Atlassian's blog. Open information sharing inside companies can take many forms. Collaboration tools like Google Docs and Sharepoint provide an easy way for people to create, edit, and discuss documents related to project work. Importantly, managers should resist the temptation to restrict access to documents and forums unless truly necessary.

Modernize tech. Collaborative technology is critical to supporting innovation and more agile ways of working, especially in this age of distributed work. And let's face it—email just isn't the best option for open, asynchronous collaboration. In addition to document collaboration, project management tools like Jira and Trello are important for ensuring that good ideas make their way to execution.

A blog post published by Atlassian explains that the software platform used to help teams collaborate matters, too. It should be open, flexible, and customizable, they say. And it should be extensible, so it can support an organization's existing assets. In addition, moving to the cloud lowers the cost of collaborating by allowing organizations to rent rather than buy computing power and to pilot emerging technologies with less investment. "Using the cloud can reduce the risk of innovation and increase the benefits of collaboration, considerably," says Mark Schwartz, enterprise strategist at Amazon Web Services.

Working with Anne's team at the foundation, we eventually got the collaboration moving in the right direction. I helped them identify a talented leader from my network to run the program and serve as our liaison. We made a lot of good progress in curating a quality dataset and executing commercial deals with biopharma. It was an innovative opportunity and set the stage for other foundation-commercial partnerships. We would like to acknowledge the vision and work of Ray and Meredith Huml, the father-daughter duo who had a big hand in the idea behind a registry for neuromuscular diseases and who also are a powerful reminder that successful collaborations aren't just limited to your office mates.

One area of innovative collaborations goes by the acronym P3. It stands for "public-private partnerships," an increasingly popular trend in many industries and particularly in public works. According to the journal *Public Works Management and Policy*, such collaborations involve the use of predevelopment agreements to enhance collaboration between the public and private sectors. Known colloquially as "progressive P3s," these agreements allow the private sector to help scope and shape the structure of projects at the front end.

This is collaboration on a massive scale—in some cases, literally the size of a city. A case in point is the city of Lynn, Massachusetts, in which a truly inspired public-private collaboration has quite literally transformed the cityscape.

CHAMPIONS OF CHANGE

Lessons from Fearless Founders and Enterprising Executives

Al Wilson
Founder and CEO, Beyond Walls

A century ago, the city of Lynn, Massachusetts, produced a million pairs of shoes a day.

Today, it produces art—huge works of outdoor art. To date, it produces an average of about thirteen large-scale works a year, many of them painted on the very walls of the buildings that once housed Lynn's shoe factories and mills.

Beyond Walls, a not-for-profit founded in 2016, is the engine behind an explosion of outdoor artistic activity that now makes Lynn one of the most distinctive skylines in New England. As of this writing, a total of eighty-seven murals painted on the exteriors of downtown buildings, ranging from single-story storefronts to nine-story apartment complexes, now give this once-drab, down-and-out city a new head-turning vitality.

Entrepreneur Al Wilson created Beyond Walls as a response to a citywide effort to increase walkability and enhance cultural offerings.

But he was most certainly not alone. Collaboration—with local community leaders, advocacy groups, government agencies, schools, and local businesses, not to mention the artists themselves—was, he says, "fundamentally critical. It would not have happened without collaborations, at every level and in almost every aspect of the project."

During a walking tour of the city, Wilson showed off some of the most spectacular—and subtle—works of art, which are commissioned and painted over a two-and-a-half-week period each year (artists are trained in safety protocols and certified to use the kinds of lifts and harnesses that enable them to spray paint or put a brush or roller to the side of a tall building).

The pantheon of Beyond Walls paintings includes some truly stunning works, such as the nine-story portrait of a young man by an Australian artist known as Smug One. The towering, photorealistic mural depicts a handsome, fit young man with a pair of athletic shoes slung over his shoulders, as if he's on his way to the gym. It's called *The Resident* because that fit, young man actually lived in the building on which his portrait is painted.

Art like that gets attention. Wilson has had interest from cities around New England and beyond looking to initiate Beyond Walls projects in their downtowns. Beyond Walls has received multiple awards for its work, including the MassInc. Gateway Cities "Innovation" Award, the HubWeek Art Award for "Most Impactful Public Art," the Rudy Bruner Award for Urban Excellence, and the American Institute of Architects (AIA) Urban Design Award, which recognizes "the best in urban design, regional and city planning, and community development." Wilson has been invited to speak at national conferences in New Orleans, St. Louis, Atlanta, and Jackson, Mississippi.

As he acknowledges, none of this would have happened without partnerships, alliances, and friendships—collaboration in every form. Here are some insights about collaboration from the founder of Beyond Walls.

Build your collaborations from the inside out.

Looking for collaborators? Start with the people around you. For Wilson, it was in the parks and on the playgrounds of Lynn. A recreational soccer player, Wilson competed in the adult leagues and pick-up games that are a fixture of many communities. Relationships formed on the field and soon migrated to informal get-togethers after the games. There, ideas were exchanged, particularly about how to make downtown Lynn safer, brighter, and more appealing. "We talked about maybe which streets could be one way, or where we could add bike lanes," Wilson said. "None of which happened then. But it was the start of something bigger."

These informal exchanges provided the nucleus of a group that eventually grew to include twenty-eight volunteers. "They were a slice of the community," he said. "Residents, business people, elected officials." And it was from this group that the larger vision of Beyond Walls arose. "The feeling of the group was, 'Let's make it epic,'" he said.

Build your collaborations gradually—and communicate frequently.

As with any bold, new idea, there were skeptics and naysayers. "No one gave us much chance," Wilson says. "But once we got rolling, it was like a snowball, pulling more and more people in."

One way people heard about the project was a weekly newsletter Beyond Walls produced that provided project updates and outlined how the work was advancing. This gave all involved and the broader community a real sense of progress and reinforced ownership and responsibility.

The mayor of Lynn received the newsletter, and Al was able to arrange a meeting with her. Al and his collaborators made a positive impression as they described their vision. "The mayor told her department heads, 'This is good for the city. Try not to get in this group's way,'" Al chuckled. "That alone was really helpful."

When Al and his volunteer committee were first starting to talk about some kind of downtown revitalization, no one had a contact in City Hall. That "friend-of-a-friend" connection to the mayor's office wouldn't have happened without a gradual widening of his collaborative circle.

Another gradually established collaboration helped remove the last major obstacle to the launch of Beyond Walls. The group needed a special license from the Massachusetts Bay Transit Authority to install much-needed underpass lighting on three downtown railroad bridges in Lynn—part of what Al calls a "designed response" to the problem. "We were trying to provide a creative response to the problem," he said. But attempts to acquire that license were stymied by a wall of regulations, lawyers, and bureaucrats.

At the time, Al had started to collaborate with the chief of staff of a local congressman, who saw the value in what the group was doing. When he heard from Al about their problems getting permission from the Transit Authority, he just picked up the phone. "It turns out he and the head of the MBTA had served in Iraq together," Al explains. "He called his friend, and in ninety seconds it was solved. We got the license. But it wouldn't have happened if this collaboration wasn't so robust."

Map out your collaborative network.

Wilson realized that the project's success rested on a stable foundation of support. And he singled out three collaborative pillars, all of them stakeholders in the project. "We identified the business community, the city, which included department heads and elected officials, and, of course, the residents of Lynn, who would be the ones most impacted by this," he said. "We recognized that all three of these 'legs of the stool,' so to speak, needed to be involved in each major decision." Having a big picture of the various allies and decision-makers who needed to be involved helped ensure smoother interaction.

Make your collaborators accountable.

Finding collaborators is one step. Establishing the terms of their collaboration is another. "You've got to keep your collaborators engaged," Al says. He did this in the early days of the Beyond Walls project by assigning people in his original group to specific tasks. This increased accountability but also weeded out those who weren't willing to put in some work. "We'd give people little assignments coming out of our weekly meetings," he said. "The people who were there to just gripe don't show up for the next meeting. Because they hadn't done the work. And we needed collaborators who were willing to contribute time and energy."

Such efforts helped make the group stronger and more effective. "It's not just kumbaya and 'Isn't this nice that we're all here together?'" he says. "You've got to hold people accountable. That's how effective innovation works."

For more information, visit https://beyondwalls.org/.

5

THE 5C's: CHANGE—INNOVATING
FOR TRANSFORMATION

I was deep into my reading when the Air France pilot—flying the Sunday afternoon Paris to Riyadh route—announced in a heavy French accent, first in Arabic and then English, that we were entering Saudi airspace. The crew, impeccably dressed in the smart Air France red and pale blue uniforms, gathered up a few remaining wineglasses and stowed away and locked the alcohol cabinet. The passengers in business class, mostly moms in their mid-thirties with school-age children, donned their abayas over their jeans and T-shirts. It was 2014, and the government of the Kingdom of Saudi Arabia (KSA) had a no-alcohol policy and women were required to wear the traditional dress—abayas and hijabs—when in public.

I deplaned at King Abdulaziz International Airport wearing black slacks and a tailored white blouse. "What is your business in the Kingdom, Mrs. Marchand?" asked the young immigration officer at passport control. "Advising an investment firm on innovative healthcare business opportunities!" I replied helpfully, wishing to be perceived as a friendly American. After he checked my visa and stamped my passport, I was hurriedly ushered into a black sedan that delivered me to the local abaya shop, where I was fitted and dressed in a calf-length black robe in under fifteen minutes. One advantage: There were no fashion decisions to make—I just required a serviceable garment to wear during my weeklong meeting with the private equity company I was advising.

The manager of human resources of the company hosting my visit accompanied me and paid the bill. She had introduced herself at the airport as Farah. She was a gracious woman in her thirties with a bright smile outlined in a festive shade of red lipstick, big brown eyes ringed by luxurious black lashes, and a black hijab wrapped snugly around her face. We climbed into the back seat, and twenty minutes later, Farah was checking me into the Four Seasons Hotel in downtown Riyadh, where I was shown a room on the women-only floor, called the Pearl. She then gave me something I hadn't heard since I was an adolescent and my mother took me aside one evening after school: instructions for how to be a woman.

More specifically, she outlined the rules and codes for being a woman staying in Saudi Arabia.

"You can wear your abaya open since you're Western," She added. I was relieved to hear that I didn't have to wear the hijab. "Just put it around your shoulders like a scarf," she advised. She then instructed me not to leave the Pearl, which had a lounge, fitness center, a separate elevator, and an all-female staff. After telling me the car would pick me up at 7:30 a.m., she bid me good night. I heard a voice on a loudspeaker outside the hotel recite the final prayer of the day. I sipped tea as I reread the board meeting materials, this time in the large three-ringed binder Farah had left in the room. I anticipated my first experience in KSA as I nodded off to sleep.

And an experience it was. During my first visit to the Kingdom, I had an opportunity to witness a slow but sure transformation in a society that so severely, if politely, limited what I—or any other woman, regardless of where she came from—could do. A campaign was taking shape to give Saudi women the right to drive. Although it may sound like a simply practical thing to do, making such a change in a society where, as recently as the 1950s, women couldn't attend college was not a decision to be made lightly.

I was on a business visa (at the time, there were no tourist visas), having been asked by a business school colleague, who was now the chief operating officer for a private equity firm, to serve on the board of advisors. My role was to advise on the firm's investments in healthcare, both in-country and abroad, and to work with Farah on modernizing HR policies.

I enjoyed the local cuisine of shawarma, kabsa, dates, and yogurt. Honestly, I felt like a celebrity while I was there—as an American businesswoman, I was treated with respect and admiration. Family businesses, like the one I was advising, were seeking to expand and invest and wanted to learn more about opportunities in the United States and Europe. I also learned something that surprised me: the restrictions on women were not simply sexist because men wanted to keep females subjugated. And women are not necessarily the second-class citizens they appear to be to outsiders. In fact, as I learned, women are highly respected in Saudi culture, and the conservative dress code is meant to preserve their dignity and to protect them from unwanted advances, according to Farah, who is Lebanese. She was in the country with her husband, who was also from Lebanon and worked for the Saudi government. I also learned that KSA was a country with strong values—religion, family, and healthy living—which meant no alcohol, illicit drugs, or entertainment. People were friendly and looked happy. Clearly, KSA was doing a lot right, but still, the traditions and policies for women and the presence of sharia law made for a restrictive environment. I wondered about the impact on innovation, where the mindset requires curiosity, problem-solving, adaptability to change, and diversity. Would such a closed society be open to new and bold initiatives?

The trip was successful. My advice seemed well received, although I realized that instilling some of the attributes necessary for innovation was going to take time. When I returned home, I continued to follow the news from KSA. And I must say I was quite happy when, in September 2017, I read that women had been given the right to drive.

It was a small but significant step toward a society where women were not only respected but also treated as equals.

During that first visit, I had formed a different view about what most Americans know as Saudi Arabia. And I was glad to see that my hopes that this society was taking positive steps forward, at least in the arena of women's rights, seemed to be confirmed.

Fast-forward to my recent visit to KSA, to a university in Riyadh in February 2024. This time, I wasn't consulting; I was teaching a program on business and entrepreneurship. On this trip, I wore a business suit, stayed at a Hilton Garden Inn, and moved about the country freely. The educational program included a mixed cohort of men and women. I quickly learned it was the first time some of the students had ever been in an integrated classroom. Yet both sexes seemed open and willing to work together, and I observed new friendships forming and an appreciation for differences of thought and approach—the innovation mindset at work, I thought! The women in my class were bright, accomplished, and energetic—studying, law, engineering, and marketing—and excited about their future careers. Even the abayas had changed. I saw women in beautiful white, tan, or navy abayas and some with beads. The women's makeup was exquisitely done, and I could tell they took pride in their appearance. The students formed mixed-gender project teams, and their assignment was to plan the launch of a new product. One of the team's projects was expanding an athleisure brand into the Middle East. The team proposed a line of athletic wear they named Modi because it was full-body clothing that reflected the modesty sought by women in the culture.

My hopes—that this vibrant society with much to offer was changing for the better—had been confirmed, at least from my limited perspective. This was innovation at a societal level. Or was it?

Economically, the main problem for the Saudis can be summed up in one word: oil.

Yes, the precious commodity that transformed these desert societies into economic powerhouses is also their Achilles heel—and they know it. Today, oil accounts for 90 percent of Saudi's budget revenues. And this oil-based economy has, at least up to now, ensured KSA's economic success. According to a 2024 *Forbes India* report, it's ranked nineteenth among the world's major economies.[1] Its people, like those in the private-equity family business I had visited, have benefited, as have the millions of ex-pats who have moved to KSA from the United States, India, Pakistan, Ethiopia, and other countries in the Middle East for oil-related jobs. (According to the *New Arab*, Saudi Arabian census data from 2022 show that foreigners made up more than 40 percent of the population— 13.4 million people in a country of 32.2 million.)

The problem is, as anyone with a business background will quickly attest to, KSA's wealth is heavily overweighted in one industry. That's very risky in the face of a global societal movement to decrease reliance on petroleum-based products and use green or sustainable forms of energy, like electricity to power vehicles. It's an ominous trend for a country so dependent on one economic pillar.

The Kingdom's leaders have recognized this and have launched what you might call a "re-org" at the national level. It's being led by the Crown Prince Mohammed bin Salman Al Saud, widely known as MBS. He and his administration are calling it Vision 2030, and it is a massive government program for economic and social transformation. The fact that Vision 2030 was announced in 2017 suggests that the leadership in the capital city of Riyadh realizes what a monumental task this will be.

How are they doing so far, in terms of economic measures? According to a report by the New Zealand Ministry of Foreign Affairs and Trade, Saudi Arabia's nominal gross domestic product (GDP) growth in 2022 was an impressive 8.7 percent, placing it first in the G20. Its tech sectors have ballooned, with the e-commerce sector alone expected to exceed $13 billion in valuation by 2025. The proportion of Saudi women in the workforce has doubled in the last four years to 33 percent, surpassing the 30 percent target laid out in the original plan.[2]

The report also notes that the plan has fallen short on several counts. It states that international tourism has proved a hard sell for wary Westerners, and the tourists that do arrive seem to be a motley crew of intrepid Christian fundamentalists and Saudi-bankrolled social media influencers. Grandiose construction projects have been plagued by setbacks upon contact with reality. And despite a ready availability of solar and wind energy, as well as an enviable uranium endowment, ambitious sustainability targets have proved infeasible and have been quietly scaled back numerous times.

Still, although this is a book on innovation and not geopolitics, my own impression, after having traveled in the Kingdom considerably over the past decade, echoes that of Alex Zhavoronkov, PhD. He offered his observations on the changes in the Kingdom in a 2022 story in *Forbes*, "The New Saudi Arabia—Vision 2030 and AI": "I believe that within the next ten years, Saudi Arabia will be better recognized as a place that leads global efforts for advanced artificial intelligence and cutting-edge innovation than as a land of conflicts."[3]

Maybe it's my natural optimism, but I'd like to think that Dr. Zhavoronkov is correct that the changes I witnessed as an American businesswoman are part of larger and more sweeping ones in what, until quite recently, was a closed and hierarchal society.

We'll come back to the future of KSA at the end of this chapter. In the meantime, let's take a look at another vision statement. I know it's hard to imagine one more audacious than recasting an entire nation's economy, but this one is equally ambitious: "to make life multi-planetary by establishing a self-sustaining city on Mars."

A city on Mars? Are they kidding? No, that statement from SpaceX is consistent with its commitment to progress and disruption in the field of space exploration and technology. Can you see the future and yourself in it? Maybe. Many of their stakeholders can. Why be satisfied with exploring only our planet Earth when you can experience other planets in the solar system? It appeals to the pioneering spirit, the adventurer, the Lewis and

Clark and Christopher Columbus explorer in Americans. And it's gaining traction. Founded in 2002, SpaceX designs, manufacturers, and launches advanced rockets and spacecraft with a purpose of revolutionizing space technology. And look at who's on board with human missions to Mars—NASA, the China National Space Administration, the European Space Agency, Boeing, and space advocacy groups like the Mars Society and the Planetary Society. Now that's a mind shift—getting us to think in a whole new way. It's an example of radical innovation that bends the curve, changing life forever. It's the same effect trains, planes, and automobiles had in the late 1800s and early 1900s, giving us the ability to explore and utilize more of our planet for societal, economic, and personal benefit. Why is this kind of change—of the SpaceX ilk—so difficult for an organization? In their book *Radical Innovation*, Gus Gruber and Wolfgang Roca examine how and why people struggle with change in organizations. They posit that most are confused by the concepts of process innovation as opposed to radical innovation.

Mark Powell, a former Oxford fellow, author, and former partner at Ernst and Young, explains, "Process innovation is about moving up the curve. Radical innovation is about changing the curve, moving things in a new direction entirely. But changing the curve is risky, because you can't guarantee it will work." Mark says that the problem in organizations is that for individuals to move the curve (Reed Hastings moved the curve in a new direction when he launched Netflix, a new way to access DVDs), they must take personal risks that organizations often punish if the new initiatives don't work. "I can teach you financial management," he says. "I can teach you basic concepts of managing a team." But what drives creativity is a shift in mindset—what I call an "innovation mindset." Mark takes a similar view. "I can't change people, much less an organization, unless I challenge their way of looking at the world."

Mark—a leadership consultant who was a professional competitive dancer for more than twenty years—describes an interesting personal experience that changed his own mindset. Mark says that, as a dancer, you are a member of various groups, but you compete as an individual not as a member of any organization. His personal goal was to get into the finals—the top six—and win. "I got to the point where I was in the top twelve of every competition, but I couldn't get any further." His coach at the time was Lynn Harmon, a world-renowned professional dance instructor ("one of the best dancers ever," Mark notes). He asked her what he should do to advance. Lynn's advice shocked him. "I'll never forget that moment," he says. "She said, 'You're gonna have to learn to breathe.'"

Mark said he laughed and remembers saying something like, "Okay, I'm pretty sure I know how to breathe." "But," she said, "you're missing the point. You're technically as good as anybody else, but you're going to have to think about different ways of creating energy." Performers create energy, whether it's singing, acting, dancing, or something else, Mark explains. "And we create energy by controlling our breathing. If you've ever done yoga, you kind of get the gist of it. A lot of power from yoga comes from how you breathe." Lynn told Mark she could teach him to use his breathing to create more energy, which in turn would give his dancing more impact and measurably improve his results.

"But then, what she said really caused me to pause—caused me to panic," Mark went on. She told me that while I was learning to breathe differently and before I mastered it, my results were going to go south. "So be prepared to start losing competitions you would have won, but you have to stick with it," Lynn emphasized.

Mark says this mind shift required a big commitment—he had to balance the idea of practicing harder and longer with practicing differently. He had to adjust his vision of success. "Lynn turned out to be right. For six months my results tanked!" Why? Mark was "playing," as he describes it, exploring, working with a new idea. "Then suddenly, I went from the top twelve to the top six finishers, but not before I bottomed out first. But it was absolutely the right thing to do to improve my performance."

The reason I'm sharing Mark's story is that making change in an organization often follows a similar trajectory. Sometimes we must stop doing something and learn a new way of doing that something—in effect going backward—before we move forward again. A lot of organizations can't cope with that concept. They can't handle the idea of potentially going off track to get on track. Mark says the idea of rehearsal, of experiment and play, is a concept that doesn't exist in many organizations outside the performing arts. Mark is emphatic on this point: "You can't innovate, you can't make meaningful change that bends the curve if you don't experiment; you are doomed to incremental innovation on the curve but not changing the curve."

How is this relevant in business? Mark says he was working with a water company in the United Kingdom that was having the same problem water companies around the world experience—30 percent of their product, water, leaks into the ground. That's a big, expensive problem. He advised them to use artificial intelligence (AI) to identify and find leaks in the underground water network, enabling the company to repair leaks earlier. Good idea, right? Well, not so fast, according to Mark, who chuckles recounting the tale. "They said, 'Yeah, but this is how we run our process. We have union workers who work in this manual way and they need to make a living; we're happy to build a slightly better tool. But why would we transform everything?'" Mark was ultimately successful in getting the water company to use AI to help detect leaks but only after they designed a pilot that didn't displace the union workers.

Let's look at one more powerful example of vision and mind shift.

Born in Spain and trained in clinical medicine and basic research, Francisco Leon, MD, PhD, was a drug developer at the Immunology/Oncology Department of Bristol Myers Squibb (BMS) when we met in 2002. I was running research and development (R&D) business operations, and we were collaborating on a company-wide educational training program called SciEx. Francisco was excited about the program and eagerly assisted in developing materials to explain drug-development simulation. I saw then he was an innovative thinker destined to shake up the world of biotech, and he's never let me down. Francisco has spent his entire professional life studying immunology, the science of how the body fights external and internal sources of disease, and he's worked for large corporations, including BMS and, later, Johnson & Johnson. His interests in immunology include celiac disease, type 1 diabetes, psoriasis, and Crohn's disease, and for the past eight years, he's been interested in the thymus gland and its potentially critical role in immune diseases.

His problem was that he couldn't interest investors in research on the thymus gland given how little was understood about it, making it too speculative an investment at the time. So Francisco did what a good innovator does. He pivoted. In 2016, he put on hold the thymus-focused company plan and instead pitched the lower-risk approach of drug repositioning. He and his business partner, Ashleigh Palmer, founded Provention Bio, a biotech company that acquired six candidate drugs that had been abandoned by other companies to reposition them for the prevention of autoimmune based diseases including one drug candidate targeting Type1 diabetes. Provention Bio never paid a single dollar in upfront fees for any of these assets. Instead, they promised the seller a return once Provention Bio successfully developed the assets and sold or commercialized them. Investors liked the sound of that deal. Francisco and his partner raised $28.4 million in a series A round of funding. Ultimately, they took the company public, and they obtained Food and Drug Administration approval for a drug that delays the onset of type 1 diabetes—teplizumab (Tzield®). They sold the company, based on this revolutionary immune-resetting drug, to Sanofi in 2023 for $2.9 billion. The press release described Provention as a leader in a new drug category of immune disease interception—a game changer for people at risk for developing type 1 diabetes and with potential in many other immune diseases.

Francisco says, "That's the innovation mindset—right? 'Let's do something that others wouldn't do.' People wouldn't touch those assets. They had no value to them at the time. So we worked on them and ultimately were able to commercialize a drug that intercepts diabetes in its tracks, earning Sanofi's commitment to enable broad access to the drug to those who need it."

Francisco's innovativeness didn't suddenly emerge while he was working in Big Pharma. He tells the story of being a boy curious about what would happen if he lit a match to a paper bag doused with alcohol. "I almost caught the house on fire," he laughs. "Fortunately, my mom wasn't too mad!" Francisco says that to create change, you need a very high degree of curiosity and a very low respect for tradition. "So many times, people accept what they're told, especially if taught by a figure of authority. But other people are always challenging the status quo." While at Johnson & Johnson, Francisco was asked to take a personality test, along with peers in his department. The test asked about one's comfort level when disregarding conventional wisdom. "It was almost embarrassing because I was off the charts in my desire to buck the status quo." Francisco says he's always believed you have to question everything, especially being in the scientific field. "Going down the wrong path can be an expensive mistake for a pharma company."

That brings us to the present—Francisco had not given up on studying the thymus gland; he just needed to create a path to continue his work. In January 2024, he founded a new biotech, Tolerance Bio, to preserve, manipulate, and regenerate the thymus gland. And he's working on a meaningful proof of concept for the new science, creating an entirely new therapeutic modality for a condition where kids are born without the thymus and succumb in two or three years to repeated infections and autoimmunity.

He explains more about the thymus gland, a soft organ in the upper chest that produces T cells and hormones. "Babies are born with a thymus gland to protect them from disease." It is largest in infants and children. After the first two years of life, he says, the thymus starts to shrink, and it nearly disappears after puberty. Only about 5 to 10 percent of its function is left in adults. "Our T cell immune repertoire has been established, and the medical dogma was that you don't need the thymus anymore as an adult," he says. "At least that was the general belief in the field. So it was totally against conventional wisdom to think that you should preserve your thymus, because if evolution doesn't preserve it, you must not need it, right?" Always ready to question authority, Francisco challenged the conventional wisdom. He created the business plan for Tolerance Bio in 2016, pitched it to a few investors, and got zero interest—"They said it was a crazy idea." But timing is everything. His moment to strike again came when a study, published in 2023 in the *New England Journal of Medicine*, showed that cardiac surgery patients who also had their thymus removed had a 300 percent increase in mortality, with significant increases in cancer and autoimmunity, in the five years after the surgery.[4] These findings published in a prestigious medical journal enabled Francisco to revisit conventional theories about the thymus. Francisco's theory is that by finding a way to simulate the function of the thymus gland, the immune system's senescence can be addressed, improving quality and duration of life for many people. He added the study's results to his original business plan and was able to secure investment with biotech venture capitalists. "Tolerance Bio wouldn't have happened if I hadn't challenged the conventional wisdom and created a vision about what was possible," he says.

What can we learn from visionary innovators like Mark and Francisco? Plenty. Here are some principles for making effective and lasting change in your organization.

PRINCIPLE 1: CREATE A BURNING PLATFORM

We're not suggesting an experiment along the lines of what Francisco did as a kid. This is different. This is about injecting urgency into your message. Leaders have to define what's wrong with the status quo and get people excited about the future. They need their employees to see the exigency—the pressing need, the urgency—that informs their idea and to recognize that the best time to change is now. They need to build a narrative explaining the need for the change, make sure it resonates with customers and employees, build alignment across the organization, and deal with resistance.

Emily O'Halloran, a former managing director in Accenture's digital business unit, explains how a burning platform (a situation in which an urgent crisis requires immediate, significant change) was created to move the consulting giant into a new direction, a direction that embraced going digital. "We needed to transition our entire organization to digital, helping our clients understand how digital technologies could either propel their businesses forward or pose disruptive challenges." How did Emily do this? She says that Accenture made several acquisitions to create the digital business unit that was responsible for leading the transition. The fact that the consulting organization was talent based meant inspiring a whole lot of people from different companies and different cultures and melding them into one. This shift marked a departure from a traditional consulting model to one that prioritizes digital platforms, customer engagement, and applied intelligence. "To lead our clients into the new digital landscape, we first had to transform ourselves. This meant becoming a digital-focused organization, challenging existing norms, and introducing fresh ideas," Emily says. "We had to create a new business unit with a new way of working and show people they were part of something important, groundbreaking, and needed by our clients."

PRINCIPLE 2: PREPARE TO BE WRONG

Sir Ken Robinson was a visionary cultural leader who challenged establishment thinking on education. In his work in his native Great Britain—and through a hugely popular 2006 TED Talk—Sir

Ken (as he was known) questioned some of the basic assumptions of schooling in the West and urged fundamental changes. "Robinson argued that children do not grow into artistic creativity but are educated out of it by school systems that prioritise academic achievement and conformity instead of liberating imagination and initiative," wrote *The Guardian* in its 2020 obituary on the educational reformer. Sir Ken pulled no punches when it came to his vision of change. "I believe our only hope for the future is to adopt a new concept of human ecology, one in which we start to reconstitute our conception of the richness of human capacity," he said in a speech in 2006. "Our education system has mined our minds in the way we strip-mined the earth for a particular commodity. We have to rethink the fundamental principles in which we are educating our children."

That same year, Sir Ken recorded his famous TED Talk, provocatively titled "Do Schools Kill Creativity?" With 78 million views, it is still referenced in discussions about innovation and change and the importance of taking risks. In it, he argues that we don't grow into creativity; we grow out of it, in large part because educational institutions snuff out creativity. Children will take chances, but they lose the capacity to take risks as they get older for fear of being wrong. Or, as Sir Ken memorably said in his TED Talk, "If you're not prepared to be wrong, you'll never come up with anything original."

But that's the biggest problem organizations face with respect to creativity in their workforce: people are just terrified of being wrong. And for good reason. Those who are wrong usually pay a price. And once again, too many organizations pay lip service to Sir Ken's ideas, but in practice, those employees who dare to think differently are often penalized if their ideas don't pan out (as can be the case with innovation) when they take a risk and do something different. Mark Powell, who we met earlier in this chapter, is a big fan of Robinson's, but he recognizes the practical problems with following his advice. He emphasizes, "People do get fired if they try to do something different and it doesn't work."

Management, he said, needs the courage to allow their employees to try. The payoff is potentially too great not to. "If you try new things," Mark says, "99 percent of them probably won't work. But the 1 percent that do work could change everything!"

Do you have the courage to allow your employees to change, grow, and perhaps find the new idea that could change everything? That's what successful innovation is based on.

PRINCIPAL 3: DELETE SOMETHING

To get people to change, you have to free up time to work on the new, more important things. Henri Richard, president and GM of Rapidus Design Solutions and advisor to several technology firms, has a framework he uses to create that bandwidth.

Hit the "delete" button—literally and figuratively.

"Every year at the beginning of the planning cycle, I would ask my team, 'What are we going to delete?'"

Henri's goal is to consciously stop doing something so that he and the team can free up their schedules to focus on priorities that matter. Bandwidth, originally a broadcasting expression referring to radio frequencies, has become appropriated, according to the *Cambridge Dictionary*, to mean the ability or time to deal with a situation, especially one that involves a large amount of information or a number of problems. It can be expressed in terms of time, people, money, or even brain cycles, Henri says. "If I say to my team, "'Oh, well, there's all this new stuff we have to do, and so we need to do more with the same people and the same hours in a day,' people resist you, and they start to feel burned out." Instead, try some addition by subtraction. "You get a lot better reception if you start by saying, 'We're all working 100 percent, but unfortunately there are new things that we need to put on the table. So let's first decide what we're taking off the table." When you follow that very simple discipline, he says, "you have a much more constructive discussion on innovation."

PRINCIPLE 4: CHANGE BEFORE YOU HAVE TO

Most leaders of innovation agree that change is easier when there is tension. Henri Richard knows this well, too. "Maybe you don't need a crisis per se," he says, "but everybody would agree that it's easier, meaning you encounter less resistance, to change when you have no choice. And it's so much better to change when things are good, because there's more money, less tension, and less stress."

So, what's the answer to this paradox?

Henri says, "If there's a tip for leaders of change, it's this: The minute you feel like things are going well, stop, step back, and start to define your change-management strategy." He shares an example of how he forced change and averted a crisis when he worked for a Fortune 500 technology company. "Despite strong performance in Europe, I decided to close operations in seventeen countries to focus resources on improving our market position in the UK. This decision was challenging, and we did it with the best interest of our employees, helping redistribute work, but aimed at achieving a better overall outcome. It's important to anticipate challenges and make change even when business is good, especially when business is good."

Tony DaRe agrees. The founder and CEO of BSI Corporation, a health benefits consulting firm with offices in Bethlehem, Pennsylvania, and Detroit, Michigan, Tony says his company has had several phases of growth since he founded it in 2003. A former college football and rugby player, Tony says he's always been competitive but, at the same time, team oriented. "I was driving the company hard right before COVID. Finances were good, we were growing, but I realized I wasn't having fun anymore, and I was pretty sure I was burning out my team." Tony sat down one weekend with his partners to discuss the situation. They asked themselves, "Do we want to keep doing this?" The answer was "yes" but with a caveat. "It had to be fun again, and we had to make sure we had a great culture and a fun place to work, where employees felt appreciated and that they were growing." In other words, Tony took a step backward to go forward—and he never looked back. "We adopted summer hours, hybrid work, more family-oriented schedules, and started doing things together." The company also became a sponsor of the annual Bethlehem music festival, an eleven-day event that is one of the biggest private music festivals in the United States.

The new initiatives have gone over well with employees. "I'm proud to say we've had one person leave the company in two and a half years, and our customer-satisfaction scores are off the charts," Tony says. "When COVID hit, we were ahead of the game because we had already incorporated a lot of the workplace changes other companies had to adopt during the pandemic. We changed before we needed to, and it really paid off." In 2023, in a culmination of the changes Tony and his team made, their company was named the number one employee benefits consulting firm in the United States.

PRINCIPLE 5: PACE YOUR CHANGE WITH THE ORGANIZATION'S CAPACITY TO CHANGE

I've seen it in almost every corporate and organizational setting I've worked in, across several industries: when companies institute changes, employees are affected on a personal level. And yet management often doesn't seem to recognize or accommodate the impact these decisions will have. It's important to show empathy and patience while people make the transition. Before assigning any new duties, have transparent conversations about new responsibilities. Gauge how people are feeling and ask how to better support them during this time of change. This might mean more one-on-one mentorship or investment in new training tools. Furthermore, set people up for as much success as possible by providing clear, structured responsibilities and measures of performance. Changing too quickly can negatively impact employee retention, cause drops in profit, and even result in business failure.

PRINCIPLE 6: THINK AHEAD AND MAKE SUSTAINABLE CHANGES

Too many change efforts are rushed. Too many change efforts last only as long as the leader does. Too many disappear within 24 to 36 months. That's been my experience in large corporations. Change that's lasting must be thoughtful and strategic, with detailed plans that evolve over time, and it must be designed to be sustainable. Change also has to fit the organization. As the world continues transforming at a rapid pace, adaptation strategy is something every leader and their team should regularly discuss. In fact, change is so constant for most companies that the change management company Gartner, Inc., reports, that "the typical organization today has undertaken five major firmwide changes in the past three years—and nearly 75 percent expect to multiply the types of major change initiatives they will undertake in the next three years." Transformational leadership guides collective groups of people toward fulfilling the purpose of the company while providing instructions on how to innovate and modernize along the way. Change initiatives also fail, according to 48 percent of the respondents to the Gartner survey, because companies lack the skills to ensure that change can be sustained over time.

When those practicing innovative leadership force change, it often turns out to be hasty and weakly implemented. This leads to change fatigue. A study published by strategyand.pwc, from the Katzenbach Center, found that 65 percent of surveyed people felt they experienced change fatigue caused by initiatives that were underdeveloped, lacked preparation, and were introduced too quickly. Creating change without purpose negatively affects an organization and those who serve it. "The costs are high when change efforts go wrong—not only financially but in confusion, lost opportunity, wasted resources, and diminished morale," warn the strategy consultant DeAnne Aguirre and writer Micah Alpern in the publication *Strategy+Business.* "When employees who have endured real upheaval and put in significant extra hours for an initiative that was announced with great fanfare see it simply fizzle out, cynicism sets in."

Although periods of flux can be uncomfortable for entrepreneurs and business owners and certainly crown princes, innovative leadership is a necessity. Without it, companies become archaic as the world progresses around them. How do entrepreneurs successfully pull off effective innovation? They create a proactive, well-formulated plan that guides companies through periods of growth and organizational change.

The programs I teach in the Kingdom do just this. I instruct Saudi college students and young managers in government agencies about entrepreneurship, innovation, and business skills. Our business programs teach these students the ropes of founding a start-up and/or launching a new business idea within their organizations. Ideas may be as diverse as new healthcare services, replicating services like Amazon and Google locally, and creating new forms of green, sustainable energy. This training helps prepare young talent for jobs of the future by helping them build new skills and acquire knowledge and understanding to launch new innovative businesses, reducing reliance on oil-related jobs.

Amer Alkana is one such example. With the support of King Abdullah University for Science and Technology, he has founded a food and wellness company in KSA called Smash, one of the first healthy food apps for a market he says is more than $1 billion and growing. Amer says, "We've built a robust network of over 300 restaurants across the Kingdom. Our technology is ready to roll, and we're now onboarding the best healthy restaurants in Saudi Arabia, with plans to expand across the GCC [Gulf Cooperation Council] in the next two years." Amer is raising his series A, appealing to investors in the Kingdom of Saudi Arabia, the United Kingdom, and the United States.

A finance student I met at Wharton who organized his own exchange program with King Abdullah University of Science and Technology exemplifies the business curiosity among today's young professionals. Hamzah Almidani is seeking a business education at Wharton to learn finance from one of the best (if not *the* best) business schools in the world. He wants to bring his newfound knowledge and network back to the Kingdom and spread it among his colleagues to inspire the pursuit of innovation and entrepreneurship. His work is a wonderful testament to the power of curiosity and the innovation mindset.

I am proud of Hamzah and Amer and the many Saudi young leaders, male and female, whom I have taught and who are paving the way for the country's future. And I hope that in the next ten years, we'll see Saudi Arabia as a leader in technology, social change, and economic growth. It all starts with the right vision, the right leadership, and the fortitude to stick with the ups and downs that inevitably accompany change. Saudi Arabia has had its ups and downs throughout its over ninety-year history but is making strong progress on a fundamental transformation that I believe will have a positive impact on future generations.

CHAMPIONS OF CHANGE

Lessons from Fearless Founders and Enterprising Executives

Aniruddha Sharma, CEO and Chair of Carbon Clean

"These young geniuses' innovation can help save the world," declared *Forbes* magazine in 2023, describing Aniruddha and his CTO and cofounder Prateek Bumb.

"His work driving the development and delivery of carbon capture and reuse technology could have a genuinely transformational impact on multiple sectors," wrote the organizers of the BusinessGreen Leader Awards when they named Aniruddha Entrepreneur of the Year in 2022. With accolades like that, it should come as no surprise to learn that Aniruddha is an enthusiastic, inspiring proponent of innovation and creativity, starting, of course, with his own company, whose mission he describes as follows: "We help decarbonize the steel, the cement, the waste, the refining petrochemical plants," he says. "Essentially, we're trying to revolutionize industrial decarbonization by bringing technology which is ten times smaller in size compared to what exists today."

And why is that so important? "It is really important," he emphasizes, "because 70 percent of the industrial sites have no space to build any decarbonization equipment."

Today, UK-based Carbon Clean is indeed a global leader in carbon-capture solutions for hard-to-abate industries, such as cement, steel, refineries, and energy from waste. According to the company's website, Carbon Clean's patented technology significantly reduces the costs of carbon capture when compared to conventional solutions. The company has been recognized with a slew of industry honors, including a 2022 BNEF Pioneer award, a Global Cleantech 100 company award (three times), and one of CEMEX Ventures Top50 ConTech Startups.

The future is bright for Carbon Clean. But when Aniruddha and Prateek started the company in 2009, it was what most new ventures are: a gamble. Aniruddha had just turned down a well-paid job from a large management consultancy. And, he notes, we were "in the middle of a global financial crisis."

He was undaunted. "I just knew I had to do it," he says. "I felt that if I didn't make that change at that precise moment, then five or ten years down the line I'd be asking myself why I hadn't. Our time on this planet is limited. So go and take the risk, make it happen!"

How does the CEO of a highly innovative organization encourage creativity and experimentation among his employees? Here are Aniruddha's tips on how leaders can successfully encourage and manage change in their organizations.

Push the envelope.

Aniruddha offers this example, one that many growing businesses face. As they say, it's a good problem but a problem nonetheless. "We'd been doubling our sales every year, and we needed new office space," he says. The company wanted to look in Central London, but of course, office space in one of the world's great capitals is not cheap. The team went out to scout some new locations in the city and then reported back to him.

"They were like, 'We've got these options. They cost x, they cost y. And the energy cost is pretty high.'" Duly noted, said Aniruddha, who then challenged them to push the envelope a bit. "I asked them, 'Why don't we actually look for a building that has its own solar panel, a building that recycles water, a building that has a high level of insulation?'" In other words, a self-sufficient building—the kind of change in location the team had not been considering. But their boss encouraged them to lift their vision beyond "just" another building. "It got them thinking," says Aniruddha. "Which of course, was the idea."

And that's how Carbon Clean found their new home in the London Bridge section of the city. They didn't just move to a new space; they moved to a newsworthy space: the team found one of the only net-zero-carbon buildings in London. Their new headquarters—at 105 Sumner Street, in a building known as The Forge—featured photovoltaic solar panels, rainwater harvesting, natural ventilation, a green roof garden to encourage bee pollination, and a commitment to 100 percent of waste diverted from landfill.

The new location represented a major change for Carbon Clean, a home base that was consistent with their brand and their mission. But it would not have even been considered unless Aniruddha had cajoled his team to think boldly. This, he says, "is an example of pushing people to make a change, and maybe encouraging them to think a bit more out of the box with how and what they're changing."

Oh and as for the extra costs of being in a self-sufficient building? "Actually not true, when you get into the details," he says. "We're making a big savings in energy costs in the long run."

The lesson is this: encourage your employees to think big and to think unconventionally. You never know where that will take them, you, and your business.

Dispel the fears.

Change can be disconcerting, even under the best of circumstances. But when one's livelihood and career are perceived to be at stake as part of the change, it ratchets up unease to terror.

"The culture of penalizing failure is actually quite big in large corporate organizations," Aniruddha acknowledges. There, he says, "everything has to be a success and things that aren't successful are considered a failure." But when it comes to innovation, "that's the wrong way to think about it."

Instead, he says, employees shouldn't be worried that any change they suggest will carry with it a high risk for them. "It's incumbent on business leaders to build a culture that encourages people to take calculated risks and doesn't penalize well-calculated risk-takers," he says. "Obviously, clear expectations must be drawn around not doing stupid things. But if people are thinking through process or possible outcomes carefully and then taking a risk to make something happen, that's different."

Loosen the reins.

Aniruddha believes that when it comes to change management, large organizations are often their own worst enemies. Not only do they take a punitive view toward new ideas that aren't successful, but they also discourage a welcomeness to change by making the inevitable "restructurings" a process that is fraught with insecurity and anxiety. "Whenever you tell an employee, 'Your team size is going to change, your reporting lines are going to be different,' people are like, 'Oh my God, I don't know what's going to happen.' To be honest, it's quite human, it's quite natural. We all invest in our relationships with our bosses and co-workers."

The answer is to make any changes in teams and reporting lines a predictable event. As Carbon Clean began its rapid growth, Aniruddha knew he had to take a closer look at his organizational structure. "I knew these structures had to change as we grew," he said. "So now we go through changes around the team every six to nine months." With that awareness, he said, employees aren't bracing for the shock of an email or the disruption of an unexpected change in their jobs. The scheduled changes, he says, "create a sort of psychological safety net. They know it's going to happen, and they know the outcome is likely to be a positive, for them and for the organization."

Leave the meeting.

Better yet—don't even attend! Most executives would assume that their place is right in the middle of the first or second brainstorming meeting to discuss new ideas. Not so fast, says Aniruddha. "In those early meetings, it's important that the senior managers remove themselves from the room." Creative change, he says, should be a "bottom-up" process. And it makes perfect sense: How many meetings have you sat through, at any stage of your career, when everyone in the room has one eye on the senior executive sitting around the conference table? People are not going to feel free to think creatively; they're going to be thinking about what the boss will think of their idea. That's no way to rev up the innovation process!

Another good reason is that the employees often know what's better. "When we have discussion around what new product features to bring in to make our customers' lives easier, I generally won't be in the room," he says. "We're more likely to have our service managers, the people who actually deal with the customers. They're the ones who can say, 'Do customers really care about this change we're proposing?'"

And senior executives shouldn't worry that their standing is somehow diminished or that they're perceived as weaker if they don't attend every meeting about change. On the contrary, says Aniruddha: "The irony is that, if you think by not being present in the room, you'll lose authority, you've probably already lost authority."

To learn more about Carbon Clean, visit https://www.carbonclean .com/about-us.

6

THE 5C's: CHANCE—INVESTING
IN RISKS

It was the first day of school in early September 1975—a typical humid, summer day in the Maryland suburbs of Washington, DC, where our family lived. My mom had pulled my long, wavy brown hair back in a ponytail with a pink bow to make my mile-long walk to school a little cooler.

It had been a busy day at school, but the most important thing I needed to tell my mother when I returned home that afternoon was the lunchroom incident. When I had unwrapped my sandwich—liverwurst and Swiss cheese on rye with mayonnaise—Sandra Sullivan was appalled. "That is gross!" Sandra shrieked, loud enough for everyone else at the lunch table to turn their attention on me and my sandwich.

And attention is, of course, what no fifth grader wants in the lunchroom.

It was the opening salvo of what turned out to be the year loud-mouthed Sandra tried my patience daily. Everyone else was munching on peanut butter and grape jelly on white Wonder bread. I thought peanut butter and jelly was for babies and loved liverwurst, but still I felt my cheeks flush in embarrassment when Sandra snickered at my lunch.

At the end of the day, when I walked in the door of my house, with my little brother close behind, both of us red-faced from the heat (despite the bow), I regaled my mother with important tidings, the most urgent of which was, of course, the lunchroom incident. I also relayed school news: what I thought of my teacher Mrs. Walker, my old and new friends in class, and oh yes, I almost forgot, the back-to-school parent folder, which I was eager to discuss. Mrs. Walker had explained that a local bank was partnering with area elementary schools like mine, Highland Elementary, to teach kids about saving money. You could open an account by filling out a request for a new savings account and bringing five dollars in cash to school by the end of the week.

"I can't wait to tell dad about it," I told Mom, who nodded.

"Good idea," she said.

Over dinner, Dad listened carefully as I explained it to him and then looked over the form. Together, we hatched a plan. He would pay me for completing tasks in his business, a small chemical manufacturing company, after school. My responsibilities would include assembling and packing plastic bottles, putting packing labels on boxes, and transcribing messages from the answering machine and helping to identify urgent customer calls. Real work, I thought. Most of my friends got an allowance for doing chores—chores that were a joke, in my opinion. I mean, should you really get paid for feeding the dog and making your bed? Give me a break, I thought, as my friend Lisa rattled off her paid chore list over the phone that night. But Lisa and I agreed about one thing—we were both going to use our new sources of income to invest in our savings accounts.

The next day, my mom sent me to school with a five-dollar bill and the completed form in a white envelope labeled "Lorraine Hudson's Savings Account." As I placed the envelope in my schoolbag, my dad, never one to waste a good teaching moment, took me aside. "You can pay us back the $5 interest free when your savings reaches $25. And that's not a small concession," he added. "The interest rate is 8.75 percent, and inflation is 13.4 percent." Then he reminded me of Benjamin Franklin's advice—"A penny saved is a penny earned"—kissed me on the forehead, and told me he'd have some paid tasks waiting for me when I got home from school that afternoon.

I'm not sure I knew what interest and inflation meant, but I liked the idea of my savings account growing larger.

Over the ensuing months, I watched that happen, slowly at first, but between money from my job and gifts—I told everyone who cared to listen that I wanted money instead of presents—and interest accumulating on the account, eventually I had enough to buy a $100 certificate of deposit (CD). That was just the first of my big financial moves: I was very proud the day I acquired a couple shares of stock in Bell Labs for $34.76, which my uncle, who was a manager in the company's Morristown, New Jersey, office helped me procure—I guess you could label that my first exposure to insider trading! I was keen to learn about investing and read books in the public library. Then, low and behold, I got inspiration from an unlikely source. At church! I listened closely to what is probably one of the earliest stories about the power of investing. It's called the Servant's Story, and it's in the New Testament in the Book of Matthew. It goes something like this, depending on the version of the Bible you reference:

[14] A man went away and put his three servants in charge of all he owned. [15] The man knew what each servant could do. So he handed 5,000 coins to the first servant, 2,000 to the second, and 1,000 to the third. Then he left the country. . . .

[19] Sometime later the master of those servants returned. He called them in and asked what they had done with his money. [20] The servant who had been given 5,000 coins brought them in with the 5,000 that he had earned. . . .

[22] Next, the servant who had been given 2,000 coins came in and said, "Sir, you gave me 2,000 coins, and I have earned 2,000 more." . . .

[24] The servant who had been given 1,000 coins then came in and said, "[25] I was frightened and went out and hid your money in the ground. Here is every single coin!"

[26] The master of the servant told him, "[27] You could have at least put my money in the bank, so I could have earned interest on it."

After hearing that, I resolved never to bury any money. But my parents made sure I understood that the real lesson from that parable was about the abilities we are born with and our need to cultivate them and use them for good. Still, it got me thinking about chance, about investing.

"How does someone double their money?" I asked my dad at dinner that night. Before he started his own business, my dad had been a sixth-grade teacher who taught geography, history, and the French language. He always jumped at the opportunity for what we now call a teachable moment. In this case, he saw an opportunity to enhance my financial literacy, which he seemed eager to do. He grabbed a yellow legal pad and pencil, pushed aside his half-eaten plate of manicotti—our family favorite, I should add—and drew a diagram of how he invested in his business. But first, he gave me the setup. Dad always had to set up the context for his lessons first.

He started this lesson with an adage engrained in my brain to this day, "If you're not growing, you're declining, and the only way you grow a business over the long haul is to invest in new areas of opportunity. You have to be creative and think like an inventor to be successful."

First, he drew a line showing how much he invested in his core business—making and selling industrial cleaning products. The main product was an oven and grill cleaner he sold to restaurants and cafeterias. The previous year, he had invested in offering the oven cleaner in a spray bottle and adding two new product lines, a window cleaner and a stainless-steel cleaner, to the core business for the same customer segment. Next, he drew a line showing how much he invested in new customer segments. He had repackaged the existing product line and sold it to two new markets: the printing and engraving and automotive sectors. Finally, he drew a line showing how he was investing in new areas of growth—the trend for environmentally friendly (now called green) chemicals was just emerging, and my dad wanted to get ahead of the curve with a new green line of products that he would create in partnership with a leading sanitation innovator in the area. My dad's diagram showed he was investing 80 percent in core, 15 percent in new markets (we can call this "adjacent" because those areas were close to his original market), and 5 percent in new solutions and new markets (what might be termed "transformative" today).

He showed me his growth forecast for the next three years based on those investments, and I saw that his growth by year three would be primarily driven by the new green product line and that revenues from the core product would be declining as buyer behaviors increasingly favored eco-friendly products. My father had received his bachelor's degree in education, not business, and I asked how he had figured all this out. "The hard way," he said chuckling. "I saw what happened to the business the couple years I held on to profits and was afraid to invest. My business didn't grow. I knew I had to do something different—take some calculated risk—and this portfolio mix has worked well."

Do something different. Take a calculated risk. Take a chance! Identify new markets, new products, new trends, new opportunities for collaboration. These are lessons I learned from my dad and my childhood that have stayed with me to this day. They have informed my views not only on innovation but also on success in business.

INNOVATION: A KEY TO CORPORATE SUCCESS

Looking back, I guess my dad was ahead of his time with his "innovation investment" plan. Back then, few management theorists seemed to pay much attention to that concept. One of the first references to innovation in corporations is found in a volume mentioned earlier in this book, one of the most important business books of the 1980s. In *In Search of Excellence*, Thomas J. Peters and Robert H. Waterman examined seven successful American companies from a list of seventy-five, highlighting what they had in common.

The authors noted that the most successful companies not only invest in innovation to keep their products and services fresh and aligned with customer needs but also have innovative cultures and organizational systems nurtured by leaders who encourage agility, adaptability, and willingness to change, all characteristics that help them create and implement innovative products and services. This blend of investing in Chance and encouraging a Culture that can manage risk is fundamental to the 5C's—in particular, Chance, which we examine in this chapter.

In a much-lauded 2012 *Harvard Business Review* article, "Managing Your Innovation Portfolio," Bansi Nagji and Geoff Tuff reported an interesting investment pattern among companies in the industrial, technology, and consumer goods sectors. Top-performing firms typically allocate about 70 percent of their innovation resources to core offerings, 20 percent to adjacent efforts, and 10 percent to transformational initiatives. As it happens, returns from innovation investments tend to follow an inverse ratio, with 70 percent coming from the transformational realm. The authors' research was inspired by Google founder Sergey Brin's now famous 2003 research and development (R&D) principle called 70-20-10 (also dubbed the Golden Ratio), in which he proved mathematically, according to an interview with his Google cofounder and CEO Eric Schmidt, that you needed 10 percent investment in R&D—things unrelated to the core business—to make the sum of the growth work. The *HBR* authors and Schmidt both admit that this formula is not set in stone and doesn't work for every industry, but still, Brin's work in 2003 and the *HBR* 2012 article have spurred discussions to this day across C-suites and boardrooms globally about the importance of investing in innovation to drive future growth.

In a survey we conducted of 120 executives as part of our research for this book, we asked respondents about the portfolio mix they thought made the most sense for their companies or companies they had worked for. The results from our interviews were interesting: a significant number of interviewees said investing in Chance— new ideas that might spur innovation—was critical for driving company growth. According to the data, the average score rating the importance of innovation investment was eight on a ten-point scale. This underscores a strong consensus around the high value placed on innovation. To test adoption of the portfolio 70-20-10 rule, we asked respondents to hypothetically allocate investments they typically made among core, adjacent, and transformative in their companies.

Their allocations highlighted the importance they placed on innovation driving company growth:

Incremental or core: 40 percent
Adjacent markets/products 30 percent
Disruptive/transformative: 30 percent

These results suggest that our respondents believe in the need to invest in R&D and transformation to an even greater degree than the Sergey Brin 70-20-10 model recommends. Clearly, respondents highly value investment in innovation. But when probed on the actual investment in innovation in their companies, while most couldn't quote the exact amount, it was far less than the ideal represented in our survey results. Why? Was irrational exuberance for innovation that doesn't align with the company's available investment pool the cause?

Mark Adams, partner at Two Bear Capital in New York, which launched a $350 million fund in 2024 for which Mark is sourcing investments from AI, life sciences, and cybersecurity companies, provided his perspective on why there may be a difference between what the C-suite considers ideal and what, in his view, is actually the best approach. Mark believes companies, at all stages of growth, have to invest in technologies to run the business and to create and support the implementation of their products and services. This technology infrastructure is critical to providing products and services and supporting future innovation. This is especially true for high-tech start-ups, where all the focus may be on investing in tech to build differentiation, media buzz, and the product suite. Even in companies the size and breadth of Google and Amazon, the investment in technology is considerable and a top priority.

In 2018, Google announced that it had invested $30 billion in cloud infrastructure to keep pace with its network's needs, a case where the technology is needed to enable the company to deliver core products and services. Mark says tech investment shouldn't be underestimated. He's seen it account for as much as 20 percent of investment dollars and for good reason. The tech is needed to maintain the core business and support new products and services, as was the case with Google. Keep that in mind as we examine the portfolio concept.

As any good financial manager will tell you, the ideal investment portfolio has a mixture of short-term and long-term positions; of stocks and bonds; of liquid assets that can be converted quickly to cash and others, like real estate, that have value but can't be quickly sold. Similarly, the assets in an innovation portfolio vary in terms of their potential payoff and timing.

Some would be incremental, meaning that the innovation is an enhancement, an evolution, or a new twist on an existing product. An example of this would be Coca-Cola adding a new soda flavor.

Others would be disruptive or radical—like Amazon, which essentially turned the entire retail marketplace upside down. A lesser-known example of being disruptive is Emulate, an organ-on-a-chip technology that helps researchers emulate human biology and predict human response. Like most savvy financial investors, smart companies invest in their innovations along a continuum of risk and reward. Their goal is to construct the portfolio that produces the highest overall return balanced with their intestinal fortitude for risk.

Nagji and Tuff share what they call the Innovation Ambition Matrix in their *HBR* article.

Let's break this down.

The bottom of the matrix highlights core innovation initiatives— efforts to make incremental changes to existing products and incremental inroads into new markets. This could be the new Coca-Cola

THE INNOVATION AMBITION MATRIX

Firms that excel at total innovation management simultaneously invest at three levels of ambition, carefully managing the balance among them.

TRANSFORMATIONAL
Developing breakthroughs and inventing things for markets that don't yet exist

ADJACENT
Expanding from existing business into new to the company business

CORE
Optimizing existing products for existing customers

WHERE TO PLAY

CREATE NEW MARKETS, TARGET NEW CUSTOMERS' NEEDS

ENTER ADJACENT MARKETS, SERVE ADJACENT CUSTOMERS

SERVE EXISTING MARKETS AND CUSTOMERS

USE EXISTING PRODUCTS AND ASSETS

ADD INCREMENTAL PRODUCTS AND ASSETS

DEVELOP NEW PRODUCTS AND ASSETS

HOW TO WIN

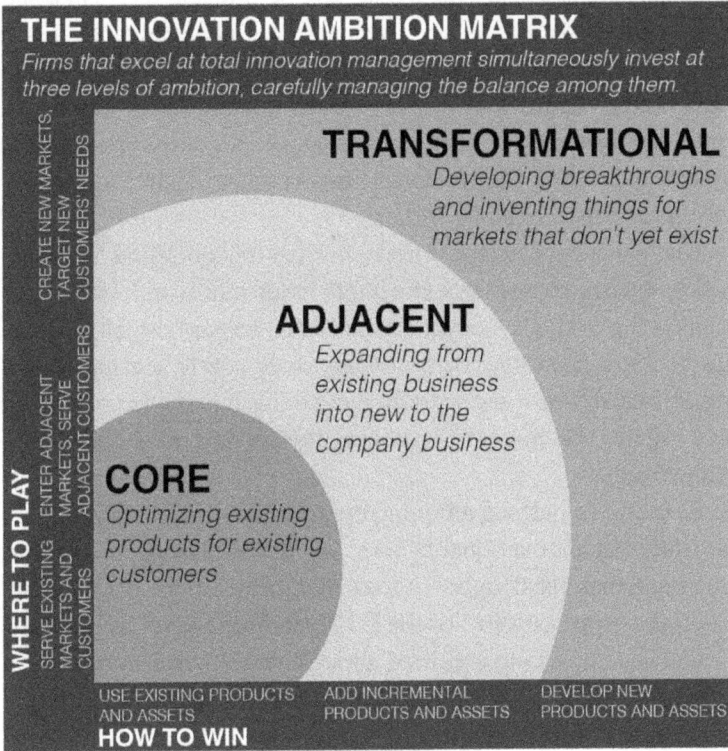

Figure 6.1 The Innovation Ambition Matrix illustrates how companies should consider investing in innovation: 70 percent core products, 20 percent incremental products, and 10 percent new products.

flavor or my dad offering two additional cleaning products to his food-service customers.

At the top of the matrix are transformational initiatives, designed to create new products—if not whole new businesses—to serve new markets and customer needs. These are the innovations that, when successful, make headlines: think of iTunes, PayPal, Spotify, Uber, and ChatGPT. These game-changing innovations require that the company build new capabilities to better understand customers, to

157

communicate about products that have no direct antecedents, and to develop markets that aren't yet mature. Understandably, this is the area companies struggle with the most. A study by the Corporate Strategy Board showed that mature companies attempting to enter new businesses fail as often as 99 percent of the time. This is because launching transformative innovations requires an organization to transform along with it!

That's not easy. As I've written in both this book and *The Innovation Mindset*, those "big game hunt" innovations—things that are really going to knock everyone's socks off—are just a small percentage of the innovations that, perhaps more subtly, end up changing an industry or a society. Often overlooked is the fact that they may require the company launching the product to change, often dramatically.

To create something different, organizations need different people, different motivational factors, and different support systems. The ones that get it right—a 2024 McKinsey report article showcased the "superpowers" of the US Magnificent Seven and the EU Granolas—think long and hard about how to invest in growth in a way that aligns with strategic goals, culture, talent, organization systems, and infrastructure.[1]

In the middle are adjacent innovations that can share characteristics with core and transformational innovations. An adjacent innovation involves leveraging something the company does well into a new space. Procter & Gamble's much-admired Swiffer is a case in point, and it's easy to understand. It arose from P&G's understanding of their customers and their need for a long-handled mop. But it used a novel technology—the trap and lock—and took the solution to a new customer set—professional housekeepers interested in innovative technologies to replace traditional wet mops, brooms, and dustpans with a faster, more efficient way of cleaning floors. While professional housecleaners were the original target audience for Swiffer, ordinary folks also loved the idea—I'm an avid Swiffer user—and the marketing campaign broadened to the masses, generating new revenue for the company. Adjacent innovations allow a company to draw on existing capabilities but necessitate putting those capabilities to new uses. They require fresh, proprietary insight into customer needs, demand trends, market structure, competitive dynamics, technology trends, and other market variables.

The portfolio approach to investing in innovation serves two purposes. First, it gives managers a framework for examining all businesses opportunities, assigning them to one of the three tiers. Second, it facilitates a discussion about the right investment strategy for the company—how to apportion risk in the portfolio. A consumer goods company like Procter & Gamble may decide it is best to invest in incremental innovations like product extensions. A high-tech company may need to take bigger risks for the chance of bigger payoffs.

This may sound obvious, but I was surprised to learn in my interviews with some of the C-suite executives who make up our Innovators' Circle, which we created as a sounding board for new ideas and best practices in organizational innovation, that few organizations think this way and even fewer achieve a well-balanced portfolio. A point Nagji and Tuff made in their article and that I confirmed in my interviews with investors is that financial analysts in the capital markets find this model attractive because it shows a company is thinking about balancing short-term, predictable growth and riskier but longer-term opportunities to drive sustainable growth.

So what are the outcomes of this model? Why does the Golden Ratio Sergey Brin designed matter? Nagji and Tuff found that the return ratio is roughly the inverse of that ideal allocation: core innovation efforts typically contribute 10 percent of the long-term, cumulative return on innovation investment; adjacent initiatives contribute 20 percent; and transformational efforts contribute 70 percent. Mathematical alignment!

Of course, every business plan or model has its caveats, and the Golden Ratio for investing in chance is no exception—there are three.

The first caveat is industry. The industrial manufacturers Nagji and Tuff studied (and our research concurs) have a portfolio of core innovations and a few breakouts. They come closest to the 70-20-10 breakdown. By comparison, technology companies spend less time and money on improving core products because their market is eager for the next hot release. Consumer packaged goods manufacturers have little activity at the transformational level and invest in incremental improvements. Nagji and Tuff's study showed that industrial manufacturers, the ones most closely following 70-20-10, collectively have the highest price-to-earnings (P/E) ratio relative to their peers, perhaps suggesting that they are closest to getting the balance right—for them.

A second variable in this model is the company's competitive position within its industry. For example, a company might want to pursue more high-risk innovation in the hope of creating a truly disruptive product or service that could dramatically alter its growth curve. A struggling Apple made this decision in the late 1990s, effectively betting its business on several bold initiatives, including the iTunes platform. A company that wants to retain its leadership position or believes the market for its more ambitious innovations has cooled may decide to do the reverse, removing some risk from its portfolio by shifting its emphasis from transformational to core initiatives.

Finally, one of the most important factors to consider in this model is a company's stage of development. Early-stage enterprises, especially those funded by venture capital, may feel that a disproportionate investment in transformational innovation is warranted, both to attract media attention, investors, and customers and because they don't yet have much of a core business to build on. As they mature and develop a stable customer base and as protecting and growing the core becomes more important, they may shift their emphasis toward that of a more established company.

Dave Evans, the CEO of Fictiv whom we profiled in an earlier chapter, amplifies this point. He explains that in the early days of a venture-backed business like his, you're putting as many dollars as you can into technology to find product-market fit. "Your first customers are going to come from word of mouth, and the best way to differentiate from the competition is to excel in your R&D and tech," says Dave. "You have to balance the road map of investment on technology and other factors that will help you scale the business over time."

The motivations around investment for an early-stage company versus a corporation are clearly different, and we compare and contrast companies at various stages of growth in an upcoming chapter. Suffice it to say that, in an early-stage company, nearly all of the budget is invested in innovation and technology infrastructure in order to create the products and services the company will provide to the market—as Dave pointed out in describing Fictiv's investment model in the early days. Compare that with the white-glove financial consulting firm Mark Adams worked for early in his career. "They probably spent only 1 percent on innovation," he says. Why? Mark laughed at that question. "Because they spent all their capital running the core business better. And the partners were getting older and wanted profits to fund their retirement. So profits that could have been reinvested in the business instead funded the partners' retirement income."

As we'll see in our chapter on organizational archetypes, companies have different life cycles and stages when it comes to planning for innovation and growth. It's key to know what stage the business is in and the type of business you want to build. Is this a venture-backed business in the technology sector, where you're looking at the high financial returns of an early-stage risky company? Or is it an older company that is private equity based and has a different return on investment (ROI), time horizon, and capital needs? Is it a homegrown, cash flow–based business where you are taking money out on a loan against your house or 401K and you're reinvesting this capital into the business with an expectation of short-term return?

Those are at least three buckets of very different company requirements for investments in innovations. Each situation has to be evaluated on its own merits.

INNOVATION INVESTMENTS IN TOUGH
TIMES—TAKING A BIG CHANCE

In addition to how they would spread their innovation dollars in the portfolio, a second question we posed to our Innovators' Circle was to solicit their views on investing in chance even when business is weak and budgets are constrained. I have been in many situations where quarterly earnings and budget constraints make senior management wary of spending any money that isn't essential. Projects designed to drive growth were put on hold or, worse, killed completely. The 2008 recession, for example, caused the pharma research services company Covance/Labcorp to replace some innovative growth initiatives with financial and operational efficiencies to better manage the bottom line. By contrast, at Bristol Myers Squibb, an ambitious R&D program to redesign the organization and change the role of the physicians resulted in a two-year slowdown in productivity before the changes were embedded in the organization and led to improved outcomes in time to market for critical therapeutics. But, as my dad learned the hard way, curbing investing out of fear (avoidance of risk, which is innate to chance) is a foolhardy way to run a business. Our experts agree: 85 percent believe companies should continue to invest in innovation during downturns. It's worth noting some of their reasons:

- Investment in chance—new ideas—during downturns is crucial for long-term success and for enhancing competitive advantage, efficiency, and customer satisfaction.
- Companies that innovate during tough times are often leaders in their sector when conditions improve.
- Innovations can vary in capital intensity; some require significant resources, and others need innovative use of existing assets. Each opportunity should be assessed according to risk-benefit.
- A few interviewees felt that innovation should remain a priority regardless of economic conditions, though some said their companies adopted a more cautious approach during financial constraints.

This last point around cautious investing is worth exploring further. "Roaring Out of the Recession," a March 2010 *Harvard Business Review* article, sheds light on how companies invested during a downturn and how it affected them once the economy rebounded. The study showed that 17 percent of companies didn't survive the 2008 recession—they went bankrupt, were acquired, or became private. Only 9 percent of the sample flourished after a slowdown. The study categorized the winners as what they call "progressive focused"—they deployed an optimal combination of defensive and offensive strategies to weather the storm and come out ahead.

For example, these companies cut costs by improving operational efficiencies rather than slashing employees. They invested in R&D, marketing, and assets like plants and machinery. Let's compare Staples to Office Depot during the 2000 recession. Staples took the opportunity to close underperforming stores but increased its workforce by 10 percent. Office Depot, by contrast, slashed employees. The progressive-focused companies also stayed engaged with their customers, which we know is the best lens through which to make investments in future growth. For example, during this same period of time, retailer Target increased marketing and sales by 20 percent and capital expenditures by 50 percent over prerecession levels. It increased the number of stores and expanded into new merchandise segments, grew its internet business, and ramped up its credit card programs. It also consolidated poorly performing brands like Dayton's and Hudson's stores under Marshall Fields, a well-known brand. Why did they do this? They were bullish on their value proposition of affordable-priced goods for the lower and middle class and figured that, in a recession, people would be more inclined to shop at their stores. Their results proved they were right.

In a more recent analysis, a HubSpot blog published on July 7, 2020, also reported on companies that thrived during the 2008 recession. Their list included TeamLogic IT, Netflix, Citigroup, Lego, Groupon, MailChimp, and Warby Parker. Let's look at what a few of these companies did right. At the time, Netflix was not the media giant it is today. They had just introduced a new product as a response to the dying video rental store market. They called it a "streaming" service—a new concept for many consumers in 2008. Over the next two years, the company continued to work on partnerships with organizations like Xbox so people could stream through those devices. These investments in innovations allowed them to grow during the downturn. In fact, some might say the recession helped catapult Netflix to the status they hold today.

Those with long memories may be surprised to see Citigroup on this list. The bank reportedly lost $32 billion in 2008 and was one of the biggest federal bailouts from the mortgage crisis. But a 2014 review by the Federal Reserve found that Citigroup was one of the only banks to have grown its assets over the six years following the recession. According to HubSpot, the difference between Citigroup and its peers was that it recognized it needed to rebuild trust in its brand. Citigroup invested in branding and improving service quality. They expanded globally, diversified their business model, and developed robust risk-management practices. And to continue building their positive brand story, in 2015, according to a Citigroup press release, they launched Community Progress Makers, a not-for-profit designed to connect low-income communities with greater economic opportunity.

After their bailout, the emphasis Citigroup placed on investing in expansion, business models, new products, and corporate marketing put the bank on a high-growth track for the next decade and a half.

Other companies may not have invested in innovation, but they were bold in launching or changing their innovative business models during a recession to bolster growth prospects. Groupon launched during the recession—the ideal time to advertise a discount service for consumers keeping a closer eye on their wallets. Mailchimp also took advantage of the recession to tweak their business model to a freemium (free) basic subscription that could be upgraded to a paid plan when the customer needed more services to help them manage budgets that were tighter during the recession. This strategy helped Mailchimp grow, and they've retained that business model. Popular eyewear company Warby Parker recognized that recession-weary customers needed affordable fashion glasses they could buy online. They marketed themselves as affordable and convenient and have gone on to become very successful.

Throughout this book, we've made this clear: it is our strongly held belief that growth—sustainable growth—depends on innovation. This kind of growth needs to be distinguished from acquisitions that inflate a company's top line, often only temporarily, and rarely lead to real innovation-based growth. No doubt budget constraints do present challenges, as does the need to meet quarterly forecasts while working with budget limitations. In many organizations, R&D has to negotiate budgets directly with key operating divisions to tie their research spending to real-world customer problems. At IBM, it's a best practice for R&D professionals to interact directly with customers, cocreating solutions in "garage" sessions—a homage to all the Silicon Valley companies supposedly starting their companies in their parents' garages. These companies—IBM, Microsoft, and Apple—are training R&D to think in business terms so the researchers will be better able to decide whether an idea is worth pursuing in the first place.

Let's examine the biopharma industry through the lens of an August 2024 McKinsey article, "Making More Medicines That Matter." The authors analyzed the top fifteen companies in the industry and found little correlation between R&D spending and value creation of new drugs. Instead, the authors showed that performance has largely been propelled by "blockbuster" medicines—drugs that achieve over $1 billion in peak-year sales. In other words, big pharmaceutical companies devote a disproportionate amount of their resources to blockbuster drugs. As we've seen, the really innovative companies don't just invest in the "moon shot" breakthrough. They spread their investment around to different types of innovations.

Given that, is it any surprise there is little innovation coming out of Big Pharma and many other large corporations? In pharma's case, its business model is to acquire biotech start-ups—the kind capable of producing that rare blockbuster—who assume early-stage risk while pharma absorbs later-stage risk (e.g., regulatory approval and marketing).

Compare that with a company like Microsoft when it "de-verticalized" the computer industry or Costco when it pioneered a new business model with its upscale warehouse stores. These are companies that, unlike many in the pharmaceutical industry, invest consistently and wisely in innovation.

MEANINGFUL INNOVATION STARTS WITH GOOD IDEAS

Studies have shown that lack of time and resources and a short-term focus are the biggest barriers to innovation in organizations. But is this so? Is innovation highly dependent on investment, and is it senior management's presumed obsession with near-term earnings that most limits a company's innovation productivity?

In fact, our survey of executives in the Innovators' Circle indicated that the number one reason for lack of innovation investment had nothing to do with money: it was because the firm lacked good ideas! And that's a direct result of not hiring the right people and training them to be problem-solvers.

The second reason was resistance to innovation in the organization. Therefore, our prescription for success addresses these areas raised by our survey panel:

- *Increase the number of innovators in your company.* The greater the percentage of employees who regard themselves as innovators, whatever their formal job descriptions may be, the greater is the innovation yield—and the less you'll encounter resistance from within the organization. (See Erez Naaman's tips on how to more effectively hire innovative people in chapter 1.)
- *Make sure the focus on radical innovation is at least 10 percent, as the 70-20-10 rule suggests.* The higher the proportion of truly radical ideas in a company's innovation pipeline, the higher is the innovation payoff. Incremental innovation, process improvements, and the like have

their benefit and are a good way to get the organization to start to innovate quickly, but they don't drive long-term, sustainable growth, as the 70-20-10 rule shows us.

- *Favor externally sourced innovation over internally sourced innovation.* The better a company is at harnessing ideas and energies from outsiders, the better its return on innovation investments will be.

- *Emphasize learning over an exclusive focus on the financial benefits of investing in innovation projects.* The more efficient a company is at exploring new opportunities and establishing a continuous learning culture, the more efficient its innovation efforts will be.

- *Focus on doing a few new things well rather than increasing the sheer volume of opportunities in the pipeline.* A firm that is deeply committed to a relatively small number of broad innovation goals and is consistent in that commitment over time will multiply its innovation resources and optimize its output.

Here are some additional thoughts on how to make your innovation investments pay off.

Hire People and Get Out of Their Way!

Years ago, J. M. Juran and W. Edwards Deming showed that companies can reap big rewards by investing in the problem-solving skills of rank-and-file employees. In other words, the best way to get more ideas into the innovation pipeline is to ask your employees for them. Jeff Bezos is known for saying he hired the best people and then got out of their way. Elon Musk says the same about SpaceX and Tesla. In fact, most innovation-focused CEOs have a similar philosophy. They also encourage and incentivize innovation among employees. Fictiv holds annual hackathons where all employees are encouraged to present new ideas to management for funding. Dave Evans says that process has helped unleash things ranging from a Fictiv cookbook to drive culture and employee morale, to new ways of servicing customers, to new offerings. Cemex, the highly inventive Mexican cement maker, devotes nine days each year to harvesting employee ideas. Each of these Innovation Days is focused on a particular business or function. In advance of the event, a sponsoring vice president personally invites hundreds of employees to submit ideas around a chosen theme—developing novel customer solutions, for instance, or dramatically improving cost efficiency. To foster innovation, the company developed an internal collaboration platform called Shift that enables employees and teams of employees with similar objectives to share opinions, thoughts, ideas, experience, and best practices. More than two hundred communities have been formed since Shift was launched with a goal of creating new value propositions for customers and improving the company's competitive edge, according to a 2010 article by Glenn Remoreras in his #Perspectives blog, "Cemex's Innovation Through Collaboration." This is a helpful example of how people will find ways to work with each other when you hire the right talent and are clear on your mission and goals.

Set Goals

Identify the number of people in your company who have an innovation role (R&D personnel, product development staff, and so on). If this group composes less than 10 percent of your employee base, commit to tripling that number over the next twelve months—not by hiring more innovation specialists but by involving existing employees in innovation processes or events.

Create a Board of Innovation

Empower a group of managers or innovation-minded employees to screen new ideas and sponsor first-stage experiments. Encourage everyone in the company to think innovatively and to submit their ideas forward to this new innovation board. (Depending on the size of the firm, you could even consider rewarding everyone who submits with a gift coupon or other incentive.) For every department and business unit, benchmark the percentage of employees who have submitted ideas or participated in innovation events.

Are Your Ideas Radical or Incremental?

The question you might be asking is "Are we investing enough in innovation?"

The question you should be asking is "Are we investing enough in ideas with the power to make a real difference to our competitive performance?"

Many companies miss this crucial distinction. The fact is that most "new" ideas are nothing of the sort. They're retreads, updates, and add-ons—modest improvements to ideas that were modest to begin with, as we've explored in this chapter and chapter 5 on change.

There's nothing wrong with that; incremental changes are vital. But it's radical ideas that yield the biggest innovation payoffs and drive above-average growth.

"Radical" is a term that's tossed around a lot in politics these days. Let's define what we mean by "radical" in terms of innovation. An idea is radical if it passes one or more of three tests:

- It changes customer expectations and behaviors. For example, PayPal's user-friendly service has changed the way people send money to one another.
- It changes the basis of competitive advantage. The proliferation of smartphones has changed the photography, news, and entertainment industries. Camera makers, for example, suddenly found themselves competing with phone companies—an idea that would have been unthinkable forty or fifty years ago.
- It changes industry economics. For example, with its simplified route structure, no-frills service, and flexible work practices, Southwest Airlines changed the traditional cost structure for airlines. (By the way, at this writing, Southwest is changing again, and many customers are torn over the airline's decision to assign seats in 2025.)

But let's be clear here: "radical" doesn't necessarily mean "risky." Risky investments are uncertain and expensive. Some radical ideas, like fusion power, quantum computing, and AI applications may be risky, but many others are not. A good example is the Starbucks debit card. The idea was radical: Who, after all, would have expected that coffee drinkers would happily pay for their daily dose of caffeine days or weeks in advance? Yet it wasn't a particularly risky idea. The technology (magnetic-stripe debit cards) was well proven, and the idea could be easily tested in a few stores before a big rollout. I call this a renovation in the world of innovation because it's a new application for an existing technology. In the first two months after the card's launch in November 2001, Starbucks booked more than $60 million in prepayments. Since then, more than 26 million cards have been sold, and they now account for about 10 percent of Starbucks's sales, according to a *Harvard Business Review* article.

Encourage Fresh Thinking

French physiologist Claude Bernard once remarked, "It is what we think we know already that often prevents us from learning." To generate radical ideas, you have to teach people to look beyond the conventional. A good way to start is by adopting a collaborative approach that is common in the world of software development: a hackathon. Ask a group of employees to deconstruct your company's business model into its constituent elements: supply chain, value proposition, product configuration, pricing, marketing strategy, and so on. The team members should then conduct a point-by-point comparison with the business models of your biggest competitors. Whenever they identify a point of convergence—and they will find dozens—they should ask, "Is there truly no other way to organize this aspect of our business, or have we become the unwitting prisoners of industry convention?" The goal here is to become conscious of the orthodoxies and the dogmas—the standard industry practices, if you will—that silently strangle radical ideas.

It's important to note here that talent matters a lot if you're going to invest in a combination of incremental and radical innovations. The skills needed for core and adjacent innovations are quite different from those needed for transformational innovations. In the first two realms, analytical skills are vital because such initiatives call for market and customer data to be interpreted and translated into specific offering enhancements. It's well documented, for example, that Procter & Gamble deploys upwards of seventy senior employees around the world to help identify promising adjacencies. These "technology entrepreneurs," as the company calls them, are responsible for researching a variety of sources, including scientific journals and patent databases, and for physically observing activities in specific markets in order to find new ideas that can build on P&G's core businesses. The company credits its technology entrepreneurs with uncovering more than ten thousand potential offerings for review.

Transformational innovation efforts, by contrast, typically employ a discovery and concept-development process to uncover and analyze the social needs driving business changes (what's desirable from a customer perspective), the underlying market trends (what kinds of offers might be viable), and ongoing technological developments (what is feasible to produce and sell). These activities require skills found among designers, cultural anthropologists, scenario planners, and analysts who are comfortable with ambiguous data. Gary Hamel describes how Samsung decided to compete based on innovative design and recognized that it needed new and different skills. The company moved its design center from a small town to Seoul to be closer to a valuable pool of young design professionals. It also teamed with a number of outside firms with strong design skills and created an in-house school, led by industrial design experts, to hone the abilities of designers who exhibited potential. The results speak for themselves: Samsung has garnered numerous design awards while evolving from a manufacturer of nondescript consumer electronics to one of the most valuable brands in the world.

Don't Panic, Just Pivot

In the entrepreneurship and venture-creation courses I teach, students get to experiment without fear of failure—and it's so liberating for them. If they go down a path and find an idea isn't resonating with the customer or the market, or is too complex to design, or just can't muster investor interest, they pivot. This was the case with one graduate team at Yeshiva University when they tried to develop a point-of-care diagnostic test for pancreatic cancer, a complex disease for which there just wasn't enough easily accessible patient data to identify disease trends and train AI. (In chapter 8, we'll meet a Harvard researcher who is developing an AI pancreatic cancer screening tool. I wish I had known him when my team at Yeshiva was working on this project!) When my team realized they were hitting a dead end, they didn't panic. They didn't throw up their hands and consider the project a failure. Instead, they designed a diagnostic for a much easier-to-identify illness—flu—to show that they could gather and analyze data and understood the process of developing an AI-based diagnostic. The student team pitched their idea to investors, an important final assignment in my course. The investors appreciated the simplicity of their minimum viable product (MVP) and saw how it could translate to screening and diagnosing more complex diseases.

Don't Let Funding Get in the Way of Innovating

As we've discussed, most efforts related to core and adjacent innovation are fairly small-scale projects that don't need major infusions of cash. They can and should be funded by the relevant business unit's profit and loss (P&L) through annual budget cycles. Bold, transformational innovations are different. Their funding should come from an entity, perhaps the executive suite, and ideally the CEO, as in the case of Cognizant Technology Solutions, which had a budget for teams to cocreate new solutions with customers. I've seen models I call the "innovation tax" approach, whereby the

C-suite asks all areas of the business to contribute a percentage of their budgets to transformational initiatives (under the theory that innovation benefits the whole company, so everyone should support it). Of course, business units rarely see their "contribution" as going to a good cause; they simply perceive that the corporate office is siphoning off 5 percent of their budgets and come to regard the innovation team as the bad guys. I've seen this method go awry in pharma companies I've worked for.

Companies might instead create a completely different funding structure for transformational innovation, one that's separate from the regular P&Ls of the business. An example is Merck's Global Health Innovation venture fund, a separate limited liability corporation that invests in interesting healthcare companies operating at the periphery of Merck's core pharmaceutical, vaccines, and consumer-health businesses. The main purpose of the fund is to place bets on components of a future business model for the company. It is also used on occasion to fund organic innovation initiatives, such as Merck Breakthrough Open, a crowdsourcing forum that solicits employee ideas for transformational growth opportunities. Many corporations with venture capital arms, including Fidelity, Verizon, Amazon, J&J, and Pfizer, have embraced this model and seen positive results.

Keep the Pipeline Flowing!

How does a company keep track of its various innovative projects as they make their way through the pipelines? Companies typically rely on stage-gate processes to periodically assess a project's viability, recalculate their projected ROI according to any changed conditions, and decide whether they should get a green light. This is effective when advancing new products that may take years to commercialize as we see in industries such as biotech, agriculture, and energy. In the case of a core product extension, projections are only as reliable as the market insight the company can glean: customers can say whether they would like a proposed product variant and, if so, how much they'd be willing to pay for it. Bissell, a company that manufactures and sales household vacuum cleaners learned its customers were willing to pay more for a vacuum that picked up pet hair. However, if the initiative involves an entirely new solution—one that customers may not even know they need— think about smart home devices NEST specializes in, traditional stage-gate processes may not work well. After all, it's impossible to predict fifth-year sales for something a customer doesn't yet know they need or want.

A lot has changed in my life and in the world of business since the day my dad sat me down and sketched out his own "innovation investment" model. Although I'm glad to see that some of the lessons I learned from him still apply, I'm also pleased with developments that are helping to fan the flames of innovation in many industries. One of the most important, to me, is the presence of more and more women in what was, when I entered the industry, a predominantly male preserve. I'm especially thrilled to see that there are now women in positions where they not only develop innovative ideas but also fund them! Plum Alley is a venture capital firm created in 2011 to provide more opportunities for women in STEM to raise capital to bring their early-stage ideas to fruition. Plum Alley was created with a dual mission of increasing financial investment acumen among women and investing in women-founded, high-tech, early-stage companies. As an investor member, I'm proud of Plum Alley's growth as an organization and the impactful, high-tech innovations in agriculture, biotech, water, and transportation we have invested in.

AN INNOVATION INDEX FOR THERAPEUTIC MANUFACTURERS

I've spent much of my career in biopharma, a trillion-dollar industry struggling with lengthy drug development timelines, exorbitant costs, and an overwhelming rate of clinical trial failures. Despite its urgent need for innovation, the industry remains risk averse due to its highly regulated and litigated nature. Traditional methods for developing new therapies rely on extensive trial and error, leading to inefficiencies that slow down progress.

For more than thirty years, I have been at the forefront of improving clinical operations to accelerate drug development. Now, with the advent of big data and AI, we finally have the tools to make a meaningful impact. My colleague, Dr. Deepak Patil, and I founded Roxi-Ai to help derisk early-stage pharmaceutical and medical device investments, improving both clinical and business outcomes. Our goal is to provide pharmaceutical executives and investors with a more precise, data-driven approach to deciding which products to advance and which to pass over—an essential consideration in an industry where more than 90 percent of drugs fail between phase 1 and approval, leading to an estimated $50 billion in annual losses.

In collaboration with Dr. Fred Ledley, professor of management and director of the Center for Integration of Science and Industry at Bentley University, we've developed an AI-powered innovation index for therapeutic products. This objective, standardized tool

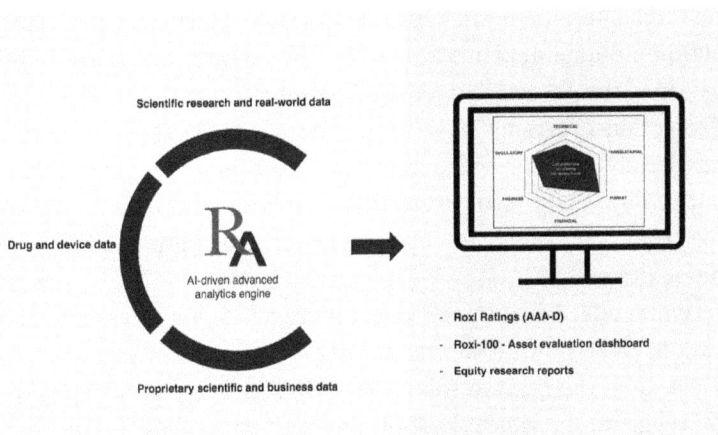

Figure 6.2 The Roxi-Ai Innovation Index helps investors assess an early-stage pharmaceutical assets' chances of commercial success.

evaluates six key categories of risk across more than a hundred criteria, offering specific, actionable insights into the likelihood of a new therapy's success. By reducing uncertainty in early-stage investments, Roxi-Ai enables pharmaceutical companies and investors to redirect R&D dollars toward projects with a higher probability of success, mitigating systemic risk while increasing returns across portfolios. Ultimately, this fosters greater investor confidence, accelerates the development of lifesaving therapies, and improves overall sector-wide efficiency in bringing new treatments to market.

CHAMPIONS OF CHANGE

Lessons from Fearless Founders and Enterprising Executives

Tracy Harmon Blumenfeld
Cofounder and CEO, RapidTrials

"Is it reasonable to expect a terminally ill patient to travel to a research site once a week for the duration of a trial?" asked Tracy Harmon Blumenfeld in a 2017 interview with *Advantage*, the publication of the Association for the Accreditation of Human Resource Protection Programs (AAHRPP). "Does it make sense to require an already sick person to come to a research site and spend an entire day trying to navigate their way around the facility, moving from department to department for imaging procedures and blood draws?"

We've talked about passion as a prerequisite for successful innovation, about how those who drive truly impactful change are laser focused on the need to solve a problem. As Tracy's rousing rhetoric suggests, she is not short on passion—or compassion for those whose only hope for combatting a serious illness (or preventing others from going through the same affliction) might be participation in a clinical trial. Critical to the advancement of medical knowledge and the testing of possible new treatments, the ClinicalTrials.gov website of the National Library of Medicine reports that, as of January 2024, there were 20,465 clinical trials recruiting patients in the United States and 65,474 trials worldwide.

It's a huge and important industry and one that Tracy completely disrupted with her company RapidTrials, which has dramatically improved the efficiency—not to mention humanity—with which trials are organized and conducted.

"It seemed to me they were running the trials in these academic centers, but that wasn't where the patient was," she said. Meanwhile, "doctors were getting squeezed by managed care and were looking for other avenues. Research seemed like such a good fit."

Indeed it was. Founded in 1996, RapidTrials emerged as a frontrunner in optimizing clinical trial efficiency for drug developers and research institutions, earning a spot on the prestigious Philadelphia 100 list of fastest-growing companies. In 2017, under her leadership, RapidTrials made a strategic decision to sell a portion of the company's proprietary assets to Medidata Solutions, Inc.

"Tracy's vision for clinical trial efficiency and the innovative methods she has developed to improve operational performance have influenced the industry," said the late Glen de Vries, Medidata's founder, at the time. "I'm excited to see what valuable insights she will generate next to help shape the clinical trials of the future."

Tracy continues in her leadership and advocacy role for both ethical and effective clinical trials, contributing numerous journal articles and working with an alphabet soup of some of America's most important medical and healthcare institutions, including the National Institutes of Health, the National Academies of Medicine, and the AAHRPP.

Not to mention the fact that Tracy has penetrating insight into the innovation process. Which is why we have asked her, as we conclude our discussion of the 5C's—Customer First, Culture, Collaboration, Change, and Chance—to offer her observations and thoughts on how these five critical aspects, and a couple of other factors, can help an organization create a culture of innovation.

Listen carefully, and don't rush to judgments.

"Sometimes I think the first thing, when you're having a conversation with a potential new customer about your new innovative solution, it is really important to make sure the vocabulary you choose to describe your solution is crystal clear. From my experience, 'patient recruitment solutions' to you could be totally different to what it means to the potential customer. So I think it is critical that you listen carefully to their language. If your solution is really innovative, the audience you're presenting to may not have ever considered it or may assume it is solving for a different problem. So make sure you're listening and don't end up with a confused customer and a lost opportunity."

You might find success in failure.

"Honestly, whether you're someone trying to champion an innovation within your company or on your own, you're going to meet a lot of people that just don't get it. So I'd say, look for failing projects. Look for the group that hasn't hit their goals. That hasn't met their obstacles. That needs to shake things up. These prospects may be more open to a creative solution."

Sell solutions, not ideas.

"The innovator needs to understand the mindset of the people they're selling to. Whether they're within your organization or outside, remember that they are getting pitched all the time. They're busy; they're under the gun. Ideas are cheap; solutions change a company's trajectory. If you're trying to do something innovative, you have to make sure that you differentiate your solution clearly and quickly. People like to categorize solutions, and put them into boxes, which goes against the mindset of the innovator. They're not going into the meeting thinking, 'What kind of innovative things are they up to?' They want to know if your solution is better, cheaper, and or faster than the one from the other vendors they just heard from."

Don't be shy.

"Create awareness of your idea and build credibility. Speak at a conference. Write papers for peer-reviewed journals. Get press for your new approach. You don't have to reveal every single detail of your innovative product or service, but you should be out there, explaining in public forums why it's a good idea, a good solution. Building awareness in the ecosystem your innovation impacts, particularly in trusted third-party venues, increases the likelihood that they might buy into your idea or, at least, take a meeting with you and be willing to learn more."

Build alliances.

"How do you get your first customer? Sometimes you just have to put your money where your mouth is. To get a customer to give you a chance to test a new solution you've created for the market, you may have to let them try the solution for free or sell it at a reduced price. We call this risk-sharing. Sometimes that's just something you have to do to build trust. Be flexible in your pricing. If you really believe in your idea, it will be worth it in the long run."

To learn more about RapidTrials, visit https://www.rapidtrials.com /about/.

To learn more about Tracy, see https://www.linkedin.com/in /tracyharmonblumenfeld/.

7

THE FOUR FACES
OF ORGANIZATIONAL INNOVATION

Just as we can distinguish, classify, and even rank organizations based on their revenues, their relative size in their industry, their technological proficiency, their community-mindedness, and their management styles, innovativeness too is a critical, if often overlooked, differentiating characteristic of organizations.

How innovative is a company? Or to use the typology we have introduced in this book, to what extent does an organization adhere to the 5C's? Do they foster a culture of innovation? Do they genuinely put their customers first? Do they reward initiative without punishing the failures that often accompany experimentation? Are collaborations and partnerships within and without the organized encouraged? And importantly, do they follow a strategic portfolio approach to investing in new ideas?

From my experience, the answers to those questions are:

Yes—and no.
More—or less.
It depends on the organization.

Over the course of my career as a corporate executive, a consultant, an entrepreneur, a coach, and an educator, I have seen a wide range of what we might call innovation-minded behaviors. Through that experience and in tandem with both my ongoing research and our Innovators' Circle (a panel of more than seventy-five innovators whom we've asked to weigh in on various questions about innovation in their industries), I have developed four archetypes for classifying companies according to their innovativeness: the Fearless Start-Up, the Adolescent Up-and-Comer, the 70-20-10 Innovator, and the Stodgy Old Bureaucracy.

- The Fearless Start-Up: When people think of innovation, these are the kind of businesses that come to mind, the kind of firms that have helped define Silicon Valley and the digital revolution. They even come with their own origin stories and mythology (Jobs and Wozniak in the garage; Zuckerberg in his Harvard dorm room; AirBnb's Brian Chesky in his San Francisco apartment). Start-ups are great at solving problems and creating solutions. But as the start-up founder we spotlight in our later case study explains, the challenges include funding, staffing, marketing—and recognizing that a good idea is sometimes not enough to ensure success.
- The Adolescent Up-and-Comer: This type of company has a high innovation score but is conscious that its progress is being held back because it lacks process, discipline, and effective ways of collaborating. It's adding organizational muscle even as it maintains a highly innovative culture that is open to talking about failure. In this chapter, we share insights from the CEO of a privately held, growing, technology-based company whose story of success and investment in scaling is a great example of how companies can professionalize their operations without compromising creativity.
- The 70-20-10 Innovator: This is the sweet spot. These companies follow the 70-20-10 portfolio approach to investing, which we explained earlier in this book, and have a process for moving worthy new projects through the pipelines efficiently. These companies report a 10–15 percent premium in price-to-earnings (P/E) ratios over their peers, and their five-year growth rates are impressive. They embrace innovation in the culture and make it safe to fail. Examples include familiar

names such as Netflix, Amazon, Google, and Tesla. One is the remarkable Tata—sometimes called "the GE of India"—a corporation that in a single two-year period showcased 3,300 implemented innovations in various digital technologies. But these big names are not the only examples of companies that get it right. In this chapter, we'll also spotlight the impressive experience of a 170-year-old French water hygiene company that has managed to grow in a sustainable way by following a formula for investing in innovation.

- The Stodgy Old Bureaucracy: The fearful, mostly risk-averse corporation is—as you might guess—on the far right of the innovation continuum. It sacrifices innovation for scale, process, repeatability, and reproducibility. In the desire to please shareholders with expected results, it increasingly loses focus on the customer, becomes more internally focused, and leaves behind its ability to change and pivot. There is an exhaustive list of companies in this category, but we should note a few, including Dupont and Hewlett-Packard, that are working hard to put the innovation mindset back into action. Companies at this stage have a choice: pivot and grow or decline and die, which is what happened to Blockbuster. Blockbuster became complacent and didn't pivot quickly enough in the face of start-up Netflix.

By examining these four innovation archetypes, we can uncover valuable insights into how an organization's culture, size, and maturity influence their approach to innovation. An understanding of these dynamics not only highlights the unique strengths and challenges faced by each type of company but also offers lessons on how to cultivate an environment of innovation tailored to the company's specific needs.

I'll offer some of my experiences with each of these types of organizations, as well as insights from leaders and senior executives. Let's start with the type that's probably the kind of company most people think about when they think of innovation.

#1: THE FEARLESS START-UP: MOVING FASTER AND FASTER

CASE STUDY: FORETRACE

I listened carefully as Nick Ascoli explained how he had founded and sold his first start-up at the tender age of twenty-nine.

Nick is a friend of my middle son (also named Nick), and he lives in Maryland with his wife. He's an expert in a trendy and complicated area—cybersecurity. He founded Foretrace in 2021, launching an innovative, trademarked product he developed called the Total Recon Engine. It's a technology that performs reconnaissance on a company's digital footprint, using the same techniques as cybercriminals to detect security weaknesses, thereby enabling the company to proactively remediate them. Mitigating security risks is a big area of need for organizations in all industries and of all sizes, but it's a particularly costly area for large companies. To underscore the point, cybersecurity was a whopping $172.24 billion market in 2023, according to a Fortune Business Insights report in August 2024. Nick's company, Foretrace, was acquired by a privately held, Canada-based global leader in a particular aspect of cybersecurity called threat exposure management for an undisclosed amount in 2024. The Canadian company, Flare, believed it could bolster their already strong growth trajectory with Foretrace's new product.

I had known Nick for ten years but in a very different context—he wasn't always a successful young start-up founder. He had been my son Nicholas's roommate at Penn State University and was now his close friend. Nicholas had been a groomsman in Nick and his wife Michelle's wedding. We had tailgated with Nick and his family at football games, attended graduation parties, and nearly crashed his wedding reception—that's a separate story—and now I was hearing a little bit about what an accomplished entrepreneur he was.

It was my son who had encouraged me to dig deeper into Nick Ascoli's story. "He wants young founders to learn from his mistakes," Nicholas said. "He says he's made a lot of them, and he'd like to help other first-timers avoid the same unnecessary errors. Maybe you can help."

"That's music to my ears," I told Nicholas. It's reminiscent of my own start-up experience, including an eye-diagnostic company where I made every mistake in the book. (All those mistakes are chronicled in my first book, *The Innovation Mindset*.) So did I want to hear Nick's story directly from him and help him share his lessons learned with others? You betcha.

Nick Ascoli graduated from Penn State's top-ranked School of Information Systems Technology in 2017 with a degree in cybersecurity. At the beginning of our Zoom discussion in July 2024, Nick expressed what he felt was a common misconception about startups: the perception that every founder is a kid barely out of college who takes a student project and parlays it into, well, Facebook. "While you certainly do see young founders in tech," Nick acknowledged, "an overwhelming majority are much later career executives who have massive networks that they leverage to raise funds. I was kinda in between, not exactly the fresh college graduate but also not the seasoned executive with a massive network. And that lack of a network was a challenge I worked hard to overcome."

Nick's start-up was typical of many new companies that, regardless of the age of their founders, tend to have similar characteristics. Before we delve further into Nick's story, let's outline, for context, the three main innovation-related characteristics of start-ups:

- They are innovation focused: Start-ups are heavily focused on innovation because that's often their core value proposition. They usually try to disrupt the market with novel ideas.
- They utilize creative investment approaches: Limited in resources, start-ups often rely on bootstrapping, angel investors, or venture capital. They invest in research and development (R&D), product development, and market fit.

- They have high risk tolerance: The risk tolerance is high because they need to establish themselves quickly. They're more willing to take bold risks to achieve breakthroughs.

Nick's first job after graduating was an analyst role in a Philadelphia-based boutique consulting firm that specialized in cybersecurity. "We served Fortune 1000 companies and, as a recent college graduate, working with them was the most valuable experience I could have had," he said. "When you're a consultant, especially at a smaller, more tactical firm, you've got to show up for a project knowing more about the tools you're working with than the person who's been using the tools for years; you're there to solve their problem. It's a fast way to learn the business."

Nick's projects involved areas like trying to build detection software for the novel techniques hackers were using against his customers. He quickly advanced to a hybrid role where he was responsible for innovation and customer delivery. In this new job, Nick was exposed to different cybersecurity software tool sets and started to see some gaps in the technologies. "There were a lot of tools that companies were using to understand their security exposure from the outside looking in," he said. "Meaning, if I'm a cybercriminal looking at our company from the outside in, what can I find—where do I start building the footprint of the person or the organization I'm targeting?"

Nick says he discovered a need for tools that used the same techniques that cybersecurity professionals and cybercriminals were employing in real-world hacks. "My idea was to create a product that leveraged the same exact techniques as cyber adversaries to give an organization the most authentic view possible of what cybercriminals might find when they are targeting them."

That idea formed the basis of Foretrace. He was accepted by a start-up accelerator called CyberTech|X Accelerator in Tampa Bay, Florida, where he did customer-discovery research to confirm customer need for his product concept and built his prototype.

(A start-up accelerator is a mentor-based program that provides guidance, support, and limited funding in exchange for equity.[1])

After being accepted to the accelerator, Nick said he reached a critical point in the timeline of any founder. He could no longer just devote nights and weekends to developing his big idea. He had to either leave his job and launch the company or not. "I went for it," Nick says, launching Foretrace in January 2021.

Nick grew the company that first year by hiring only contractors. He continued his own consulting gigs because, he said, "I needed to put bread on the table." It would be quite some time before he made his first full-time hire (a decision he would regret delaying).

Eventually, Nick built his advisory board to include a couple of senior people in the industry who helped him get the first paying customers in the door. That enabled Nick to hire a seasoned cyber-security executive as CEO, giving the company the experience and gravitas required to raise capital to fund its growth.

"I was not able to raise any funds as a solo founder with no cofounders or employees," he said. But once he had built a team, he was able to secure a half-million-dollar investment from the state of Maryland's Technology Development Corporation (TEDCO), which funds early-stage, technology-driven start-ups. Soon after that, in 2023, he says, "We started conversations with Flare, our Canadian older brother of sorts, who was growing very, very quickly."

Nick met Flare's CEO at a big cybersecurity conference in Las Vegas. What started as a casual, friendly conversation blossomed into an acquisition. Foretrace accepted Flare's offer to acquire them in early 2024. "I was happy to be acquired. I wanted to be part of a fast-growing cyber company, and there were a lot of synergies between us. Looking back, it was a good decision."

Nick gained decades of start-up experience in a few short years. Before he was even thirty years old, he had learned what it takes some serial founders a lifetime to learn. So the big question is: What would he have done differently?

FEARLESS START-UP: TIPS FOR SUCCESS

Build a team, faster. Nick now says he wished he'd brought on three or four cofounders and given them a healthy stake of equity. "I came from a technical background and thought the business side of the company was easier than the technical side," he admitted. "I learned how difficult leadership is. I also learned how difficult it is to get leads. Business development is extremely difficult. If I had had a team that complemented my strengths and weaknesses, we could have moved faster."

Pivot faster. Initially, Nick relates, he was focused on the wrong customer, and it took him a while to realize that and pivot to the right customer—in his case, the head of security operations. "If you have a strategy that's not working, contract terms and licensing models that aren't hitting, then you have to move on real fast," he says. "You don't have the luxury of time, because there is a competitor out there who's well-funded and whose strategy is working."

Learn humility faster. For many months, Nick stubbornly refused to change or pivot. "Shedding my ego is also something I learned in consulting, but still I wish I had moved on faster in the face of data that contradicted my wishful thinking."

Figure out what you're really selling. "Initially, I was trying to push my product to simulate a hacker to an audience that wasn't necessarily able to operationalize it," he admits. "It was only when we pivoted to using it in security operations, as an alert system, that people started listening. That's when we started getting more demos. That's when we started to find a fit. And I waited way too long to acknowledge that, because it meant acknowledging that my original approach was the wrong one."

Aggressively grow your network. "Who you know affects your ability to raise money. How much money you raise affects your ability to get customers, and the size of sales—in our case, software licenses—affects customer retention," Nick reflects wisely. He adds that he took every meeting and attended every event he could afford and always tried to secure a speaking role (advice that is consistent with Tracy Harmon Blumenfeld's advice from chapter 6). He advises first-time founders to become comfortable with public speaking and going to networking events. Whether it's a formal networking event or an informal get-together over pizza and beer, he says, "You should network like crazy, because you never know where that important lead might come from."

Derisk financially as much as you can. Nick says that if he had hired his CEO sooner, they would likely have been able to fundraise earlier and been in a stronger position to negotiate the terms of deals they entertained. "My tip? You want to be in a position where you don't need to fundraise for as long as you can. It gives you the control to say, 'We're happy with our growth and can wait for better terms.' "

As a founder of start-ups myself, I have two additional tips to share:

If you do need to raise capital, raise as much as you can when you have the opportunity. This will help you to derisk your financial position. In one of my start-ups, I made the mistake of turning away investment for fear of dilution only to face the capital markets drying up the following year, making it impossible to raise the funds needed to continue running the company.

Find creative ways to preserve cash to reduce your burn rate and prolong your ability to operate. Ways to do this include hiring contractors. For example, in one start-up, I hired very talented clinical scientists, biostatisticians, and project managers as contractors so that

I could expand and contract the talent pool and budget according to need. I also identified vendors who were interested in strategic partnerships and willing to be compensated in equal parts cash and debt, which they could convert into equity or cash at a later stage, once the company was generating revenue. While this doesn't work for everyone, it enabled me to slow the burn rate while the company was still in the proof-of-concept stage.

#2: THE ADOLESCENT UP-AND-COMER: BALANCING INNOVATION AND GROWTH

CASE STUDY: ProSci TECHNOLOGY COMPANY

Nothing like an 8 a.m. Zoom to start your day! On a chilly morning in early April 2024, from my home office in the suburbs of Philadelphia, I met with Adam, the CEO of a protein-science technology company. Based in Tampa Bay, Florida, Adam was an early-morning runner like me, and we had agreed to meet at 8 a.m. after our respective runs.

A small, privately held laboratory that provides protein-based products and services to biopharma manufacturers and academic research, ProSci had been established in 2014 by an entrepreneur who had recently transitioned the company to his son, Roger. The company was in the protein-purification sector, which involves isolating a specific protein from a complex mixture containing many contaminants so that it can be used in biomedical research. (In 2022, protein science including purification was an $8.3 billion market, according to Global Market Insights.)

Adam had been recruited by the founder to professionalize the operation and drive new growth. The founder's son, the majority shareholder and head of the board, was eager to grow the company more aggressively. An ex-military officer who had been CEO of several small companies, Adam wasn't an expert in protein science, but he had highly qualified scientists on his staff. What he was good at was fixing businesses and driving growth. He was seeking advice on expansion. After we shared our morning running results—I had run five miles and he three and a half (in the same time it took me to run five, I might add sheepishly)—we got down to business. He spoke with the urgency and precision of a military officer.

"We've built something truly special here," Adam told me. "We're a start-up in many ways but poised for breakout growth if we can achieve the right balance of scale and innovation." But to grow sustainably, Adam knew he had to figure out how to scale the business globally, open up new customers and markets, and at the same time keep current customers happy. "Can you help us get the balance right between innovating and scaling?" he asked. "And can you guide us on establishing an advisory board? We sure could use some commercial expertise."

I assured Adam I would do my best. We started by reviewing employee and customer feedback; analyzing market trends in the United States, India, and China for the protein-purification market; and assessing the best approach to investing in growth while maintaining the core business and a solid customer base. "It all starts with asking the right questions," I reminded Adam, "so we know what problems we're solving for." Our work together over the next six weeks involved answering questions about the business—how to create and tap into customer demand; what kind of purified proteins would be best to add to their product portfolio; what geographies were optimal for expansion; and where they needed to invest in talent and processes to support functions including accounting and project management. In the spirit of the portfolio approach to innovation, we also examined how to optimize the company's portfolio for investment in innovation and create a road map for growth in the short, medium, and long term.

- How much do we invest in core technology to offer more existing products and services to the current customers?
- How much do we invest in adjacent markets or therapeutic areas by taking our solutions to new customers and by creating new products and services?

- How much do we invest in transformation or new opportunities as yet unexplored to drive growth for five years and beyond?

The answers to those questions helped us create a road map and action plan for prioritizing opportunities and investments over the next three years. When Adam presented the road map to the broader team, excitement surged. They quickly rallied behind the notion of blending the entrepreneurial spirit of the company with the need for scalable solutions. To ensure that this innovative direction aligned with their growth ambitions, I helped Adam recruit an advisory board.

By the end of the fiscal year, ProSci had successfully balanced its innovative ambitions with the realities of commercial growth. This included adding talent and improving processes and systems. We found some immediate opportunities to offer existing clients new services, increasing revenues quickly. And a new customer in India had an urgent need that the company was able to address with a short turnaround. These new sales caught the attention of several potential investors the company was courting. They became eager to support a company that not only had promising products and services but also demonstrated a strong commitment to customer-centric innovation.

I called Adam recently to check in. "We've shown that scaling doesn't have to come at the expense of our creativity," he said, proudly. "By staying true to our mission and embracing user feedback, we've built something extraordinary."

Adolescent Up-and-Comer: Tips for Success

As our case study of ProSci demonstrates, the Adolescent Up-and-Comer has a high innovation score but is conscious that its progress is being held back because it lacks process, discipline, and effective ways of collaborating. It's adding organizational muscle as it maintains a highly innovative culture that is open to talking about failure.

Still in the throes of rapid development, this archetype may grapple with its identity, much the same way Adam and ProSci did. As it scales, it must balance the desire for innovation with the need to establish processes, often leading to growing pains that can stifle creativity if not managed properly. Emerging companies balance innovation with scaling, maintaining a high but more cautious risk appetite.

Invest in growth. At this stage, companies typically have more resources than start-ups but are still lean enough to invest significantly in innovation. The best approach is to invest in growth with a balance of incremental and breakout growth. Cocreating and piloting ideas and solutions with key customers is an excellent way of conducting customer research and ensuring there is a customer willing to pay for your new product or service when it's launched.

Focus on efficient scalability. At this stage of growth, companies are focused on scaling their operations. This focus inherently drives innovation as they seek more efficient ways to expand their market presence, optimize their processes, and enhance their product or service offerings to meet growing demand. As you scale, ensure that your operations are efficient. Invest in systems and tools that automate repetitive tasks, freeing up time for your team to focus on strategic initiatives. This allows you to maintain innovation efforts without becoming bogged down by operational challenges.

Leverage strategic partnerships. Consider forming alliances with other companies or organizations that complement your offerings. Partnerships can provide access to new markets, resources, and expertise that enhance both your scaling efforts and your innovative capabilities, allowing for shared growth without diluting your core mission.

Make innovation a priority! Organizations at the emerging-growth stage can still maintain an entrepreneurial culture that encourages risk taking and creativity. This starts from the top: leaders in emerging-growth companies typically prioritize innovation as a key driver of success. You should be willing to invest in long-term innovative projects while maintaining the agility to pivot as necessary.

As a consultant to this and other Adolescent Up-and-Comers, I have one additional tip.

Focus on hiring the best talent at the right time and not just in time. Too often, these companies are still operating by the seat of their pants, and hiring is more just in time than a thoughtful strategy of assessing what talent they need and when they will need it and then hiring the best talent that fits with the culture. When I was working with C2i Genomics—a New York–based cancer diagnostic tool company that was recently sold to the global diagnostics company Veracyte—we worked to professionalize the management team and hire top talent that could help us accelerate the company's growth and exit potential, and it worked!

#3: THE 70-20-10 INNOVATOR: SPINNING GOLD FROM WINDMILL BLADES

CASE STUDY: VEOLIA NORTH AMERICA

On an unseasonably warm October morning in Philadelphia, I met on a Zoom call with Bob Cappadona, President and Chief Executive Officer, Environmental Solutions and Services, a division at Veolia, a France-based energy recycling company. Bob was calling in from a conference room in northern New Jersey, where he was visiting a client. Bob wore a dark suit and tie, looking every inch the corporate executive with his distinguished silver hair, slim stature, and a big, broad smile that lit up his face.

I could see his rollaboard in the background against the white conference room wall, so I knew he was heading to the airport after our meeting. Such is the life of the CEO!

Bob's company, founded 170 years ago, takes pride in the fact that it helped deliver some of the first clean drinking water directly into the homes of nineteenth-century France. Today, Veolia is what many would call a purpose-driven organization: their stated mission is "to contribute to human progress by firmly committing to the Sustainable Development Goals set by the UN to achieve a better and more sustainable future for all."

They do this by outside-the-box thinking in the three areas of their business: water, waste, and energy.

Bob has worked for this idealistic and innovative global leader for more than thirty years. Considering that Veolia was founded in 1853 and that, instead of being an old fogy of a firm, it is still vital, growing, and innovative, my first question was easy:

"Bob," I said, "how do you do it?"

He laughed. One way, he explained, was to do something that many companies give lip service to—genuinely encourage new ideas and create an environment where employees feel safe to express those ideas.

Innovation can't be mandated, like some new set of employee parking regulations, or demanded, like a call for greater productivity on the assembly line. Bob recalls attending a workshop in innovation where he saw dramatic proof of that. "We were discussing how to create a more innovative culture," explained Bob, "and one of the leaders was in front of the room, literally pounding the table, asking why no one was sharing new ideas. 'How can anybody say we're not a company that's built for innovation?' he demanded." Bob sat listening, shaking his head. "I remember turning to the person sitting next to me and saying, 'I don't even think he realizes what he's doing. He's created such a volatile environment that people are fearful of bringing their ideas forward, fearful of failing or of being humiliated that their idea was crazy.' "

At Veolia, thinking in an innovative way is kind of baked into their business: they don't have off-the-shelf solutions. Each customer that comes to them has a distinct challenge that requires a singular, customized solution. Or, as Bob describes it, "People send us crazy stuff in five-gallon containers, and we try to figure out what to do with it."

One particularly unusual example of such "crazy stuff" landed Veolia on *CBS News* in 2023.

It involved recycling windmill blades. One morning, Bob got a call from General Electric. "They said they had 300-foot-long windmill blades from renewable energy farms that their customers were depositing in landfills—clearly not a very green solution, and thus a problem, given that the renewable energy farm's goal was to create green electricity. They wanted to know if we could help."

Bob laughs as he recalls what he thought at the time—but didn't articulate. "I wanted to say, 'I'm not sure what you expect us to do with a 300-foot-long windmill blade,' but of course, I didn't."

Instead, Bob told GE, "Send us a five-gallon bucket of windmill blade pieces, and we'll take a look at it."

They did take a look, got their innovative juices going, and before long, Bob's team had created a process for recycling windmill blades. Today, 6,500 windmill blades later, the company's method of using the material in the blades as a feedstock into other materials has led to a truly green solution.

"We have recycled more than 6,500 windmill blades from industrial windmill farms, where we take that material and incorporate it as a feedstock into other materials and create a truly green solution."

For those curious about the specifics of this creative recycling solution, Bob is delighted to explain. Some of the blades are made from fiberglass, which has silica in it. Veolia extracts the silica and sells it to customers who manufacture reusable products from it.

Bob also adds that he has learned more about windmill blades than he ever thought would be possible—or necessary.

They key takeaway is not that silica is our friend: "More importantly, we empower our employees to take crazy ideas and translate them into very good ideas that help our business and the client's business, and make a difference in the world."

Those employees who are able to spin gold from, well, windmill blades deserve a little credit, Bob says. And Bob is happy to give it to them. "I probably get an eye roll from about half of our employees, but I enjoy putting people up on stage at our events and recognizing them for the work that they do." Half of the group, he says, are embarrassed or uncomfortable with the attention bestowed on them. "But the other half will whisper in my ear, 'I'm going to be up there next year.'"

Another reason I chose Veolia to exemplify the archetype of the 70-20-10 rule is their innovation-investment strategy. At Veolia's North American division, Bob has 3,000 employees looking for opportunities to dream, tinker, and create. And while much of what they produce is related to some of Veolia's core products, the company also has an annual "moon shot" program where they solicit ideas from the employees. Last year, a total of 160 different ideas were presented and reviewed by management. The employees who present the best ideas get a trip to Paris and the opportunity to present their brainstorms at Veolia's corporate headquarters. Many of these ideas are actually implemented. And, says Bob, "They can range from a new, innovative idea for our Human Resources group, to a physical asset or business line implementation, or maybe a service line that we haven't had before."

These innovations represent 20 percent investment in adjacent technology and 10 percent in disruption—new ideas that drive future growth.

Veolia's organizational structure also emulates the 70-20-10 formula. And it represents a process that allows the best ideas to filter to the top. The company has an Emerging Markets Group—a department dedicated to nurturing innovative ideas that could represent growth opportunities for the business. "So we take it from a start-up, 'moon-shot' idea, with a few people dedicated to it, and then ramp that up to the point that it can move from our emerging business units into one of our core business investments," Bob says. "It follows a natural process."

THE 70-20-10 INNOVATOR: TIPS FOR SUCCESS

Reward the problem-solver. "Keep in mind that the thing that seems so innovative today is going to be obsolete someday," Bob advises. "And five years from now, our business will be bigger than it is today. At the same time, it will also likely be addressing a different challenge than we're addressing today. We need people looking ahead to solve problems we don't even know we will have."

Never stop listening to the customer. "We've all heard this advice, but it's worth restating," says Bob. "By truly listening to and understanding customer challenges, we can make a difference. It enables creativity within the business and allows our business to change a little bit faster than the environment around us."

Encourage small improvements. "Try to create an environment where people are excited about bringing new ideas forward, no matter small or big. As we know at Veolia, many of the innovations in large companies, like Veolia, are small, or they occur over a long period of time. But they can be just as valuable in the long run."

Build the right team. "You need to build the team with people who are going to support the idea, because you may or may not be in the position to sell the idea. Make sure you get the group on board so that they are able to sell the idea." Bob says, "Today, I'm probably that person. I'm the person who now must put the idea forward and sell the idea and work with people who are planting those seeds within our group. What I do is make sure that I'm fostering the development of those seeds as well as selling them moving forward, so that our organization supports them, our customers support them, and we give them the opportunity to develop new products and services that have meaningful impact."

#4: THE STODGY OLD BUREAUCRACY: WHEN INNOVATION IS NOT TOP OF THE AGENDA

CASE STUDY: BUSINESS VETERAN COLIN FOSTER ON HOW CORPORATIONS INNOVATE

As you might have guessed, the fearful, mostly risk-averse corporation is on the far right of the innovation continuum, sacrificing innovation for scale, process, repeatability, and reproducibility. In the desire to please shareholders with expected results, they increasingly lose focus on the customer, become more internally focused, and lose their ability to change and pivot.

In general, the Stodgy Old Bureaucracy often represents the antithesis of innovation. Rigid structures and entrenched processes can stifle creativity, creating an environment where new ideas are met with skepticism and slow adaptation. Corporate companies invest heavily in innovation but with a focus on incremental improvements and low-risk approaches.

That doesn't mean every large, established corporation is an innovative foot-dragger. Netflix, Amazon, and Tesla are prime examples of big organizations working hard to keep the innovation mindset alive.

I met with Colin Foster in early January 2024 over Zoom in our respective home offices. Colin is an executive in residence at Yale and Columbia universities. He's CEO of a Yale spinout called Cytosolix. "An oncology therapy company in stealth mode" is how he describes it. Yale and Columbia universities are institutions that some might say are the educational epitome of stodginess and bureaucracy (it is Yale that achieved the dubious distinction of a university having more administrators than students). But surprise!

Cytosolix and Saatient (a startup Colin spun out of Columbia in 2024) aren't his first rodeos. He was a senior executive for a decade at Bayer Pharmaceuticals and, from 2002 to 2004, served as CEO and president of North America. Additionally, Colin has been a board member and CEO of several life sciences companies, both private, early-stage, venture-backed and public.

I had sought out Colin because I was interested in his thoughts on innovation, thoughts that were cultivated during his corporate experience—and that he now had an opportunity to test in his current roles as CEO of Cytosolix and Saatient.

His response made me feel that I should have been in one of the Yale lecture halls, taking copious notes (which I did!).

"Innovation is change that can happen in increments, but not because it's incremental in itself," Colin opined. "It can be a big change, a big leap forward, like the electric car, but it happens with a series of discoveries. In corporations, innovation is more incremental around improving things like cost efficiency. In this case, it occurs on a continuum. But it's only helpful if it causes dissatisfaction that propels people to make small changes. The world needs to embrace and adopt your change, your innovation—they have to need it."

There is a big difference between big and small companies when it comes to their approach to innovation, according to Colin. Big companies win in the market with innovation that comes in increments. They win by controlling the market. They use their size as a benefit to gain and maintain that market control. They tend to be risk averse, preferring investments that offer predictable returns. Their approach to innovation is structured and involves lots of marketing testing. Small companies win in the market with innovation and speed. They also benefit from their size, being small, which allows them to be nimble and make quick decisions. You see more impactful innovation, like the electric car Colin referred to earlier, in smaller companies where they have the risk appetite for trial and error, which are critical ingredients for innovation to thrive and flourish.

But even within a conservative and sometimes rigid structure, innovation is possible in large companies, Colin says. He proved it, achieving measurable growth in several corporations during his tenures. So what metrics matter? Quality, speed, and money, according to Colin. Those are also metrics that involved the balance sheet, income statements, people and promotions, and capital raised.

"If you're not hitting your numbers, you're not innovating," Colin underscores.

In my own experience (especially in Big Pharma), corporations focus on incremental innovation to improve efficiency, expand their market share, and respond to competitive threats. They may pursue transformational innovation but usually at a slower pace. They have significant resources so they can invest heavily in R&D, innovation labs, and strategic partnerships. But as was the case with some of the pharmaceutical firms I worked with, they may also decide that the easiest way to innovate is to acquire new technologies through start-ups (how and whether those start-ups can keep their creative mojo under the ownership of a storied bureaucracy is a separate question).

The Stodgy Old Bureaucracy: Tips for Success

Define your innovation. Corporations want innovations that create value, that can move needles. Yours must be more than simply a "good idea." To help better describe your innovation—as you inevitably will as it moves up the hierarchy—Colin has developed a list of six characteristics. Think about these as you frame the description of your big idea—or as you develop new and even bigger ones!

- Is it credible? (Is it grounded in reality?)
- Is it meaningful? (Is it a "must have"?)
- Is it unique? (Is this a new product in the market, one that can drive growth—and grow?)
- Is it sustainable? (Is it enduring given the competitive landscape and the evolving market?)
- Is it simple? (Can it be shared and widely understood, and does selling it come "clean" or with a litany of conditions?)
- Is it accessible? (Can it be put into customers' hands easily and quickly without contractual or other related delays?)

You don't have to have all the answers. "Absence of knowledge is my superpower," says Colin. "I ask basic questions based on my lack of knowledge, and it gets people on their toes." If you are pitching the idea, perhaps you don't need to have every detail explained or figured out. But you do need to be able to anticipate those basic questions. On the other hand, if you're in management, and you're the one on the receiving end of the "I have an idea" pitch by your employees, testing the underlying premise of the idea, asking the basic, if obvious, questions—how/where/when/whether/why this idea could be implemented—will get them to rigorously think through their idea and its feasibility.

Don't assume more money means greater innovation. "In good times, you tend to spend faster and spend more, but that doesn't mean the ideas are bigger, better," he says. "With money you may move faster. But money doesn't create greater or more innovation." I like Colin's point. More money doesn't correlate with better innovation. In fact, I might argue that it's just the opposite. The best innovations grow out of constraints like limited budget, resources, and time. I like to share the story of Phil McKinney, former CTO of Hewlett-Packard's innovation lab, who insisted on a lean budget and team to force the team to think more creatively and work faster.

Colin concurs. He says new ideas don't flourish when budgets are overflowing. "Innovation occurs when the stress of budget constraints forces people to think," he says, "to do their best." I agree. Stress takes us from "nice to have" to "must have." If something is really going to innovate, it won't be taken off the table. It will survive the filter. You may have less data to back it up and it may take longer, but you'll get there.

Maria Boulden, former head of sales at DuPont, a behemoth in the chemical industry, adds some interesting perspective. DuPont, she says, has had its ups and downs as an innovative company. "Up until the 90s, we listened to customers, innovated around their needs, created categories and enjoyed market leadership.

Company Types

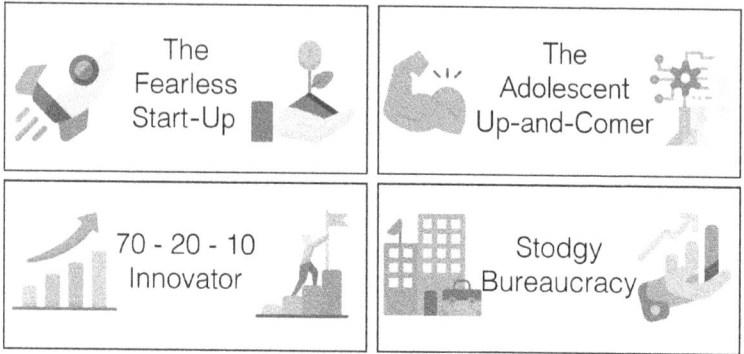

Figure 7.1 Most organizations fall into one of four innovation categories based on their innovation mindset and not their chronological age: the Fearless Start-Up, the Adolescent Up-and-Comer, the 70-20-10 Innovator, and the Stodgy Bureaucracy.

As the company grew and corporate executives emphasized consistency in stock performance, we became more focused on quarter-to-quarter performance, and innovation became an expensive afterthought. We stopped listening to customers as closely and started to lose some of our prowess in the industry. When we let down our guard, it allowed competitors to take some of our market share. That's always a dangerous thing and, in some markets, we never recovered from it. That forced us to get more innovative in our go-to-market strategies, where we could afford it. But imagine the possibilities if we had innovated on the front end and the back end."

LORRAINE'S SURVIVAL GUIDE FOR INTRAPRENEURS

Here are my tips on how to stay innovative no matter what size or stage company you are and for keeping innovation top of mind and communicating effectively no matter what kind of organization you're working at. Innovation has to be a mindset, and leadership has to embrace and inculcate it in the culture.

Be persistent, not insistent. You've got a good idea on how to improve efficiency in your department, or division, or corporate-wide. You have at least some of the data to prove it can work, and in your innovative heart, you know it will work. That's great—but don't expect everyone in management to drop what they're doing and give you a round of applause or immediately take steps to initiate your brilliant idea. And don't react badly if you discern foot-dragging on the part of upper management. Remember, organizational behavior is complex, regardless of the kind of organization we're talking about. Be patient—try pitching it again in a couple of months or look for an alternative path to a decision-maker. Some people who are confident of the value of their ideas can border on the insistent—the subtext of which is "How could you be so stupid as to not see the brilliance of my idea?" Resist the impulse to be insistent. Really good ideas eventually rise to the top. But shepherding those ideas may take time and persistence.

What's in it for them? Here's the question that everyone will be asking, regardless of the organization: "What's in it for me?" (WIIFM). In this case, "me" is your customer or key audience. My students learn the importance of WIIFM in the business communications course I teach at Wharton. It means tailoring your message to the interests and priorities of your audience. It means telling them what they need to know and not what you think they need to know.

A necessary correlate of WIIFM is crafting a compelling narrative. Develop a clear and engaging story around your idea. Articulate not just the idea itself but the problem it addresses, the proposed solution, and the anticipated benefits. Use data and case studies to reinforce your narrative, making it more persuasive.

Understand the organizational landscape. Familiarize yourself with the company's strategic objectives, priorities, and decision-making processes. This contextual understanding allows you to align your ideas with broader organizational goals, making them more compelling.

Build relationships. Cultivate strong relationships with senior leaders and key stakeholders. Networking within and outside your organization can create advocates for your ideas. Engage in informal conversations to gauge their interests and concerns, which can help tailor your pitch.

Focus on return on investment. Senior managers are concerned with the bottom line. Clearly outline the potential return on investment of your idea, including cost savings, revenue generation, and improved efficiency. Quantitative data can significantly bolster your case.

Encourage feedback. Present your ideas as works in progress rather than final solutions. Solicit feedback from senior managers, demonstrating your openness to collaboration and refinement. This approach fosters a sense of ownership and increases buy-in.

Demonstrate quick wins. If possible, implement small-scale pilot projects to showcase the viability of your ideas. Presenting tangible results from these initiatives can effectively illustrate their potential impact.

Leverage formal channels. Utilize established channels for idea submission, such as innovation committees or strategic planning sessions. Ensure that your ideas are presented in a format that aligns with these processes, demonstrating your understanding of organizational protocols.

Engage in continuous learning. Stay informed about industry trends, innovations, and best practices. This knowledge not only enriches your ideas but also positions you as a credible resource, enhancing your influence within the organization.

Advocate for a diverse perspective. Highlight the importance of diverse viewpoints in driving innovation. Position yourself as a champion for inclusivity, which can resonate well with senior leaders committed to fostering a diverse workplace.

CHAMPIONS OF CHANGE

Lessons from Fearless Founders and Enterprising Executives

Angela Mangiapane
President, Mars Global Services

In her thirty years at Mars, Angela strengthened the organization's talent pipeline and powered the evolution of the business, pushing boundaries to inspire innovation. From the beginning of her journey until now, Angela's contributions amplified and energized the transformation of Mars, a privately held company based in McLean, Virginia. Once a purveyor of candy bars, it is now a global organization with more than $50 billion in annual sales with an expanding portfolio of leading pet nutrition, veterinary services, and quality snacking and food products—M&M'S®, PEDIGREE®, and BEN'S ORIGINAL™, to name a few.

Throughout her career, Angela has played an invaluable role in driving change across the business, evolving into a more innovative mindset during her time as president of Mars Global Services (MGS). Behind the most loved brands of Mars are 3,000 MGS associates under Angela's leadership who are working to enable easier work throughout Mars by providing innovative services and solutions across digital technologies, procurement, human resources, finances, and more to over 150,000 associates in more than seventy operating markets worldwide.

With a focus on operational excellence, Angela empowers her team to drive the adoption of cutting-edge technologies, use data analytics and automation to unlock business inefficiencies, and streamline processes that save money, time, and effort for internal customers. In other words, she inspires MGS associates around the world every day to forge ahead in their pursuit to do things differently and better. Here are a few lessons she's learned about facilitating change in a large global enterprise.

Listen up and down the line.

"So many people believe answers come from the top, but innovation can come from anywhere and anyone," says Angela. "If you listen to the people in your organization who are on the assembly line, on the showroom floor, or answering the phones, you'll learn a lot—in fact, you may find the big idea you're looking for. But to get to that point, you need to create an environment where leaders facilitate opportunities for people to voice their concerns, not one where leaders are thought to have all the answers."

Innovation is portable.

Angela's experience at Mars shows that an aptitude for innovating is transferable. Originally from Canada, Angela has served in roles that have taken her from finance in the United States to human resources (HR) in Latin America and France, and ultimately to her current role at MGS—and innovation accompanied her at every turn. Someone with an innovative mindset can foment change across different departments, different functions, and different situations within their organization. "When I worked in our former Mars Coffee and Tea business, I was granted an opportunity to explore innovation in HR," she says. Angela led the HR division to become an early adopter of competency training and development plans. In her current role, she's taken MGS from what used to be considered a transactional IT shop to what is now a "business within a business," with six expanded service lines that integrate artificial intelligence (AI) and process intelligence into its daily work across Mars.

Tap into your "intrapreneurial" spirit.

"What I've learned in my career is that we are limited by our core beliefs," says Angela. "If you believe you're just a cog in the wheel, you'll only ever be a cog in the wheel. If you believe, however, that you are an intrapreneur—someone who behaves like an entrepreneur while working within a large organization—you've already won half the battle. Have confidence in yourself. If you have a great idea, make the case for it to your boss—and if there is a high ROI, explain to them exactly what's needed to make it happen."

MGS launched a project that would free up time for internal customers called "My Hub." "It's a personalized, digital workspace that brings together processes, tools, and resources that our Associates use every day, decreasing time spent on locating them and maximizing time for value-add work," says Angela. "It meant transforming ways of working that have existed for years—and, inevitably, there was some initial resistance to the idea—but my team effectively proved the value of the project and got approval for funding before showing the return."

"We took a leap of faith, and it paid off in dividends," Angela says. "If you've got a sensible idea or initiative in mind for your organization, and you've thought it out—I encourage you to do the same!"

Find your purpose.

Innovation doesn't start in the C-suite or only while you're in the office. It starts with a state of mind—one that Angela encourages. "Approaching things with awe and a childlike wonder inspires a fresh perspective, which leads to innovation," she says. "I encourage everyone to remain curious and fascinated."

She also believes in a life and an organization that are purpose driven—a term that is used frequently these days.

Mars defines purpose as its inspiration for pushing boundaries and challenging itself to transform the way it does business every day. At Mars, purpose is what drives business. It offers an opportunity to stand for more and make a positive difference. Mars has very clear metrics, guiding it to achieve growth that has a positive impact on people and the planet, starting with clarity of purpose. "The world we want tomorrow starts with how we do business today."

The company is also guided by some key concepts. "At Mars, we are driven by our Five Principles, which are Quality, Responsibility, Mutuality, Efficiency, and Freedom. These guide us to make better decisions, big and small," Angela shares. "After thirty years with a purpose-driven company, I firmly believe that making a positive impact alongside achieving business success should be a high priority for every organization."

She leaves us with this: "Working for Mars has given me insight into the value of purposeful leadership and what's possible with purpose at the center, and one thing is abundantly clear—purpose and principles lead to a more innovative workplace."

To learn more about Mars, visit https://www.mars.com.

To learn more about Angela, see https://www.linkedin.com/in /angela-mangiapan.

8

AI: DOOM OR DELIVERANCE?

The title of this book is *No Fear, No Failure.*

Fear.

Failure.

I can think of no other innovation in my lifetime that has provoked more of the former and more predictions of the latter than artificial intelligence (AI).

Our society seems to be gripped by both a collective excitement and a deep terror over this new technology. Organizations and individuals alike are in awe of AI's potential but are, at the same time, fearful of imminent or on-the-horizon failures of potentially epic dimensions due to jobs lost and entire industries becoming outmoded or redundant when AI takes over everything (as some seem to think it inevitably will).

As with any new technology of this sweeping scale, there is plenty of serious and sober thought that needs to be given to the development, applications, and governance of AI.

There are two things I know for certain, however. First, some of what we say about AI in this chapter will probably be outdated by the time you're reading it. The other thing I firmly believe is that, for organizational innovators, AI represents a dazzling array of possibilities, an innovation opportunity the scale of which we might not see again for decades (save for our pursuit of interplanetary exploration, of course).

It is in that spirit that I write this: not a spirit of fear or one of trepidation about failure. Rather, I write in a spirit of curiosity, which, as so many of our champions of change have underscored, is central to successful innovation at any level.

And although I recognize that AI is likely to change a lot of things, there are some things it won't alter. I also know it will take longer than we think for many AI applications to reach the market, much less disrupt it. My observation, as a student of innovation for more than thirty-five years, is that we overestimate the impact of new technologies in the short term and underestimate their impact in the longer term. As we explore AI in this chapter, keep in mind two very important requirements that make AI useful:

- The quality and breadth of data from which it generates information
- The quality and intelligence of the prompts constructed to query it

At this moment, both are governed by humans who can limit or enhance the power and usefulness of AI.

Right now, I think they're limiting it. If companies continue to develop their own proprietary AI to generate insights from their internal datasets, the crowdsourcing of data required for ChatGPT to grow in usefulness will be curbed. And if we want to make AI smarter, we need humans to develop new competencies in AI design and development and prompt generation, which are all opportunities for new types of jobs that didn't exist before.

There are many scenarios for how AI might evolve, and one of them was drawn out for me by a member of our Innovators' Circle, Eric Schultz, cofounder of four companies that successfully exploit various flavors of AI—QuantiaMD, COTA, Ocean Genomics, and SageForce—and advisor to a portfolio of others.

Trained in computer science at Harvard in the early 1980s, Eric worked on early AI languages, including Lisp and Prolog, and has since employed several forms of AI, from machine learning, natural language processing, graphs, and networks to, now, generative AI in his work and companies. I met Eric seven years ago when I was working at IQVIA, a clinical research technology company, and he was at the oncology data and analytics start-up COTA. IQVIA had made an investment in COTA, and we were partnering on the design of a cancer data program on behalf of our client the Multiple Myeloma Research Foundation in Connecticut. I know that upon reading this, he'll retort with an Eric-ism, as I call them—something like, "Holy smokes, that's nice of ya"—but Eric is one of the smartest and nicest people I know. He grew up in Buffalo, New York, the youngest of five children born to working-class German immigrants. After graduating from Harvard in 1983, his first job was with the software developer Lotus, which was creating the first software for the (at the time) undisclosed and unreleased, super-secret IBM personal computer (PC). A very simplified form of today's Microsoft Excel, Lotus "took off like a rocket ship, was a lot of fun to work on, and, importantly, ushered in the PC industry," according to Eric.

After Lotus, Eric created a company that was bought by Microsoft; he moved to Seattle, running the Enhanced Platforms Products Division, which involved the commercialization of innovative products coming out of the company's research and development (R&D), including mobile. He then led the creation of Microsoft's joint venture with Qualcomm to exploit the first applications of mobile data transfer in the United States. From there, he helped found COTA, which became one of the largest real-world data companies in oncology. That's where I met him. At COTA, Eric used humans, combined with AI and natural language processing technology, to pull data out of the clinical notes that doctors scribbled in electronic medical records, creating a large oncology dataset that could be used by healthcare organizations and pharma alike to better understand cancer and treatments and to aid in the discovery and development of new drugs.

Eric has absolutely no plans to retire. Instead, he cofounded an AI-based "multiomic" discovery company, Ocean Genomics, spun out of the famous Carnegie Mellon University, with Carl Kingsford head of the computational biology department. Carl and Eric founded Ocean Genomics to create a platform that allowed researchers to build and exploit extremely large databases of sequencing (DNA and RNA) and clinical data to explore biology and discover and develop drugs. Of course, in addition to advanced discovery AI engines, they also built in generative AI so that researchers, as he puts it, "can talk to their data" directly, instead of waiting for someone to write code. Most recently, he founded SageForce, a platform technology company that provides digital human assistants focused in healthcare and life sciences where knowledge is complex and compliance and factual accuracy are essential.

In the fall of 2024, I invited Eric to be a guest speaker in my class, Digital Transformation in Business, at Moravian University. As you might imagine, I was excited to introduce him to my class and looked forward to plenty of insights and Eric-isms. My students and I got both. "Eric is our AI guest speaker," I said to them. "Ask all the questions that come to mind. Remember, you have the opportunity today to learn from someone who's been involved with AI from its inception, is applying it to solve real-world problems in healthcare, and has his finger on the pulse of where this technology is going and how fast it will change our lives."

Eric simply responded, in characteristic fashion, "Yup, let's have some fun."

The students were eager to listen and learn. Phones were put away, cameras were on, and eyes were glued to the screen as Eric pulled up his first slide, a map of AI's evolution, which he proudly admitted he had made with the help of ChatGPT.

Although I had encouraged my students to ask questions, I knew the one that was most important to them. Like many people, they're worried about their future and how AI might impact it. Based on the media coverage of this new revolution, I don't blame them.

"Eric, we can start with the big picture and then walk through your map of AI's evolution yesterday, today, and tomorrow,"

I said. "But I want to get at the question that's on everyone's minds first. Once we deal with it, I think the students and I will be able to settle back and listen with open minds. I did a count, and last week alone, according to a Google search, 1,400 articles were published on the impact of AI on jobs. Most of that coverage was negative!"

No doubt you're familiar with this perspective, too. For example, in a screaming headline in a 2023 *Forbes* article, Goldman Sachs prognosticators predicted "300 Million Jobs Will Be Lost or Degraded by Artificial Intelligence."

A recent LinkedIn post opined that we will no longer need lawyers, accountants, and human resources (HR) professionals because "AI will take over professional services."

But wait, there's more! The International Monetary Fund predicts that 40 percent of all jobs around the globe will be affected.

Workers, young and old, are paying attention. Only 31 percent of US employees doubt that AI will impact their jobs in the future, and half believe that gaining AI skills will help their careers progress, according to LinkedIn's latest Workforce Confidence survey. The survey found that the youngest and the oldest workers have more doubts about AI impacting their jobs. Four in ten Gen Zers said they doubted AI would impact their roles, followed by 36 percent of Baby Boomers. Just 29 percent of Millennials and Gen Xers agreed. Meanwhile, midcareer employees are more likely to be focused on gaining AI skills to get ahead. A well-known tech educator told a class of undergraduates at a liberal arts college in Boston where I was teaching a business skills seminar, "AI will be smarter than humans. In the future, there will be two types of people—those controlled by AI and those who tell AI what to do."

In a recent TED Talk, the head of Microsoft, Satya Nadella, envisioned a similarly AI-dependent future: "Everyone will have a personal robot assistant in the future, and these robots will help you make decisions from what to wear for the weather on a given day to telling you it's time to replenish your family's paper products."

Are workers—or, like some of my students, those about to enter the workforce—worried about AI in the workplace? They sure are.

"Are those fears justified?" I asked Eric to kick off his presentation to my class.

Eric smiled. It wasn't the first time he'd been asked the jobs question in relation to AI.

"Yes," he acknowledged. "AI will automate many roles, especially repetitive or routine tasks. That's where much of the fear comes from. For example, generative AI—like ChatGPT—can generate text, images, and code, automating things people currently do in fields such as professional services, the arts, and even science."

But he added, there's a bigger picture here that many have overlooked. Automation doesn't mean elimination. "It often shifts what humans do, creating opportunities to focus on higher-value tasks," Eric said.

Such fears about the impact of new technologies, he points out, are nothing new. "When computers first started entering the workplace in the mid-twentieth century, people were terrified that they would destroy jobs," Eric said. "Typists, accountants, and even office managers thought they'd be replaced. Instead, computers created an entirely new industry—software development, IT, and eventually the internet economy—that led to an explosion of jobs and opportunities. Far from wiping out work, computers transformed industries, enabling people to work faster and smarter. AI will follow a similar path. It will disrupt some roles, yes, but it will also create new industries and countless jobs we can't even imagine yet."

I noticed my students leaning forward in their seats. I didn't see anyone looking at their phone. A good sign, I thought.

Eric continued, "Another critical thing to remember is that AI is a tool—its value depends on how humans use it. Ask AI the right questions, and it can help you solve problems or speed up work. Ask poorly framed questions, and the results won't help you at all. That's why we're seeing new fields like 'prompt engineering,' where people specialize in designing effective queries for AI systems. These roles didn't exist a few years ago and now pay very well."

"I can vouch for that," I interjected. "I can't tell you how many times AI told me, 'it depends' when I first started using it. You need humans to write intelligent queries."

Eric provided an example from Klarna, a Swedish financial technology company. "Their AI replaced the work of 700 customer service reps, handling two-thirds of customer interactions. That's disruptive, yes—but it also created new jobs for those building, maintaining, and improving the AI. The challenge is making sure displaced workers have access to the training they need to transition to these new roles."

Here, Eric underscores what he calls "one of the most transformative aspects of generative AI": accessibility.

Think back to the early computer days, if you're old enough to remember. Technology had much to offer but was difficult to operate. It still is for many people.

That is not a problem with AI. "You don't need a technical background to leverage its power," said Eric. "Just a clear idea and a well-crafted prompt."

Whether it's a student brainstorming for an essay, a small business owner drafting marketing copy, or an event planner generating creative themes, generative AI adapts to countless applications. "By framing the right questions, anyone can unlock valuable insights and put AI to work for them."

Eric concluded, "Yes, jobs will be displaced. But over time I envision that many more will emerge as we adapt and innovate. Humans are resilient. AI will augment what we do, making work smarter and more efficient. Our focus shouldn't just be on what's lost, but on preparing for what's next. Remember, the future isn't bleak—it's evolving."

This was certainly a brighter look at AI. I could see my students liked what Eric had to say.

But now we wanted to get to the other aspect of AI that brings out the dystopians. Forget about job losses—we could lose our humanity! That, of course, is another confident prediction by the AI doomsayers: AI-enabled robots taking over the world and that sort of thing. But as Eric pointed out, the ways that AI is going to be integrated into the workplace may be far more subtle. In fact, that's happening now. "AI is already woven into the fabric of many businesses, often in ways that go unnoticed. Most of it comes in the form of packaged tools tailored to specific functions, making you a user. But the next step is becoming an AI power-user—someone who goes beyond prepackaged tools to leverage platforms like ChatGPT to enhance workflows and solve problems. This doesn't require building AI from scratch but involves learning how to unlock its full potential for your specific needs."

That was reassuring for our students, and a little research showed that Eric's views backed up those of a well-known authority on AI, Jennifer Golbeck. A computer scientist at the University of Maryland College of Information who studies AI and social media, Jennifer did a TED Talk MidAtlantic presentation, in June 2024, in which she shared a story about the impact of AI on jobs. "Let's imagine this," Golbeck said in her talk. "A company can only afford one software engineer, but now we have AI, which can cut the work of the software engineer in half, and he can spend time generating new ideas because he can produce more innovation in half the time and therefore generate more revenue for the company."

She goes on to posit that this new way of working is so efficient that the head of the company says, "I'm saving money and generating more income, so now I'm going to be able to invest in two software engineers who can generate twice the products and twice the revenue."

Jennifer's conclusion is that "AI could help companies create new jobs and hire more people with greater productivity."

Yet many professionals don't see the kind of potential AI blue skies that Eric and Jennifer Golbeck describe. They see AI as a zero-sum game, meaning that it's just going to eliminate jobs, careers, and entire industries. I recently spoke with the owner of a small legal firm who's not using AI. He told me he'd rather hire a good attorney who's great with people, can collaborate with their peers, and can create a strong relationship with customers than invest in AI to do tasks and replace an assistant or paralegal. He explained that these people have more value to him because they generate income through the relationships they build. "If AI can help them do low-level tasks better to make more time for high-level relationship-building, than I'm all for it," he said. "But I won't use it to replace people."

Eric helped reassure my students—and me!—that AI was not necessarily an innovation to be feared. But what about its use to help encourage and discover innovation? Well, that's what Dinko Franceschi, a doctoral researcher in the renowned Debora Marks Lab at Harvard, is exploring. Dinko's research focuses on developing novel AI models to understand the genetic basis of human diseases and enhance early cancer detection. He also holds an Associated Researcher appointment at the Broad Institute of MIT and Harvard. I sat down with him to understand the work he and his colleagues are doing.

The lab, led by Debora Marks, a professor of systems biology at Harvard Medical School, is looking to use AI to develop a screening tool for pancreatic cancer, one of the most aggressive forms of cancer and one that typically presents at later stages with poor outcomes. There is a strong need for early detection, but until now, the limiting factors have been access to the right data and a computer algorithm that can help shed light on who is likely to develop the disease. Once those individuals can be identified, disease onset and progression can be monitored and treatment administered early to increase chances of survival. According to a paper Dinko's colleagues published in the May 8, 2023, issue of *Nature Medicine*, a research team from Harvard Medical School applied AI methods to clinical data from six million patients (including 24,000 pancreatic cancer cases) in Denmark's National Patient Registry and three million patients (including 3,900 cases) in the US Department of Veterans Affairs. They trained machine learning models on health insurance disease codes from patients' medical records and evaluated the models' ability to predict cancer occurrence over various time intervals. The results demonstrated an improved capability to identify individuals at increased risk of pancreatic cancer, paving the way for designing surveillance programs for patients at elevated risk. These programs have the potential to improve lifespan and quality of life through early detection and intervention. "The model analyzes data from patients diagnosed with pancreatic cancer within a timeframe of three to twelve months and compares their symptoms to those of control groups," Dinko explains. "By aligning these two datasets—healthy controls and pancreatic cancer patients—we can identify patterns that distinguish the groups. AI has enabled us to accomplish in weeks what would take a human months to analyze."

The next step in their work, he says, is to incorporate medication and genetic data to enhance the dataset and refine diagnostic criteria. "This will significantly improve the model's predictive accuracy," Dinko says. This work will probably take several years to complete, but Dinko believes the model can already be used by physicians to help screen people at high risk for developing pancreatic cancer. The challenge, of course, is that there is nothing you can do for someone before the cancer develops, so physicians are left to watch and wait. Still, if patients are vigilantly followed, they can start treatment sooner, when they show the first signs of cancer. There is a long road ahead to get approval for this screening tool and to get insurers to pay for it. But it's a promising advance for patients and a compelling example of how AI can be used in something of enormous value to humans.

That's just one example. There's a lot of money flowing into AI right now and a lot to be gained from learning how to use it right and, by that, I mean by using it in an innovative way—the way others, in the past, used the then-game-changing technologies of steam, electricity, and computers to build new worlds.

Maybe with AI, you can, too!

Let's return to our 5C's of organizational innovation, which can help you to steer your company into an AI-enabled future.

AI AND THE 5C's: CUSTOMER FIRST

AI has the potential to improve customer engagement and market growth by enabling companies to deliver highly personalized experiences, optimize marketing, and improve customer satisfaction. I'd like to point out that these examples are retail shopping experiences and related customer interactions, which is where AI appears to have the most benefit.

Personalized Customer Experiences

AI-driven systems can analyze customer data, including purchase history, browsing behavior, and demographics, to help companies deliver personalized experiences. For instance, recommendation engines, like those used by Netflix and Amazon, suggest products or content tailored to individual preferences, enhancing engagement and encouraging repeat purchases. This personalized touch can strengthen customer loyalty and boost retention—that is, if you don't find it annoying or downright creepy!

Predictive Analytics for Customer Insights

Related to customized experience, predictive analytics allow companies to forecast customer behavior, segment audiences, and identify high-value prospects. AI models can assess patterns in data to predict which customers are likely to buy certain products, allowing companies to target them with relevant offers. For example, because I recently purchased a gently used SUV, WeatherTech and GM conspired to offer me weatherproof floor mats as winter approached. That wasn't so creepy. In fact, I think it was a pretty good suggestion.

Chatbots and Virtual Assistants

I personally despise chatbots, LOL, but I realize they can efficiently provide 24/7 customer support, answer common questions, and process transactions. Ostensibly, according to the companies that use them as a first-line triage in place of humans, they can engage customers in real time across platforms (websites, apps, social media), improving response times and customer satisfaction. With natural language processing, these bots should be able to understand and respond to customer inquiries in a conversational manner, fostering a smoother customer experience. I'll leave it to our readers to ponder their own chatbot experiences and imagine how AI might improve them.

Enhanced Customer Journey Mapping

AI tools can be used to help companies map out and optimize the customer journey by analyzing touchpoints across channels. This enables businesses to identify bottlenecks, reduce friction, and potentially ensure a more seamless experience from initial interest to purchase. For example, AI can detect where customers drop off on a website or app and suggest optimizations to the company to achieve higher conversion rates and better customer retention.

Dynamic Pricing and Offers

AI can enable companies to adjust pricing based on demand, competition, and customer willingness to pay. Airlines and e-commerce platforms frequently use this approach to optimize revenue while maintaining customer interest. Additionally, AI can create targeted promotions and offers for specific customer segments, incentivizing purchases and encouraging loyalty.

AI AND THE 5C's: CULTURE

How is AI impacting culture? It may be too early to tell, but certainly fostering more efficient ways to collaborate and share information is one way. Some of these benefits are redundant with collaboration, but suffice to say, they have dual benefits.

Data-Driven Decision-Making

A big plus is that AI can enable organizations to base decisions on data and insights rather than on intuition or tradition. This shift encourages a culture where data are valued and evidence-based practices are prioritized. With AI analyzing complex data and forecasting trends, employees across the organization are encouraged to use data in their daily tasks, which improves transparency, accountability, and outcomes.

Increased Innovation and Agility

Similar to our discussion earlier in this chapter, by automating routine tasks and generating insights quickly, AI can allow employees to focus on high-value, creative work. This can foster a culture of innovation where experimentation is encouraged and teams are agile in adapting to new challenges. With AI's ability to rapidly analyze results and provide feedback, employees may be able to generate and enhance ideas faster, leading to a more dynamic, forward-thinking culture that embraces change.

Enhanced Collaboration and Knowledge Sharing

AI-driven collaboration tools make it easier for teams to share information and work together efficiently, fostering a more cohesive and collaborative environment. AI-powered knowledge-management systems help break down silos, allowing employees from different departments to access shared resources and insights easily. This can promote a culture of teamwork and continuous learning.

Focus on Continuous Learning and Skill Development

As AI automates many tasks and requires new skill sets, organizations are increasingly prioritizing continuous learning to improve the skills of their workforce. Employees are encouraged to develop skills in data analytics, AI literacy, and digital tools to stay competitive. This emphasis on lifelong learning can help cultivate a growth mindset across the company and reinforces a culture that values adaptability and career development.

Ethics and Responsible AI Practices

With AI use on the rise, organizations are becoming more aware of the ethical implications of AI technologies. Issues like data privacy, algorithmic fairness, and transparency are becoming part of company cultures as leaders strive to establish responsible AI practices.

AI AND THE 5C's: COLLABORATION

AI is a good tool for fostering administrative methods of collaborating within and between teams and companies by facilitating communication, streamlining workflows, and improving data sharing. Here are some examples.

Automated Communication Tools

AI-powered communication tools, such as chatbots and virtual assistants, can help with internal communication by scheduling meetings and summarizing conversations. For example, AI assistants can organize team meetings by analyzing everyone's availability, which reduces time spent on coordination. Personally, I love my Otter.ai, my note-taking assistant for this book. I interviewed more than seventy-five people, and Otter kept accurate records when it came time to fact-check quotes. I laugh sometimes when people tell me Otter got to my meeting before me or even attended in my place. Thanks, Otter.

Data Integration and Analysis

AI can help aggregate and analyze data from different sources, making it easier for teams to share insights across departments or with partner companies. Shared access to real-time insights fosters a collaborative, data-informed culture. For example, online retailers share customer data in real time to help teams determine when and where to place advertising, lower prices, or offer special, time-bound promotions.

Enhanced Knowledge Sharing and Learning

AI-driven knowledge-management systems, such as natural language processing–based search engines, may allow employees to access and share information across the organization. Some systems can analyze previous project data, documents, and reports, helping employees find relevant information quickly. AI can also suggest training materials, resources, or experts within the company, promoting a culture of continuous learning and collaboration.

Improved Project Management and Workflow Automation

AI-powered project-management tools can automate repetitive tasks, track project progress, and identify potential delays. By providing teams with real-time updates and insights, these tools improve transparency and help members stay aligned on project goals. Some tools use machine learning to forecast project timelines or suggest efficient resource allocation, which supports collaboration by enabling teams to work more efficiently together.

Facilitating Cross-Company Collaboration and Partnerships

Finally, AI can enable companies to collaborate with external partners by providing secure and efficient data-sharing platforms. For instance, blockchain-based AI systems can ensure data integrity and transparency between companies while protecting sensitive information.

AI AND THE 5C's: CHANGE

Companies are increasingly implementing strategies to manage the changes AI brings to work processes, budgets, and workforce dynamics. Here's how they are addressing these shifts.

Improving and Expanding Workforce Skills

AI is changing job roles by automating repetitive tasks and creating new demands for specialized skills in data analysis, AI ethics, and digital literacy. To adapt, companies can invest in training programs to help employees develop new competencies. This includes workshops, online courses, and partnerships with educational institutions. Initiatives to expand and enhance workers' skills will ensure employees are equipped to work alongside AI systems and take on roles that require critical thinking and creativity.

Budget Reallocation to Support Digital Transformation

Adopting AI technologies often requires significant financial investment, from purchasing new tools to hiring AI specialists. To manage these costs, companies can allocate budgets to prioritize digital transformation, reduce spending in other areas, or improve efficiency in routine tasks to free up resources. By investing strategically in AI, companies can enhance productivity and achieve long-term cost savings, even if it means initial budget adjustments.

Process Automation and Workflow Redesign

AI-powered automation can streamline workflows by reducing manual work in areas like data entry, reporting, and customer support. To make the most of this, companies are redesigning workflows to incorporate AI where it can deliver the most value. This often means reevaluating and reengineering end-to-end processes, moving from traditional models to agile ones where AI supports faster and more adaptive operations. In many cases, companies create hybrid workflows that combine human oversight with automated steps.

Change Management and Cultural Transformation

AI adoption often impacts company culture, requiring a shift toward a data-driven mindset and a willingness to embrace new technology. To facilitate this cultural shift, companies should apply change-management strategies, which include clear communication about the purpose of AI, transparent discussions on potential impacts, and efforts to reassure employees about job security. Engaging employees early and regularly, offering support, and promoting a collaborative atmosphere can help ease the transition and reduce resistance to change.

Developing Ethical Guidelines and Governance for AI Use

With AI's growing influence, companies need to implement governance structures and ethical guidelines to manage its impact responsibly. This could involve creating policies around data privacy, fairness, and transparency to ensure AI is used responsibly and in alignment with company values. Companies can form internal AI ethics committees or create dedicated roles to oversee compliance and guide AI practices. By prioritizing ethical AI, they help build trust both within the organization and with external stakeholders.

AI AND THE 5C's: CHANCE

Ernst and Young outlines ways businesses can leverage AI to guide strategic innovation investments.[1]

Customer Sentiment Analysis

AI-powered sentiment analysis enables companies to sift through massive volumes of customer feedback and social media to identify emerging needs and dissatisfaction trends. For instance, companies like Spotify use AI to analyze user feedback, revealing insights that help prioritize new features or services that align closely with customer demand. This approach ensures that innovations align with market needs, reducing the risk of misaligned product investments.

Predictive Demand Modeling

AI models can forecast product demand by analyzing historical and real-time data, helping companies allocate resources toward innovations with higher future demand. For example, in retail and consumer goods, AI-powered demand modeling can anticipate shifts due to seasonality or regional preferences, allowing companies like Amazon to adjust product offerings in response to predicted trends and improving the accuracy of innovation-related investments.

Automated Competitive Analysis

AI can help businesses analyze competitors' product launches, patent filings, and market moves to spot trends and gaps in the market. This analysis informs where to invest in innovation by pinpointing high-potential areas less saturated by competitors. Start-ups specializing in AI, like Luminance, are also developing tools to automate legal document review and patent landscape mapping, reducing R&D investment risks by providing a clear view of innovation landscapes.

Smart Prototyping and Testing

AI is streamlining product prototyping by simulating various design and performance scenarios quickly and at lower costs. Manufacturing companies, for example, are using AI-driven simulation to test prototypes digitally, allowing quicker iterations and enhancing the quality of final products. This approach reduces the costs and time associated with traditional product testing, allowing companies to focus resources on the most viable innovations.

Innovation Portfolio Management

AI tools enable companies to analyze and manage their portfolio of innovations to focus on the most promising initiatives. By evaluating factors such as potential return on investment, project timelines, and resource allocation, companies can make more informed decisions on which projects to advance. Let's look at a few examples.

BlackRock. Through its AI-driven platform, called Aladdin, Black-Rock uses machine learning for comprehensive risk analysis and portfolio management. Aladdin processes vast datasets to provide portfolio managers with predictive insights on risks and returns, helping to refine investment strategies across markets. This platform also offers scenario analysis to anticipate potential outcomes, which aids in adjusting investment portfolios based on evolving market conditions.

Goldman Sachs. The firm uses its AI-based Marcus platform for retail investment decisions, integrating AI across more traditional portfolio management activities as well. By applying machine learning to analyze consumer data and market trends, Goldman Sachs offers personalized investment recommendations that consider each client's financial goals and risk tolerance. This approach allows for more customized, real-time investment advice and portfolio adjustments.

TradersAI. Developed as a specialized model for equity trading, this AI model focuses on market timing, choosing when to trade based on volatility. TradersAI avoids high-risk events and performs optimally in high-volatility markets, which allows it to deliver returns above market averages during bear markets. This kind of AI use helps investors make data-driven decisions on when to engage in or stay out of certain trades.

CHAMPIONS OF CHANGE

Lessons from Fearless Founders and Enterprising Executives

Shih-Yin Ho
Health IT CEO and Entrepreneur

Merriam-Webster defines humanism as devotion to the humanities and literary culture. It's also characterized as a devotion to human welfare and dignity and as a doctrine, attitude, or way of life centered on human interest or values.

The humanities.

Human interest.

Literary culture.

These are not words typically used in any discussion of AI.

So when Shih-Yin Ho describes herself, as she does on her LinkedIn profile, as an AI humanist, just what does she mean? Humans and AI? Aren't they diametrically opposed? Isn't AI our existential enemy? Isn't the big fear the possibility that AI could erase our humanity and take over the world?

Yes and no.

We should first point out that Yin is not an AI neophyte, nor does she lack in more traditional and impressive credentials.

Dr. Shih-Yin Ho, MD, MBA, has more than two decades of entrepreneurial and executive experience in digital health, data analytics, and clinical research, having supported numerous companies in developing information technology products for pharma services or shifting their model from services to software-as-a-service (SaaS). She has also held senior management roles in many start-ups and mature life sciences companies; most recently, she was the interim CEO of Veradigm (formerly Allscripts), one of the largest ambulatory electronic health record companies in the United States.

In short, Yin is a serial entrepreneur, healthcare executive, and industry expert—as well as an "AI humanist."

Meaning?

"I came up with that sort of title or moniker, largely because I felt that the AI discussions were not being framed appropriately," says Yin. "You hear a lot about how 'One day AI will be smarter than us, and then they'll take control of the world.' That's the wrong way to look at it."

A better way, she believes, is through a more, well, humanistic lens.

"The idea of the AI humanist is to try and be someone who stops and says, 'Wait, what are we doing here?'" Yin says. "Instead of seeing AI as a force we have to fully trust or fear, we need to remember that we're in charge, but only if we continue to push for its development of things that allow us to be more human."

An example is ambient scribes.

Ambient AI scribes are a new application that converts the patient-physician visit into a clinical note using generative AI. That recording can be of a conversation with a patient or just a summary of the visit. According to a 2023 *New England Journal of Medicine Catalyst* study, these scribes "use machine learning applied to conversations to facilitate scribe-like capabilities in real time."[2] The use of an AI scribe, the researchers concluded, "has great potential to reduce documentation burden, enhance physician–patient encounters, and augment clinicians' capabilities."

Yin describes the benefits for physicians in a more evocative way. By giving the physicians more time—time saved from transcribing and analyzing the notes—"they're able to focus on their patients, empathize with their patients. They can spend more time and work through things with patients."

And AI, Yin says, has the potential to take that further. Using the example of the AI scribe, she points out, "It's not just time saving. The notes themselves might be of a high quality, which means the physicians can do more with them. There are downstream effects that come from this, but the upstream effects—allowing these physicians to exercise their humanity—are very compelling, and that's how we should be looking at AI solutions."

What about that dark side, though? Yuval Noah Harari warns of a "Silicon Curtain" descending between us and the algorithms we have created, "shutting us out of our own conversations—how we want to act, or interact, or govern ourselves."

"I understand what he's saying," responds Yin. "Everyone worries about that. But I think this is all the more reason to push forward a more hopeful perspective. What if we are more deliberate? What if we recognize that AI agents don't have ethics or intention? Collectively, we humans are the ones who determine what the bounds are."

Although these are provocative ideas, we are certainly veering into the province of philosophy. Yin also offers some practical advice for organizational innovators looking to figure out how to use AI.

"It's not necessarily about you or your employees going out and getting certifications in various AI applications," she says. "It's about thinking about the problem you're trying to solve. It still goes back to fundamentals. Is this a problem that would be better addressed by humans or could we use some tools that might make your workers a little more efficient or better?"

As for using AI to develop a more innovative corporate culture, here, again, she invites us to look beyond the features of one technology or AI agent or another. "I think that part of how you create a more innovative culture is to make the organization a bit more of a safe space. I know that might sound silly, but sometimes we have too many risks in the mix that hinder our ability to really think in an innovative way."

Any of us who have worked for an organization know what those perceived risks are and how they can hold us back. And it's not just the fear of AI.

It's "Oh, we can't do that; we'll get sued."

It's "Oh, we can't do that; we'll get in trouble with a regulatory agency."

It's "Oh, we can't do that because we haven't done that before."

Sound familiar? "Put all that aside," says Yin. "Is there a way to solve the problem? Let's focus on that first, and then let's look at the risks."

Yin says she has seen organizational cultures where the risk is automatically assumed to be too high to move forward. "I've seen organizations where the thinking has been so legal, so risk-averse, so fearful, not just about AI, but about any new technology or idea. There is nothing illegal about thinking and discussing new ideas."

Indeed, one might say, such freedom to imagine is part of what makes us human.

To learn more about Yin, visit https://www.linkedin.com/in/yin-ho/.

9

INTEGRATING THE 5C's INTO YOUR ORGANIZATION

Throughout this book, we've shared the stories of dozens of innovators who have embodied the 5C's of Customer First, Culture, Collaboration, Change, and Chance. Whether they are start-ups, growth-stage companies, or corporate behemoths trying to transform themselves, we've learned how they have influenced and led their teams to be innovative and embrace the change adaptability needed to grow.

In this concluding chapter, we pinpoint some of the specific practices and behaviors a leader can follow to manage and maintain an innovation mindset and to encourage a climate of change among their teams. Are there things the most innovative leaders do well that we can model and learn from?

We went to Steve Hardek for some answers. Steve is one of the most creative and innovative leaders I know. He was a founding member of the executive team at a company called Zoomessence, formed fifteen years ago. Zoomessence has a proprietary technology that transforms the way flavors and fragrances are manufactured with a focus on cost and efficiency. Steve took the CEO helm early in 2024 and has been working to expand the company into new applications of their room-temperature drying technology, including coffee, probiotics, and pharmaceuticals. Clearly, his work is not the subject of most cocktail party conversations, but as technical as it may be for the lay person, Steve is passionate about his business. He's always exploring new ways to communicate and apply what he's learned. Importantly, he is avid about studying other innovators to learn how he can get better at his job of running the company, his team and communicating with clients and his investors.

I asked Steve who his favorite innovator of all time was, who had inspired him the most during the fifteen years in which he took Zoomessence to new levels of performance and growth. "It's not one innovator," he said, citing Bill Gates, Michael Jordan, the Wright brothers, and Elon Musk, to name a few. "Parts of each of their stories help me find new ways to craft the Zoomessence story better." He chuckles and says, "I mean, how do you get people to go work in the middle of nowhere to launch rockets on Omelek Island, 4,800 miles from California, like Musk with SpaceX? Because they believe in the vision."

Steve, who is a voracious reader, has studied the biographies of many great innovators throughout history and draws from a wide range of personalities. He notes that Milton Hershey went bankrupt a few times before he made it. Michael Jordan had the vision to become the brand. "I've read about remarkable innovators like Walt Disney and comedian Lucille Ball. What have I learned? They never do it alone. They share the vision and create passion and get a whole team behind them."

Hmm, I thought. Anyone who can connect the dots between Milton Hershey, Michael Jordan, Walt Disney, and Lucile Ball is certainly looking at innovation through a broad lens. And he's right! All of the great innovators had vision and passion, but they had something else that was equally important: the right team of people behind them to translate that vision into a reality.

No one has ever done that alone.

A lot of leaders have had to learn that lesson the hard way, including me. The first time I had to lead a team through a period of change and innovation—creating a new service offering in a multinational corporation—I blew it. When I joined the prestigious public relations firm Porter Novelli's Washington, DC office with a mission to create new solutions to enable pharmaceutical companies to recruit patients for clinical trials, I was gung ho. I had developed and tested my marketing-based approach for human clinical trial recruitment at the National Institutes of Health over a five-year period. I was ready to commercialize my model. My boss at Porter Novelli-DC, Rob Gould, was open-minded, committed to healthcare and the public good, and keen on expanding the business to pharmaceutical clients, which had been the bastion of the New York office for many years. (Did I mention Rob was highly competitive?) With his guidance, we created a division called Patients1st, secured some capital from our parent company Omnicom, and set off to develop a new offering for the burgeoning pharma research and development (R&D) departments at big corporations like Pfizer, GlaxoSmithKline, Merck, and Bristol Myers Squibb.

I had a model, a business plan, consultants, an advisory board, and marketing materials. Now all I needed was the right team to make my vision a reality.

Surely that wouldn't be too hard, right? Porter Novelli was filled with bright, creative minds. And I was confident we could recruit more—folks who would take my vision and march into action.

I knew my model would work because I had tested it at the National Institutes of Health (NIH). As the senior vice president of healthcare at Porter Novelli, I had a team of a dozen healthcare marketing specialists I had overseen for a couple years. We did standard types of projects for healthcare clients, launching and promoting new brands. These were the people I first spoke with when assembling my new team for Patients1st. I assumed all of them would join my new business unit with its mission of helping to advance clinical research and get therapies to patients fast.

I was wrong.

"I appreciate you thinking of me, Lorraine," said Brooke, an assistant account executive who had joined the company fresh out of college. "But I don't want to limit myself to patient recruitment at this stage in my career. I want to get broader exposure to clients and the work we do."

Okay, fine. Surely Elizabeth, an account executive I had recently promoted, would be willing to follow me into battle. Nope. "I'm grateful for what you've done for me, Lorraine," Elizabeth said. "I like healthcare, but I want to work on launching new products in pharmaceutical. I'm not really interested in R&D."

After speaking with a few more team members, I learned why no one seemed nearly as excited as I did about what I thought was a great new opportunity.

Well, no one except Diane, that is. Diane, smart and thoughtful, had been with Porter Novelli for five years. She loved the work but was itching to do something new and exciting. She was inspired by the vision and mission that I described to her, and she agreed to join the new unit to focus on getting it up and running. "Do you have a job spec for the role?" Diane asked me when we sat down to plan the new team. "Can you tell me what I'll be doing?"

"That's something we will figure out together," I responded cheerfully. "The cool part of this new business unit is that we get to create everything from scratch: the roles, responsibilities, job specs, client relationships, and all the new solutions we'll be offering our clients." I paused, waiting for her to jump for joy over this.

"Isn't it exciting?" I asked with a glimmer in my eye.

"Well," Diane said hesitantly. "It is exciting. But, Lorraine, to be honest, I've never done this before, and I don't know how to get started. Where do I go to learn how to do the new job? I love the vision and the mission, but I don't know how to create a new business like this."

The truth was that I didn't either.

I didn't have a clear picture of the future state we were driving toward. Sure, I had a business plan, and I knew the roles and responsibilities of the team, how many offerings we needed to sell, and what those offerings entailed, but I didn't know how to implement this change or how to execute the new company's plan. I was still operating from a project mindset, organizing the team around completing a project for the client, not creating a new operating model. As I learned, it was hard work to develop the operating model, business model, job specs, processes, client delivery specifications, and processes—the guts of the new company.

At first, I felt frustrated with Diane's questions. "Pushback," she called it—a term for a healthy debate with your manager when you don't think what they are asking you to do is realistic. And she was right. But I didn't understand why Diane—my star player—couldn't just take a leap of faith and help figure all this out. I spoke to Juanita in human resources for advice.

"Diane is on board, and I'm happy about that," I said when we sat down in her office. "But she needs a lot of hand-holding. She seems to want a recipe card for how to do her job. But that's not how it works in a new business. We have to figure all this out together. That's what I need help with. I'm stuck and not sure how to move forward from here."

With Juanita's help and a consultant I trusted, we started to build the new business. We crafted roles, responsibilities, job specs, processes, standard operating procedures, and ways of working with the clients. It took a lot of time, a lot of thought, and a lot of work that only I could do because the vision and mission had emanated from me. We eventually got the business off the ground and recruited a team of people who were really passionate about our mission and who were "doers," who helped me make the unit a success. But it took twice as long and cost twice as much as I had originally anticipated. Why?

It turns out change can be painful, and it's the leader's job to make it less so. How do you do that? Well, first, recognize that organizational change invokes six questions in people's minds:

- What does this change mean to me?
- Why is it happening?
- What will it look like when it's done?

- What is my role?
- How will my job and compensation change?
- Will I be better off?

Why is change so hard even for people like Diane who want to get on board?

A 2022 *Harvard Business Review* article by Erika Andersen explains that change is hard because of our history as a species. "Until the past few generations, most people's lives stayed very much the same from beginning to end," she wrote. "People grew up where their parents had grown up, did the work their parents had done, believed and knew things the previous generations had known. Change was generally an aberration and a danger."[1]

So juxtapose our learned behaviors with the environment we live and work in today. As is often noted, the only thing that's constant these days is change. Look at the dynamic environment we live in socially, politically, and organizationally. The pace of change is faster and more intense than ever—maybe faster and more intense than humans can adapt to. It requires rewiring ourselves to be more comfortable and open to change. But being "change-capable" as Erika points out, and being resilient, adaptable, and not afraid of failure, as this book has posited, are harder than we think it will be.

This book is about having no fear and accepting no failure. So how do you create an environment that embraces change and rebukes fear?

A good leader has to have the vision—as I did at Porter Novelli; create the mission—as I also did at Porter Novelli; and win the hearts and minds of the people—as I failed to do at Porter Novelli, at least at first. So how does the leader create a picture of the future and a road map in a way that allows people to clearly see where they fit and why—to allay their fears of failure?

It starts with a shift in attitude that Erika Andersen describes in her book *Change from the Inside Out: Making You, Your Team, and Your Organization Change-Capable*. The shift takes place as we alter how we see change. There are a variety of ways a leader can help the team view change so it's not so scary. Among them are shifts in attitude:

- From difficult to easy: "This change is doable; I think it can work."
- From costly to rewarding: "I can see how I can benefit from making this change."
- From weird to normal: "It feels uncomfortable, at first, to be making this change that is taking me out of my comfort zone, but, okay, this is now starting to feel like a normal, regular way of working."

No matter whether you are recruiting people to a start-up or trying to reorganize your way to a business transformation, how can leaders support the transition to easy, rewarding, and normal?

Here are seven approaches that have worked for me.

INCREASE UNDERSTANDING

Show employees what the future state looks like and how they fit in.

In my own example of launching a new business unit at Porter Novelli, I thought everyone would line up behind me because I had an inspiring vision and a compelling mission. I mean, who wouldn't want to improve medical research and get therapies to patients faster? But my cheerful superficial "let's change the world" pitch didn't cut it for most of the people I was trying to attract. The senior executives "got it," so to speak, but my team needed fundamental information on what we were doing, why we were doing it, what it meant for them, how their jobs would change, what they would be doing, and why it was better. Once I was able to concretely answer those questions, they felt better armed with the information they needed. Some of them still declined my offer, but others came forward and joined the new business. Regardless of whether they stayed put or went with me, they all felt like they were making an informed decision—not just taking a speculative leap of faith.

I also changed my message strategy. Instead of talking about how exciting this all would be—when, as I later learned, the idea of jumping into a new and untried business might have sounded less exciting and more terrifying to them—I tried communicating with more details and greater clarity. I also made sure they knew that upper management was on board with this and that they were not putting their jobs at risk.

CLARIFY AND REINFORCE PRIORITIES

As important as it is to communicate what is changing, it's also important to say what *isn't* changing. In my case, I emphasized that the role and type of work the team would be doing would be unchanged. The roles and responsibilities of the account managers and delivery coordinators would be the same.

Steve Hardek at Zoomessence points out that this kind of clear messaging applies not just to employees but to the board—whose support in any growing company is critical. "For investors to stay confident and take the journey with you to grow the company," Steve says, "they have to believe you have an innovation mindset and that you're doing something they can understand. Even if the details behind it are complicated, you must reduce it to something they understand, and you have to be very clear on your focus and your priorities."

This communication to the board isn't a one-time event, either. "You must always be selling to those investors and communicating with them both the successes and the failures so they stay on the journey with you," Steve says. "I simplify our technology by making parallels to where it fits in the industry, who the competitors are, what performance bars we're setting."

GIVE EMPLOYEES SOME CONTROL

Especially when people work in a large organization and undergo large-scale change, employees can feel powerless, as if they have no say in the change. Give people as many choices as you can. By doing so, you can reduce fear and discomfort and increase the chances of engagement and buy-in.

A few years back, I was working on a consulting project with the pharmaceutical company Takeda. Our job was to help the leader of their oncology division reorganize her team around a new way of working globally. We brought the team together in a workshop and gave them ownership to run the workstreams responsible for determining how the new department was going to operate with other internal departments.

A lot of money was spent flying people in to the headquarters from around the world. But the oncology team leader knew it was critical for them to have control over creating their future state. She gave them the latitude to create new processes, workflows, and metrics to enable their new model to work. People left the meeting feeling energized and excited about the change and their role in it, and the end results were positive and lasting.

PROVIDE SUPPORT TO EMPLOYEES
WHEN THEY NEED IT

Too often, leaders ignore employees' concerns, figuring they will eventually figure it out and "get with the program." I was that kind of leader early in my career. I realized later that this was a traditional hierarchical and bureaucratic approach used by large organizations in the 1950s and 1960s. "Theory X" management, it was called, and thankfully, it's changed. Today companies practice collaborative leadership, standing behind their employees and helping them succeed.

That's a welcome change. But still, far too often, leaders fail to recognize that we have had a lot more time to process and engage in the change than our teams have. We've been thinking and discussing and developing these changes for months, even sometimes years. Potential team members can't be expected to make a decision the moment they are presented with our new initiatives. They need time to process the change. They likely have questions. Here's where we leaders need to tamp down our excitement and try listening—*active* listening, as we call it in the business communications course I teach at Wharton. This means giving them room to express their concerns, fears, and doubts. Don't label it as resistance. Instead, recognize that it's normal and healthy to question, even to be skeptical. Do we really want them to "get on board" with something they don't understand? That doesn't make good business sense, does it? If you give people support without being dismissive and condescending but instead by being open and reassuring, you will have a greater likelihood of influencing them. I tell my students that when it comes to leading change in an organization, you have early adopters who you can use to influence the fence-sitters; you need to move those who are neutral to positive; and although you'll move some of the resistors over time, you may not change everyone's way of thinking. That's okay. You'd rather have those who understand where they're being led and are ready to take the plunge with you.

COMMUNICATE (MORE THAN YOU NORMALLY WOULD, EVEN IF YOU DON'T HAVE ALL THE ANSWERS)

A common mistake when creating an innovation culture and managing through change is to think that we shouldn't communicate with employees unless we have something big—a major, stop-the-presses announcement.

In fact, the better course of action is to maintain a regular communication cadence, whether it's weekly, Friday, ten-minute wrap-up meetings, monthly team meetings, or whatever communication cadence the team is used to. Be transparent about where the change stands, whether it's delayed or on hold, or whatever it might be. People are more likely to trust you and work with you if they know you are including them in the communications through the good, the bad, and the ugly. Remember that for people working in large organizations, change is a constant, but many changes, especially dramatic ones, can tend to fizzle out when management changes its mind, gets new information, or encounters resistance.

I once made the mistake of not communicating during a time of change at IBM because a new product we were releasing was undergoing financial scrutiny by the CFO. When several weeks went by and the team didn't receive updates, they assumed the project was dead, and teams even redeployed resources we had lined up to support the new product release. It caused confusion and frustration. I learned then that some news, even if it's "stay the course" while we work things out, is better than no communication at all.

CELEBRATE WINS

Humans need reassurance, recognition, rewards, and celebration to stay motivated. It's hard work staying engaged in your company, your team, and your job on a good day with competing demands on your time and interests. Especially during times of change, when you can be feeling doubt, the need to spend time rewarding and recognizing the team is more critical than ever.

Over the course of my career, I have had the opportunity to work with managers who were good at motivating the team by celebrating success with a team lunch or dinner, outing, or bonus. I have also worked with others who were terrible at it. At a technology company I worked for, our only celebration was the annual sales meeting. During the rest of the year, it was an ongoing barrage of belittlement. Our manager called team meetings on Sunday mornings to shame the team into doing better. There were no clear goals, and the bar kept changing. All she did was drag down morale and drive people from the team.

On the other hand, I have had managers who rewarded the team even when we didn't hit the target but tried very hard. "You all worked hard and it shows," he'd say. That manager won hearts and minds, and eventually, we did achieve our targets; it just took a little longer than management would have liked because the forecasts were unrealistic.

ENCOURAGE CONTINUOUS LEARNING
BY REVIEWING AND ADJUSTING THE PLAN

Finally, innovation is all about the pivot—adjusting the plan, but not the vision, when the current strategy isn't working. It's important to recognize these shifts, call them out, and create a culture of continuous learnings. At one company, I held Fail-free Fridays so the team could talk about what hadn't worked well that week. This is the spirit of creating a learning culture where we "try, fail, and learn" in the spirit of continuous improvement.

KEEP THE FOLLOWING IN MIND
AS YOU ESTABLISH AN INNOVATION MINDSET
AND EMBED THE 5C'S IN PRACTICE

- Normalize failure and reframe it as learning. Leaders should openly discuss their own mistakes and celebrate teams that take calculated risks, even when outcomes aren't successful.
- Implement "innovation time," in which employees spend 15–20 percent of their time exploring new ideas outside their core responsibilities. Provide resources and mentorship to develop promising concepts.
- Design physical and virtual spaces that enable random collisions between people from different teams and backgrounds. These serendipitous interactions often spark novel solutions.
- Establish innovation metrics beyond traditional key performance indicators. Measure factors like number of experiments run, speed of iteration, and cross-functional collaboration. What gets measured gets managed.

- Create dedicated innovation funding pools with streamlined approval processes. Give teams autonomy to quickly test hypotheses without excessive bureaucracy.
- Rotate talent across departments and geographies to encourage fresh perspectives and prevent organizational silos. This cross-pollination of ideas drives creative problem-solving.
- Model curiosity by regularly engaging with external thought leaders, start-ups, and academia.
- Share insights broadly to inspire new thinking throughout the organization.

Fear of failure. Fear of change. Fear of trying.

In this book, we've offered insights, principles, case studies, and personal perspectives on how to banish these fears to achieve success. "As the pace of change increases," wrote the great management theorist and author John Kotter, "there is naturally a greater need for effective leadership."[2]

I want you to be that leader, that manager. I want you to be the one to spark or sustain a culture of innovation, that welcoming attitude toward change and new ideas in your organization. Embrace it, encourage it. And maybe you'll end up changing the world.

THE CREATION OF THE INNOVATORS' CIRCLE

The process of building the Innovators' Circle began with an idea to connect exceptional individuals who were shaping the future of their industries through creativity, vision, and of course, innovation. The circle was not designed to be a static group of people but rather a dynamic collection of forward-thinkers from a diverse range of fields, including healthcare, technology, life sciences, artificial intelligence (AI), and more. The goal was to curate a group of innovators who were not only achieving success but also redefining what innovation could look like in their respective domains.

THE INTERVIEW PROCESS

Finding the right people for the Innovators' Circle was an intentional and multistep process. First, I sought out leaders who were actively driving change within their organizations and industries. The interviews were informal conversations, allowing me to gauge each individual's approach to innovation, their ideas on leadership, and their ability to think outside the box. I prioritized those who could share a compelling and specific story, whether it was about disrupting their sector, creating new paradigms, or revolutionizing long-standing practices. After interviewing each person, I had a sense of their alignment with the goals of the Innovators' Circle and where they could fit in within the 5C's as well as the stories I share in the book. I then delved deeper into understanding how their work intersected with broader themes of innovation. This wasn't about choosing people based on current success alone but on the ideas they represented and their potential for future impact. Many of these individuals were not followers of industry trends but were actively creating those trends, blending expertise with forward-thinking visions.

HOW I DISCOVERED THE INNOVATORS

The people selected for the Innovators' Circle were found through a combination of my network, prior industry events I've participated in, recommendations from peers, and personal research. I reached out to a wide array of industry leaders, asking for suggestions and insights on individuals who were doing the hard work of innovating, both in established organizations and emerging start-ups. I personally curated this group of innovators and believe that each epitomizes the innovation mindset and has made a unique contribution to advancing innovation in their field or industry.

A CROSS-SECTION OF INDUSTRIES

What stands out about the Innovators' Circle is the broad and diverse representation of industries. It spans healthcare, technology, AI, pharma, cybersecurity, life sciences, and even global consumer products. The group includes executives from global companies like Angela Mangiapane of Mars Global Services, who leads innovation in digital services across a $50 billion company, as well as founders like Tracy Harmon Blumenfeld, who transformed clinical trials to be more patient centered. It also includes tech leaders like Shih-Yin Ho, who brings together AI and humanism, and entrepreneurs like Mark Adams, whose firm Two Bear Capital invests in cutting-edge AI, life sciences, and cybersecurity companies.

The diversity of industries was a conscious choice because I wanted the circle to represent an exchange of ideas. Innovators are not limited by the sector they come from; instead, they leverage their unique insights and solutions to influence the broader business sector. By connecting healthcare executives with tech entrepreneurs, researchers with investors, and corporate leaders with thought leaders, the circle creates ground for new ideas to flourish.

Commonalities Among the Innovators

Despite their varied backgrounds and areas of expertise, the members of the Innovators' Circle share several key attributes.

Visionary Mindsets: Each member is deeply engaged in long-term thinking, driven by a desire to solve complex problems and create lasting impact. They are not simply content with incremental change; they are pushing the boundaries of what's possible in their respective fields. Whether it's disrupting traditional business models or advancing technology to improve lives, they are reshaping the future.

Commitment to Human-Centered Innovation: A common thread in the group is a focus on human-centered innovation, where each member prioritizes solving real-world problems with solutions that directly benefit people. This approach ensures that innovation is not just about technology or efficiency but also about enhancing human experiences, improving well-being, and fostering sustainable growth in communities.

Risk-Taking and Resilience: Innovators often face skepticism and resistance. What unites the members of the Innovators' Circle is their resilience in the face of challenges and their ability to turn failure into opportunity. For example, Angela Mangiapane's journey at Mars involved navigating change in a massive global corporation, and Mark Adams thrives by embracing uncertainty and seeking undervalued opportunities in emerging sectors.

Cross-Disciplinary Thinking: Many members of the circle excel at thinking across disciplines. Whether it's blending healthcare with AI, technology with business, or human resources with innovation, they approach problems from multiple angles. This cross-disciplinary thinking is what allows them to create solutions that are not only effective but also transformative. The Innovators' Circle is more than a group of individual success stories; it's an evolving ecosystem where each member brings their unique perspective and expertise to the table. As the world rapidly changes, the members of the circle are committed to adapting, collaborating, and driving the kind of systemic transformation that will define the future of business, healthcare, technology, and beyond.

The circle represents an interconnected web of leaders who don't just talk about change but are actively creating it. You can learn more about our members through the monthly LinkedIn lives that I began hosting in September 2024, with Angela Mangiapane being our first guest speaker. We plan to continue to work with curated network of innovators through other forms of conversation such as guest lectures, panel discussions, annual innovation conferences, and more.

CHAMPIONS OF CHANGE

First Champion Erez Naaman (Chapter 1)
Cofounder and Chief Technology Officer, Scopio Labs

Erez Naaman's passion for innovation started in his youth when he would write down a new invention idea daily. After serving as a major in the Israeli Air Force and working in business development at OrCam, Naaman cofounded Scopio Labs in 2014. The company focuses on revolutionizing microscopy by providing digital solutions for rapid diagnostics.

What Makes Them Innovative

Naaman emphasizes the importance of hiring creative people and allowing them to explore ideas without micromanagement. He creates frameworks for innovation and encourages brainstorming without rejecting even the most far-fetched ideas, believing that a "yes, and" mindset is crucial for fostering creativity.

LinkedIn: https://www.linkedin.com/in/erez-naaman-8654972/

Second Champion Catherine Reynolds (Chapter 2)
Chairman and Chief Executive, Catherine B. Reynolds Foundation

Catherine Reynolds is a renowned entrepreneur and philanthropist who revolutionized higher education financing. Three decades ago, she identified a gap in the education financing system, particularly for middle-class families, and set out to create a solution. Through EduCap, she developed an innovative financial infrastructure that created today's $200 billion U.S. private student loan industry.

What Makes Them Innovative

Catherine's work disrupted the higher education finance space, making it more accessible and affordable for students. By partnering with entities like the U.S. Chamber of Commerce, she created a sustainable business model that provided student loans as an employee benefit, expanding educational opportunities for many families across the United States.

Website: https://cbrf.org/about/

Third Champion Dave Evans (Chapter 3)
Chief Executive Officer and Cofounder, Fictiv

Dave Evans is the CEO and cofounder of Fictiv, a company revolutionizing on-demand custom manufacturing. Before founding Fictiv, he worked at Ford's Silicon Valley Innovation Lab, focusing on advanced manufacturing research. With a mechanical engineering background from Stanford, Dave created Fictiv to streamline the sourcing of custom parts, enabling rapid, high-quality prototypes in days, not weeks.

What Makes Them Innovative

Dave Evans is the founder and CEO of Fictiv, a company revolutionizing custom manufacturing through a culture-driven approach. He built Fictiv with a focus on creating a value-based culture that fosters innovation, agility, and collaboration. By leveraging technology to connect manufacturers with customers, Dave has transformed how parts are produced, emphasizing speed and creative problem-solving as key drivers of success.

LinkedIn: https://www.linkedin.com/in/evansda11/

Fourth Champion Al Wilson (Chapter 4)
Founder and CEO, Beyond Walls

Al Wilson is the founder and executive director of Beyond Walls, a nonprofit transforming Lynn, Massachusetts, with vibrant public art. Since launching in 2016, the organization has revitalized the city by commissioning large-scale murals on downtown buildings, turning Lynn into an artistic destination. Under Wilson's leadership, Beyond Walls has spurred cultural and economic revitalization, gaining national attention and fostering collaborations with local businesses and artists.

What Makes Them Innovative

Wilson's innovation lies in combining public art with urban renewal to strengthen community identity and engagement. Through strategic collaboration with residents, business leaders, government officials, and artists, he has transformed Beyond Walls into a model for community-driven change. His approach uses art to address social, cultural, and economic challenges, revitalizing Lynn and inspiring similar initiatives across the region.

LinkedIn: https://www.linkedin.com/in/alfredwilson1/

Fifth Champion Aniruddha Sharma (Chapter 5)
Chief Executive Officer and Chair, Carbon Clean

Aniruddha Sharma is the CEO and chair of Carbon Clean, a United Kingdom–based leader in carbon capture technology. Since cofounding the company in 2009, Aniruddha has played a pivotal role in revolutionizing industrial decarbonization, focusing on sectors such as steel, cement, refineries, and waste-to-energy. Under his leadership, Carbon Clean has developed cutting-edge technology that significantly reduces the cost and space required for carbon capture, making it viable for hard-to-abate industries. Carbon Clean has garnered multiple accolades, including the 2022 BNEF Pioneer Award, and has established itself as a key player in global sustainability efforts.

What Makes Them Innovative

Aniruddha's innovation is in redesigning carbon capture technology to be ten times smaller and more cost effective than traditional solutions, accelerating decarbonization across key industries. His leadership at Carbon Clean fosters a culture of creative risk-taking, pushing his team to embrace bold, unconventional ideas. By championing experimentation and bottom-up innovation, Aniruddha drives the company's growth and success in a rapidly evolving industry.

LinkedIn: https://www.linkedin.com/in/aniruddhasharma/?originalSubdomain=uk

Sixth Champion Tracy Harmon Blumenfeld (Chapter 6)
Cofounder, President, and Chief Executive Officer, RapidTrials

Tracy Harmon Blumenfeld is the cofounder and CEO of RapidTrials, a leader in optimizing clinical trials for improved efficiency and accessibility. Founded in 1996, the company focuses on overcoming barriers to patient participation in traditional research. Under Tracy's leadership, RapidTrials earned a spot on the Philadelphia

100 list and made a strategic move in 2017 by selling a portion of its assets to Medidata Solutions. Tracy's passion for improving clinical trial access has made her a recognized thought leader, collaborating with top health organizations like the National Institutes of Health and the National Academies of Medicine.

What Makes Them Innovative

Tracy's innovation lies in making clinical trials more patient centered and accessible by optimizing their operations and decentralizing the process. Her work has improved the efficiency of drug development while addressing the human side of research, making trials more adaptable to patients' needs. Through her leadership, Tracy has driven significant changes in how clinical trials are conducted, enhancing both ethical standards and operational effectiveness.

LinkedIn: https://www.linkedin.com/in/tracyharmonblumenfeld/

Seventh Champion Angela Mangiapane (Chapter 7)
President, Mars Global Services

With over thirty years of leadership at Mars, Angela Mangiapane has played a key role in transforming the company from a traditional candy maker to a global powerhouse with $50 billion in annual revenue. As president of Mars Global Services, she oversees over three thousand associates who drive innovation across digital technologies, procurement, human resources, and finance, helping Mars operate more efficiently. Angela's focus on data analytics, automation, and AI has helped streamline processes and position the company for long-term success in a rapidly changing market.

What Makes Them Innovative

Angela Mangiapane's innovation at Mars lies in her ability to foster a culture of intrapreneurship, transforming Mars Global

Services into a dynamic business unit through AI, automation, and process intelligence. She encourages employees to think like entrepreneurs, driving change and aligning innovation with Mars's values of responsibility and sustainability. By creating an open environment where ideas flow freely, Angela has led the company to impactful, practical solutions through curiosity, collaboration, and embracing new technologies.

LinkedIn: https://www.linkedin.com/in/angela-mangiapane/

Eighth Champion Dr. Shih-Yin Ho (Chapter 8)
CEO, Health IT Entrepreneur and AI Humanist

Dr. Shih-Yin Ho is a serial entrepreneur, healthcare executive, and AI expert with over two decades of experience in digital health, data analytics, and clinical research. She has led multiple companies through transitions to software as a service (SaaS) models and held senior roles in startups and established healthcare organizations. She served as interim CEO of Veradigm for over one year. A strong advocate for ethical AI, Dr. Ho coined the term "AI humanist" to emphasize the importance of integrating AI into healthcare in ways that enhance human care and preserve dignity.

What Makes Them Innovative

Shih-Yin Ho's innovation lies in using AI to enhance human potential, rather than replace it, as seen in her work with Ambient AI Scribes, which automates documentation to allow physicians more time with patients. By reframing the AI narrative through her concept of AI humanism, she advocates for solutions that prioritize human welfare and improve work life. Yin encourages organizations to foster innovation through safe spaces for new ideas, ensuring that AI is developed ethically and with compassion, particularly in healthcare.

Quoted Contributors

Nitesh Bansal—chapter 1

- CEO, R-Systems
- LinkedIn: https://www.linkedin.com/in/niteshbansal1/

Laurence Blumberg, MD, MBA—chapter 1

- Biotechnology executive and cofounder of Syntimmune
- LinkedIn: https://www.linkedin.com/in/laurence-blumberg-md-33b870a/

Deirdre Letson-Christofalo, EdD—chapter 2

- Associate Provost and Dean, Moravian University School of Professional Studies and Innovation
- LinkedIn: https://www.linkedin.com/in/deirdre-letson-christofalo-ed-d-70374712/

Matt Wilkerson—chapter 2

- Founder and CEO of Extern
- https://www.linkedin.com/in/mattwilkerson/

Geoffrey M. Roche—chapter 2

- Director of Workforce Development, Siemens Healthineers
- LinkedIn: https://www.linkedin.com/in/geoffreymroche/

Christopher Harrison—chapter 2

- Board Director, External Advisor—Bain & Company, Consultant
- LinkedIn: https://www.linkedin.com/in/christopher-a-harrison-b4002613/

Jack Weiss—chapter 3

- Former CEO, WAM Systems; Lecturer Wharton MBA Program
- LinkedIn: https://www.linkedin.com/in/jack-weiss-a228242/

Armin Spura, PhD—chapter 3

- Chief Executive Officer at Bioduro-Sundia; Board Member; Angel Investor
- LinkedIn: https://www.linkedin.com/in/armin-spura-215348/

Iris Wilson-Farely—chapter 3

- Vice President, HR Innovation at Komatsu
- LinkedIn: https://www.linkedin.com/in/irisfarley/

Clay Shedd—chapter 3

- Executive Coach, Double Bridges Leadership LLC
- LinkedIn: https://www.linkedin.com/in/clayton-shedd/

Terri Hall Zecchin—chapter 4

- Executive Partner at Gartner Research, Board Member
- LinkedIn: https://www.linkedin.com/in/terrihall/

Brian Elliott—chapter 4

- CEO at Work Forward; Advisor, Speaker, and Bestselling Author; Startup CEO
- LinkedIn: https://www.linkedin.com/in/belliott/

Mark Powell—chapter 5

- Former Oxford Fellow, Author, and Former Partner, Ernst & Young
- LinkedIn: https://www.linkedin.com/in/marc-powell-aba39797/

Francisco Leon, MD, PhD—chapter 5

- Immunologist, Entrepreneur, Chief Executive Officer, Tolerance Bio
- LinkedIn: https://www.linkedin.com/in/francisco-leon-5951685/

Emily O'Halloran—chapter 5

- Former Accenture Managing Director
- LinkedIn: https://www.linkedin.com/in/emily-m-ohalloran/

Henri Richard—chapter 5

- President and General Manager, Rapidus Design Solutions
- LinkedIn: https://www.linkedin.com/in/henrir/

Hamzah Almidani—chapter 5

- Student, King Fahd University of Petroleum and Minerals, KSA and the Wharton School, University of Pennsylvania
- https://www.linkedin.com/in/hamzah-hazem-a-91a410140/

Tony DaRe—chapter 5

- Agency Principal, Founder, and Chief Executive Officer, BSI Corporate Benefits LLC
- LinkedIn: https://www.linkedin.com/in/tony-dare-17785a3/

Mark Adams—chapter 6

- Venture Capital Partner—Artificial Intelligence, Life Sciences, and Cybersecurity
- LinkedIn: https://www.linkedin.com/in/rmarkadams/

Nick Ascoli—chapter 7

- Director of Product Strategy, Flare; Former Founder and CEO, Fortrace
- LinkedIn: https://www.linkedin.com/in/nick-ascoli-28a78b93/

Bob Cappadona—chapter 7

- President and Chief Executive Officer, Environmental Solutions and Services, a division at Veolia
- LinkedIn: https://www.linkedin.com/in/bob-cappadona-3978b3b7/

Colin Foster—chapter 7

- Executive in Residence and Chief Executive Officer, Cytosolix
- LinkedIn: https://www.linkedin.com/in/colinjohnfoster/

Maria Boulden—chapter 7

- Former Vice President, Executive Partner, Head of Sales, Gartner
- LinkedIn: https://www.linkedin.com/in/maria-boulden-8a778b11/

Eric Shultz—chapter 8

- Cofounder of Ocean Genomics, Inc., Sageforce, Former CEO, COTA
- LinkedIn: https://www.linkedin.com/in/eric-schultz-01/

Dinko Franceschi—chapter 8

- Doctoral Researcher in the Debora Marks Lab at Harvard University
- Website: https://sites.harvard.edu/dinko-franceschi/

Nita Sanger—chapter 8

- CEO, Idea Innovate Consulting
- LinkedIn: https://www.linkedin.com/in/nita-sanger/

Steven C. Hardek—chapter 9

- CEO, ZoomEssence, Inc.
- LinkedIn: https://www.linkedin.com/in/stevehardek/

Contributed Their Insights
William Ashton

- Senior Executive in Healthcare Technology and Innovation and Strategic Consultant
- LinkedIn: https://www.linkedin.com/in/william-ashton/

Joyce Avedisian, PhD

- President, Avedisian Management Consultants
- LinkedIn: https://www.linkedin.com/in/joyceavedisian/

Scott Ballenger

- Head of Business Development, Crescendo Health
- LinkedIn: https://www.linkedin.com/in/scott-ballenger-59030b1/

Jabril Bensedrine, PhD

- Managing Director and Founder, The Triana Group
- LinkedIn: https://www.linkedin.com/in/jabrilbensedrine/

Steve Brazell

- Global Brand Strategist and Reputation Risk Expert, Founder of Hitman, Inc.
- LinkedIn: https://www.linkedin.com/in/steve-brazell/

Lisa Buettner

- Founder, President, and Senior Consultant, Anchor Consulting, LLC
- LinkedIn: https://www.linkedin.com/in/lisa-buettner/

Charles Cathlin

- CEO, Polaris Genomics
- LinkedIn: https://www.linkedin.com/in/charlescathlin/

Bill Darcy

- Global President and Chief Executive Officer, NKBA
- LinkedIn: https://www.linkedin.com/in/billdarcyjr/

Mack Dube
- Managing Partner, Drakensberg
- LinkedIn: https://www.linkedin.com/in/mahluli-dube/

Stephen Goodman
- Founder and Managing Director, Madrone O/A
- LinkedIn: https://www.linkedin.com/in/goodmanse/

Nisheet Gupta
- CFO/Board Member, driving innovation through M&A
- LinkedIn: https://www.linkedin.com/in/nisheetcfo/

Liz Hamburg
- Founder and President, Candoo Tech
- LinkedIn: https://www.linkedin.com/in/liz-hamburg/

Yee Ling Hayden
- Founder and Owner, Hayden Properties
- Website: Hayden-properties.com

Vicki Hildebrand
- Chief Information Office and SVP, Blue Cross Blue Shield, Massachusetts
- LinkedIn: https://www.linkedin.com/in/vicki-hildebrand/

Gabe Holdsman
- EVP, Global General Counsel, PTC Therapeutics
- LinkedIn: https://www.linkedin.com/in/holdsman/

Dr. Raymond A. Huml, MS, DVM, RAC
- Vice President of Rare and Orphan Strategy, Sciensus
- LinkedIn: https://www.linkedin.com/in/raymond-a-huml-4729b923/

Meredith Huml
- North Carolina Director, FSHD Society
- LinkedIn: https://www.linkedin.com/in/meredith-huml-79231272/

Deborah Juantorena

- Former Vice President, Enterprise Data Solutions and Engineering, Pfizer Inc.
- LinkedIn: https://www.linkedin.com/in/debbie-juantorena-4328219/

Karen D. Kaufman, MSOD

- Author and Founder, KPartners
- LinkedIn: https://www.linkedin.com/in/karendkaufman/

Rana Khan, PhD

- Inaugural Director, Bioscience Research and Training Center, Hood College
- LinkedIn: https://www.linkedin.com/in/rana-khan-1611981/

Ondrej Krehel, PhD

- Cyber Warrior and Innovator
- LinkedIn: https://www.linkedin.com/in/ondrejkrehel/

Fred Ledley, MD

- Director at Center for Integration of Science and Industry, Bentley University
- LinkedIn: https://www.linkedin.com/in/fred-ledley-6264876/

Bruce Leicher

- Legal and Strategic Advisor to Chief Legal Officers and C-Suite Executives; Biotechnology Law Professor
- LinkedIn: https://www.linkedin.com/in/bruce-leicher-8904766/

Ryan Manney

- Real Estate Agent, COMPASS
- LinkedIn: https://www.linkedin.com/in/ryanmanney/

Eric Mattson

- Partner, Excellere
- LinkedIn: https://www.linkedin.com/in/eric-mattson-882a723/

Joanne Moretti

- Chief Revenue Officer, Fictiv
- LinkedIn: https://www.linkedin.com/in/joannemoretti/

Kurt Mueller

- Managing Director, Digital and AI, Boundless Life Sciences Group
- LinkedIn: https://www.linkedin.com/in/kwmueller/

Simon Nynes, DBA

- CEO, Nynens LLC
- LinkedIn: https://www.linkedin.com/in/simonnynens/

Anouk Pappers

- Founder, Signitt
- LinkedIn: https://www.linkedin.com/in/anoukpappers/

Deepak Patil, MD, MBA

- Founder, Roxi-AI
- LinkedIn: https://www.linkedin.com/in/deepakdpatil/

Aris Persidis, PhD

- President, Biovista
- LinkedIn: https://www.linkedin.com/in/aris-persidis-7761492/

Eric Piscini

- CEO, Hashgraph
- LinkedIn: https://www.linkedin.com/in/ericpiscini/

Alicja Plonska

- Senior Vice President, Morgan Stanley
- LinkedIn: https://www.linkedin.com/in/alicja-a-plonska-cepa-cdfa%E2%84%A2-9171138/

E. William Podojil

- Vice President and Executive Partner, Gartner
- LinkedIn: https://www.linkedin.com/in/e-william-podojil-7857332/

Amit Rakhit, MD, MBA

- Chief Medical Officer, BlueRock Therapeutics
- LinkedIn: https://www.linkedin.com/in/amit-rakhit/

Avi Rosenbaum, PhD

- Biotech Consultant
- LinkedIn: https://www.linkedin.com/in/abraham-rosenbaum/

Maarten Schaefer

- Founder, CoolBrands People and CoolTravel
- LinkedIn: https://www.linkedin.com/in/maartenschafer/

Natasha Shtrazient, PhD

- CEO and Founder, Frezent Biological Solutions
- LinkedIn: https://www.linkedin.com/in/natasha-shtraizent-phd-9a1b9122/

Sylvana Sinha

- Founder and CEO of Praava Health
- LinkedIn: https://www.linkedin.com/in/sqsinha/

Ezra Softer

- Cofounder, CEO—MBA/CPA
- LinkedIn: https://www.linkedin.com/in/ezrasofer/

Natasha Srulowitz

- Director, Innovation Lab, Yeshiva University and Cofounder, WayFind
- LinkedIn: https://www.linkedin.com/in/natashasrulowitz/

Francesca Tuazon, PhD

- Founder and CEO, Science&
- LinkedIn: https://www.linkedin.com/in/francesca-tuazon-phd/

Bill Voltmer

- VP and Executive Partner, Gartner
- LinkedIn: https://www.linkedin.com/in/voltmer/

Lynn O'Connor Vos

- Chairperson of the Board, OptimizRx
- LinkedIn: https://www.linkedin.com/in/lynn-o-connor-vos/.

Rich Wartel

- Founder and CEO of One Lab Innovations, LLC
- LinkedIn: https://www.linkedin.com/in/rich-wartel-26b4449/

Mitchell Weinstock

- Venture Partner
- LinkedIn: https://www.linkedin.com/in/mitchellweinstock/

Sonia Winner

- President and CEO at Cleveland Museum of Natural History
- LinkedIn: https://www.linkedin.com/in/sonia-winner-2699123/

Linda Zhang

- Executive Director, Commercial and Investment Bank—Data and Analytics Technology, JPMorgan Chase & Co.
- LinkedIn: https://www.linkedin.com/in/linda-lei-zhang/

ACKNOWLEDGEMENTS

This book has been an outgrowth from my work on *The Innovation Mindset*, inspired by my earliest experiences as a youth contributing to my father's inventions and my own start-ups. I developed a passion for problem-solving in new and innovative ways—and helping others do the same. After my first book was published, I conducted consulting projects and workshops for companies looking to incorporate innovation into their way of thinking and working. Time and again, I was asked, "I love that *The Innovation Mindset* gives us a framework for getting our big ideas to market. But first, our organization needs to do a better job coming up with ideas. Can you help?" Well, that's just the challenge we tackled with *No Fear, No Failure*. In these pages, you'll learn how to imbue the innovation mindset into your organization in a way that creates change that sustains a culture of innovation and drives growth for the long haul.

I've been fortunate to be an innovation practitioner through my start-ups and the many roles I've held in corporations including Porter Novelli, Bristol Myers Squibb, Covance, Cognizant Technology Solutions, IQVIA, and IBM Watson Health. I've also had an opportunity to teach undergraduate and graduate students at Columbia Business School, Princeton University, Wharton, Yeshiva

University, and Moravian University and executives at organizations such as Novartis, Hewlett-Packard, and Johnson & Johnson.

The best part of writing this book was interviewing 120 innovators in different geographies and industries. I learned so much and am grateful for the time and effort all these colleagues, many now friends, invested in helping me write their stories and case studies for this book. To all the creative and innovative minds I have had the pleasure to interview and work with—in the classroom, the start-up lab, and the corporate world—thank you for your inventions, your insight, and your inspiration.

John Hanc, my extraordinary cowriter, helped me bring this book and the stories of the innovators we interviewed to life. Importantly, he made this twelve-month marathon fun.

I thank my research assistant Angel Madera Santana, a student at Fordham University studying prelaw with a focus on social justice. You worked closely with me conducting interviews, translating notes, analyzing survey results, gathering bios and photos, creating our Innovators' Circle, and being an important contributor to this book in so many ways. I couldn't have done this without you, Angel!

To my colleague and friend Anouk Pappers, an exemplary branding strategy consultant. You encouraged me to write my first book and were by my side as my strategic advisor as I wrote this one—thank you for your wisdom, support, and encouragement.

To Myles Thompson, Brian Smith, and Miriah Ralston, my editors at Columbia University Press, thank you for your belief in the need for an innovation book like this—and one of the few on this topic written by a woman—and for your guidance and support throughout this experience.

Thank you to the faculty and students at Columbia Business School for giving me an opportunity to share my knowledge and experiences and for all you have taught me about innovation and entrepreneurship.

My gratitude to my longtime colleague and friend Arda Ural, for writing an inspirational foreword to this book.

I thank each of the innovators in the Champions of Change profiles: Erez Naaman, Catherine Reynolds, Dave Evans, Al Wilson, Aniruddha Sharma, Tracy Harmon Blumenfeld, Angela Mangiapane, and Shih-Yin Ho. To all the members of the Innovators' Circle named in the Appendix, thank you all for sharing your stories, your wisdom, and your tips on innovation. I look forward to our work together in the future. Thank you Sandi Goldfarb, Andy Hoagland, Katie Desiderio, Mike Eng, Anouk Pappers, Tommy Beaudry, and Nick Marchand for making introductions to some of the innovators who were interviewed for this book.

Thank you to Nitesh Bansal, Maria Boulden, Deborah Juantorena, Eric Piscini, Paul Bailo, Benjamin Newland, Nisheet Gupta, Paul Russo, Mark Adams, Deborah Y. Cohn, Rana Khan, Natasha Srulowitz, and David Venezuela for your endorsement of this book.

Finally, to my family who have supported and encouraged me through the years and during the development of his book, especially my husband Don, mother Polly, sons Joe, Nick, brother Greg, and Matt, and my daughters-in-law Anna Marchand and Tanya Shroff—thank you. This book is dedicated to my grandsons Nolan and Isaac, to whom I emphasize the message I share with all of you: try, fail, learn—and repeat.

Lorraine Marchand, Yardley, Pennsylvania, March 2025

NOTES

INTRODUCTION

1. Scott D. Anthony et al., "Breaking Down the Barriers to Innovation," *Harvard Business Review*, November–December 2019, https://hbr.org/2019/11/breaking -down-the-barriers-to-innovation.

2. Amy C. Edmondson, "Strategies for Learning from Failure," *Harvard Business Review*, April 2011, https://hbr.org/2011/04/strategies-for-learning-from-failure.

3. Jeannine Mancini, "Jeff Bezos Says Amazon Has Had 'Plenty of Practice' with Failure but Believes It Is 'The Best Place in the World to Fail,'" Benzinga, January 10, 2024, https://finance.yahoo.com/news/jeff-bezos-says-amazon-had -170926395.html.

1. FEAR OF FAILURE AND THE 5C's—LESSONS FROM THE RISE AND FALL OF IBM WATSON HEALTH

1. John Markoff, "Computer Wins on 'Jeopardy!': Trivial, It's Not," *New York Times*, February 17, 2011, https://www.nytimes.com/2011/02/17/science/17jeopardy-watson.html.

2. Steve Lohr, "Whatever Happened to IBM's Watson," *New York Times*, July 16, 2021, https://www.nytimes.com/2021/07/16/technology/what-happened -ibm-watson.html.

3. "IBM's Rometty: 'Health Care Will Be Our Moon Shot,'" *Charlie Rose*, April 16, 2015, YouTube video, https://www.youtube.com/watch?v=46MYhalt7EU.

4. Lizzie O'Leary, "How IBM's Watson Went from the Future of Health Care to Sold Off for Parts," *Slate*, January 31, 2022, https://slate.com/technology /2022/01/ibm-watson-health-failure-artificial-intelligence.html.

5. Rob Markey, "Are You Undervaluing Your Customers," Harvard Business Review, January 2020, https://hbr.org/2020/01/are-you-undervaluing-your -customers#.

2. THE 5C'S: CUSTOMER FIRST—ASKING THE RIGHT QUESTIONS

1. Lance Dinino, "Death by a Thousand Emails: How Administrative Bloat Is Killing American Higher Education," *Bowdoin Review*, February 7, 2024, https:// students.bowdoin.edu/bowdoin-review/features/death-by-a-thousand-emails -how-administrative-bloat-is-killing-american-higher-education/.

3. THE 5C's: CULTURE—INNOVATION FOR THE LONG HAUL

1. "Culture: Everything, We as People, Are," accessed August 5, 2025, https:// web.stanford.edu/~hakuta/www/archives/syllabi/E_CLAD/sfusd_cult_03 /melissa/Culture%20Defined.htm

2. Emily S. Weinstein, "Beijing's 'Re-innovation' Strategy Is Key Element of U.S.-China Competition," Brookings, January 6, 2022, https://www.brookings .edu/articles/beijings-re-innovation-strategy-is-key-element-of-u-s-china -competition/.

3. Jason Miller, "The Power of Diversity and Inclusion: Driving Innovation and Success," Forbes.com, August, 16, 2023, https://www.forbes.com/councils /forbesbusinesscouncil/2023/08/16/the-power-of-diversity-and-inclusion -driving-innovation-and-success/.

4. "7 Keys to Creating a Culture of Innovation," Big Think +, May 10, 2023, https://bigthink.com/plus/creating-a-culture-of-innovation/.

5. THE 5C's: CHANGE—INNOVATING FOR TRANSFORMATION

1. Forbes India, "Top 20 Largest Economies in the World in 2025: GDP Rankings and Key Insights," https://www.forbesindia.com/article/explainers /top-10-largest-economies-in-the-world/86159/1.

2. New Zealand Ministry of Foreign Affairs and Trade, "Saudi Arabia: The Fastest Growing Economy Fighting for Its Future," November 2022, https://www.mfat.govt.nz/assets/Trade-General/Trade-Market-reports/Saudi-Arabia-the-fastest-growing-economy-fighting-for-its-future-November-2022.pdf

3. Alex Zhavoronkov, "The New Saudi Arabia—Vision 2030 and AI," *Forbes*, July 14, 2022, https://www.forbes.com/sites/alexzhavoronkov/2022/07/14/the-new-saudi-arabiavision-2030-and-ai/.

4. Noah Brown, "Study Reveals Unexpected Importance of the Thymus in Adults," Massachusetts General Hospital, August 2, 2023, https://www.massgeneral.org/news/press-release/study-reveals-unexpected-importance-of-the-thymus-in-adults.

6. THE 5C's: CHANCE—INVESTING IN RISKS

1. Brad Mendelson et al., "Building a Superpower: What Can We Learn from the Magnificent Seven?," McKinsey and Company, June 25, 2024, https://www.mckinsey.com/capabilities/growth-marketing-and-sales/our-insights/building-a-superpower-what-can-we-learn-from-the-magnificent-seven.

7. THE FOUR FACES OF ORGANIZATIONAL INNOVATION

1. James Wilson, "How Do Startup Accelerators Work?," Silicon Valley Bank, https://www.svb.com/startup-insights/startup-growth/how-do-startup-accelerators-work/.

8. AI: DOOM OR DELIVERANCE?

1. Dan Diasio and Traci Gusher, "Execs Double Down on AI: Explore 5 AI Adoption Strategies for Success," Ernst and Young, July 15, 2024, https://www.ey.com/en_us/services/emerging-technologies/five-ai-adoption-strategies-survey/.

2. Aaron A. Tierney et al., "Ambient Artificial Intelligence Scribes to Alleviate the Burden of Clinical Documentation," *NEJM Catalyst* 5, no. 3 (2024), https://catalyst.nejm.org/doi/full/10.1056/CAT.23.0404.

9. INTEGRATING THE 5C's INTO YOUR ORGANIZATION

1. Erika Andersen, "Change Is Hard: Here's How to Make It Less Painful," *Harvard Business Review*, April 7, 2022, https://hbr.org/2022/04/change-is-hard -heres-how-to-make-it-less-painful.

2. Deborah Blagg and Susan Young, "What Makes a Good Leader," Harvard Business School Alumni Stories, February 1, 2001, https://www.alumni.hbs.edu /stories/Pages/story-bulletin.aspx?num=3059.

INDEX

Page numbers in italics represent figures or tables.

This QR code gives you access to the No Fear No Failure page on Lorraine's website where you will find additional materials including a sample syllabus and instructor's guide, links to those featured in and interviewed for the book, additional innovators and case studies Lorraine adds to the website based on her ongoing research on innovation.

https://www.lorrainemarchand.com/no-fear-no-failure/.

This URL and the associated QR code direct to the author's own website which is neither under the control of nor the responsibility of Columbia University Press. The content which may be accessed there is provided as is and as available.

GPSR Authorized Representative: Easy Access System Europe, Mustamäe tee 50, 10621 Tallinn, Estonia, gpsr.requests@easproject.com